MARVEL KNIGHTS
SPIDER-MAN

MARVEL KNIGHTS

SPIDER-MAN

F I G H T   N I G H T

WRITER
MATT KINDT

ARTIST
MARCO RUDY

COLOR ARTIST
VAL STAPLES

LETTERER
VC'S CLAYTON COWLES

COVER ARTISTS
MARCO RUDY & VAL STAPLES

ASSISTANT EDITOR
FRANKIE JOHNSON

EDITOR
TOM BRENNAN

SENIOR EDITOR
STEPHEN WACKER

COLLECTION EDITOR: ALEX STARBUCK   **EDITORS, SPECIAL PROJECTS:** JENNIFER GRÜNWALD & MARK D. BEAZLEY
SENIOR EDITOR, SPECIAL PROJECTS: JEFF YOUNGQUIST   **SVP PRINT, SALES & MARKETING:** DAVID GABRIEL
BOOK DESIGNER: RODOLFO MURAGUCHI

EDITOR IN CHIEF: AXEL ALONSO   **CHIEF CREATIVE OFFICER:** JOE QUESADA
PUBLISHER: DAN BUCKLEY   **EXECUTIVE PRODUCER:** ALAN FINE

MARVEL KNIGHTS: SPIDER-MAN — FIGHT NIGHT. Contains material originally published in magazine form as MARVEL KNIGHTS: SPIDER-MAN #1-5. First printing 2014. ISBN# 978-0-7851-8407-2. Published by MARVEL WORLDWIDE, INC., a subsidiary of MARVEL ENTERTAINMENT, LLC. OFFICE OF PUBLICATION: 135 West 50th Street, New York, NY 10020. Copyright © 2013 and 2014 Marvel Characters, Inc. All rights reserved. All characters featured in this issue and the distinctive names and likenesses thereof, and all related indicia are trademarks of Marvel Characters, Inc. No similarity between any of the names, characters, persons, and/or institutions in this magazine with those of any living or dead person or institution is intended, and any such similarity which may exist is purely coincidental. **Printed in Canada.** ALAN FINE, EVP - Office of the President, Marvel Worldwide, Inc. and EVP & CMO Marvel Characters B.V.; DAN BUCKLEY, Publisher & President - Print, Animation & Digital Divisions; JOE QUESADA, Chief Creative Officer; TOM BREVOORT, SVP of Publishing; DAVID BOGART, SVP of Operations & Procurement, Publishing; C.B. CEBULSKI, SVP of Creator & Content Development; DAVID GABRIEL, SVP Print, Sales & Marketing; JIM O'KEEFE, VP of Operations & Logistics; DAN CARR, Executive Director of Publishing Technology; SUSAN CRESPI, Editorial Operations Manager; ALEX MORALES, Publishing Operations Manager; STAN LEE, Chairman Emeritus. For information regarding advertising in Marvel Comics or on Marvel.com, please contact Niza Disla, Director of Marvel Partnerships, at ndisla@marvel.com. For Marvel subscription inquiries, please call 800-217-9158. **Manufactured between 2/7/2014 and 3/17/2014 by SOLISCO PRINTERS, SCOTT, QC, CANADA.**

10 9 8 7 6 5 4 3 2 1

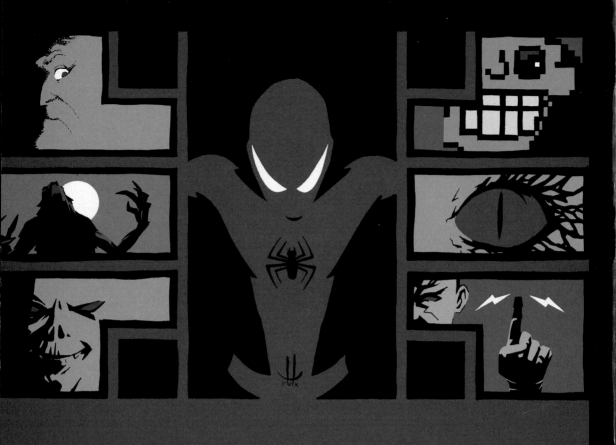

1

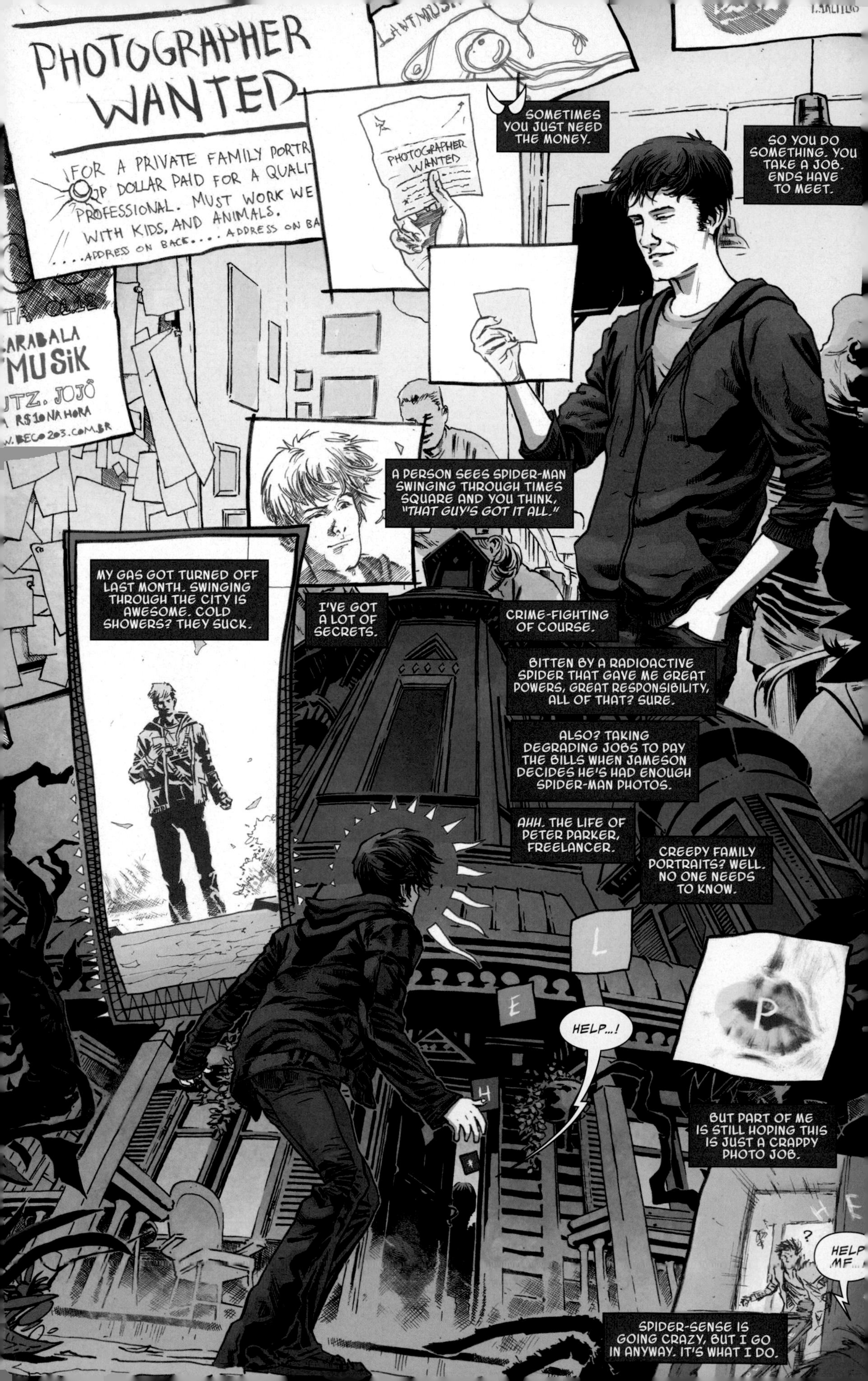
PHOTOGRAPHER WANTED
FOR A PRIVATE FAMILY PORTR
P DOLLAR PAID FOR A QUALIT
PROFESSIONAL. MUST WORK WE
WITH KIDS, AND ANIMALS.
....ADDRESS ON BACK.... ADDRESS ON BA
SOMETIMES YOU JUST NEED THE MONEY.
SO YOU DO SOMETHING. YOU TAKE A JOB. ENDS HAVE TO MEET.
PHOTOGRAPHER WANTED
ARABALA MUSIK
TZ. JOJÔ
R$10 NA HORA
W.BECO203.COM.BR
A PERSON SEES SPIDER-MAN SWINGING THROUGH TIMES SQUARE AND YOU THINK, "THAT GUY'S GOT IT ALL."
MY GAS GOT TURNED OFF LAST MONTH. SWINGING THROUGH THE CITY IS AWESOME. COLD SHOWERS? THEY SUCK.
I'VE GOT A LOT OF SECRETS.
CRIME-FIGHTING OF COURSE.
BITTEN BY A RADIOACTIVE SPIDER THAT GAVE ME GREAT POWERS, GREAT RESPONSIBILITY, ALL OF THAT? SURE.
ALSO? TAKING DEGRADING JOBS TO PAY THE BILLS WHEN JAMESON DECIDES HE'S HAD ENOUGH SPIDER-MAN PHOTOS.
AHH. THE LIFE OF PETER PARKER, FREELANCER.
CREEPY FAMILY PORTRAITS? WELL. NO ONE NEEDS TO KNOW.
L
E
P
HELP...!
H
BUT PART OF ME IS STILL HOPING THIS IS JUST A CRAPPY PHOTO JOB.
H E
?
HELP ME...
SPIDER-SENSE IS GOING CRAZY, BUT I GO IN ANYWAY. IT'S WHAT I DO.

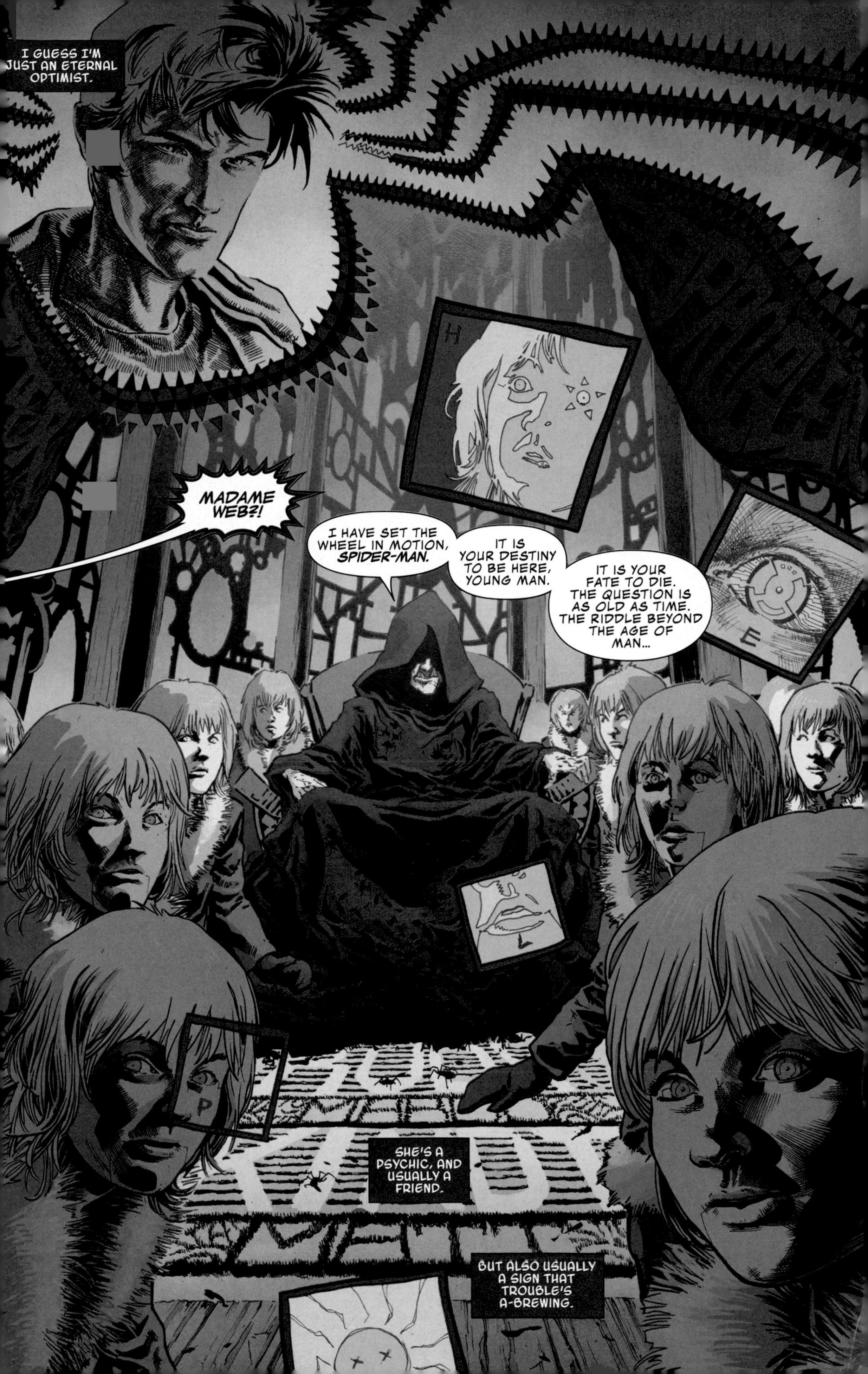
I GUESS I'M JUST AN ETERNAL OPTIMIST.
MADAME WEB?!
I HAVE SET THE WHEEL IN MOTION, SPIDER-MAN.
IT IS YOUR DESTINY TO BE HERE, YOUNG MAN.
IT IS YOUR FATE TO DIE. THE QUESTION IS AS OLD AS TIME. THE RIDDLE BEYOND THE AGE OF MAN...
SHE'S A PSYCHIC, AND USUALLY A FRIEND.
BUT ALSO USUALLY A SIGN THAT TROUBLE'S A-BREWING.

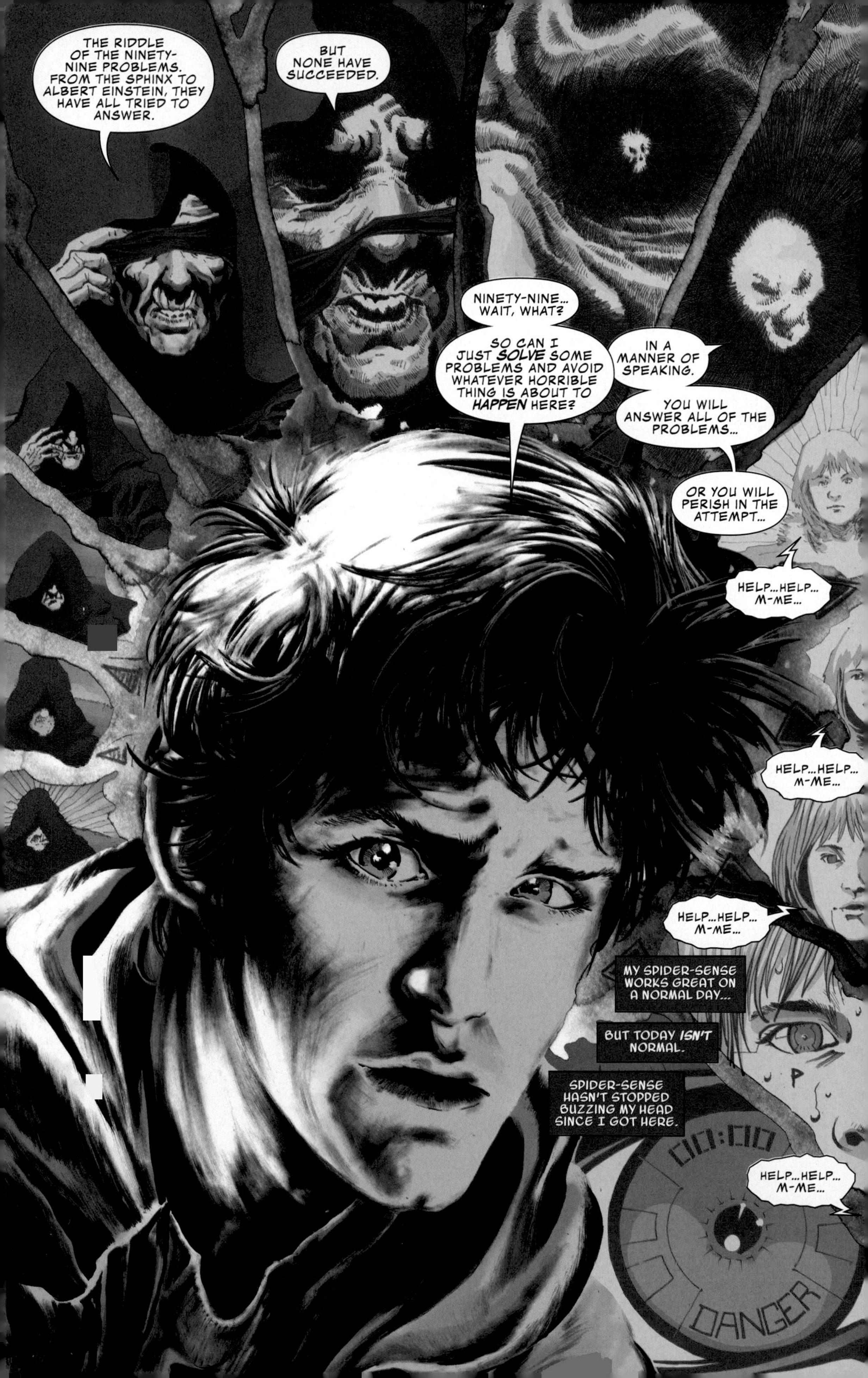
THE RIDDLE OF THE NINETY-NINE PROBLEMS. FROM THE SPHINX TO ALBERT EINSTEIN, THEY HAVE ALL TRIED TO ANSWER.
BUT NONE HAVE SUCCEEDED.
NINETY-NINE... WAIT, WHAT?
SO CAN I JUST SOLVE SOME PROBLEMS AND AVOID WHATEVER HORRIBLE THING IS ABOUT TO HAPPEN HERE?
IN A MANNER OF SPEAKING.
YOU WILL ANSWER ALL OF THE PROBLEMS...
OR YOU WILL PERISH IN THE ATTEMPT...
HELP...HELP... M-ME...
HELP...HELP... M-ME...
HELP...HELP... M-ME...
MY SPIDER-SENSE WORKS GREAT ON A NORMAL DAY...
BUT TODAY ISN'T NORMAL.
SPIDER-SENSE HASN'T STOPPED BUZZING MY HEAD SINCE I GOT HERE.
HELP...HELP... M-ME...
00:00
DANGER

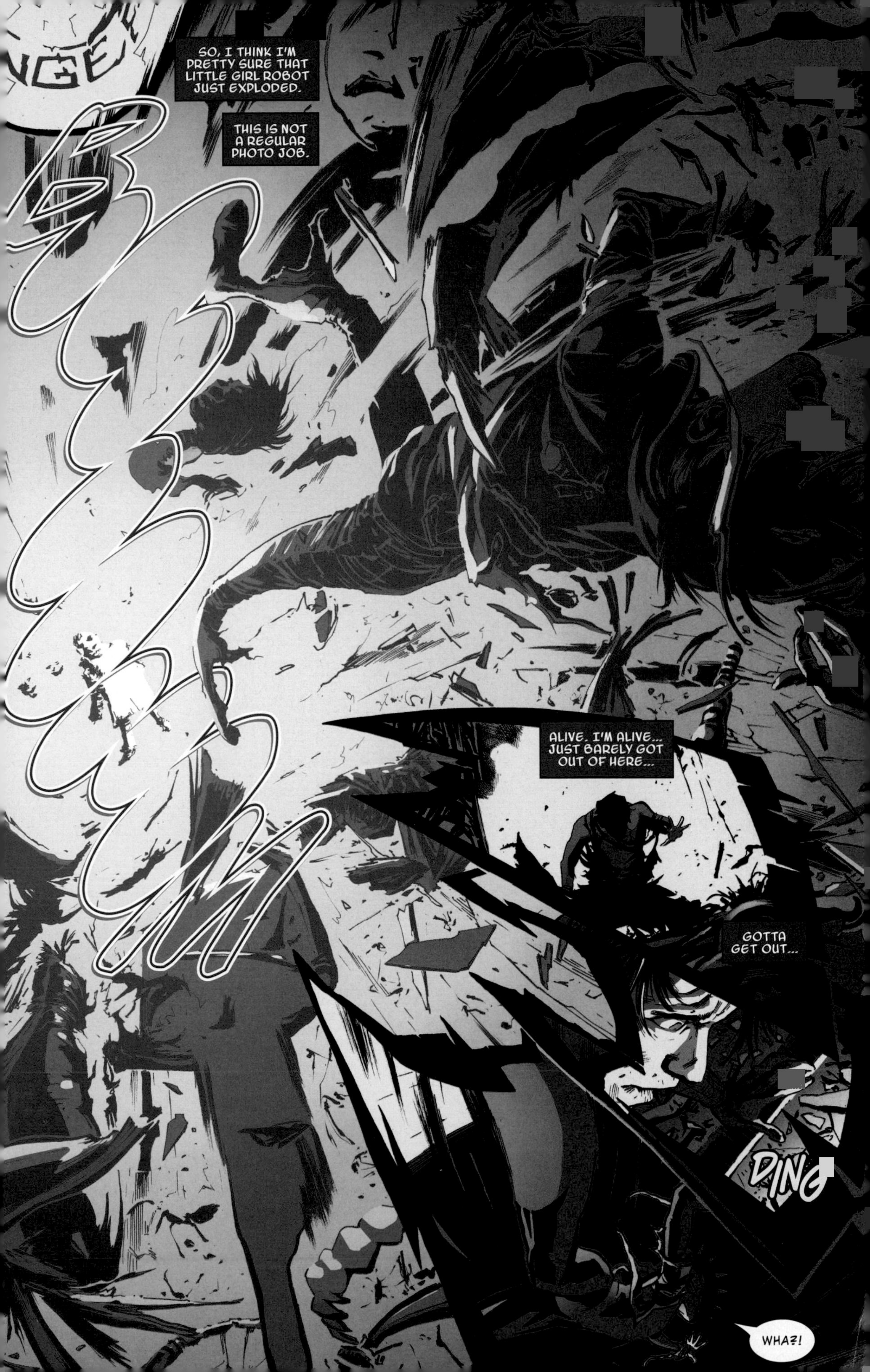
SO, I THINK I'M PRETTY SURE THAT LITTLE GIRL ROBOT JUST EXPLODED.
THIS IS NOT A REGULAR PHOTO JOB.
ALIVE. I'M ALIVE... JUST BARELY GOT OUT OF HERE...
GOTTA GET OUT...
DING
WHA?!

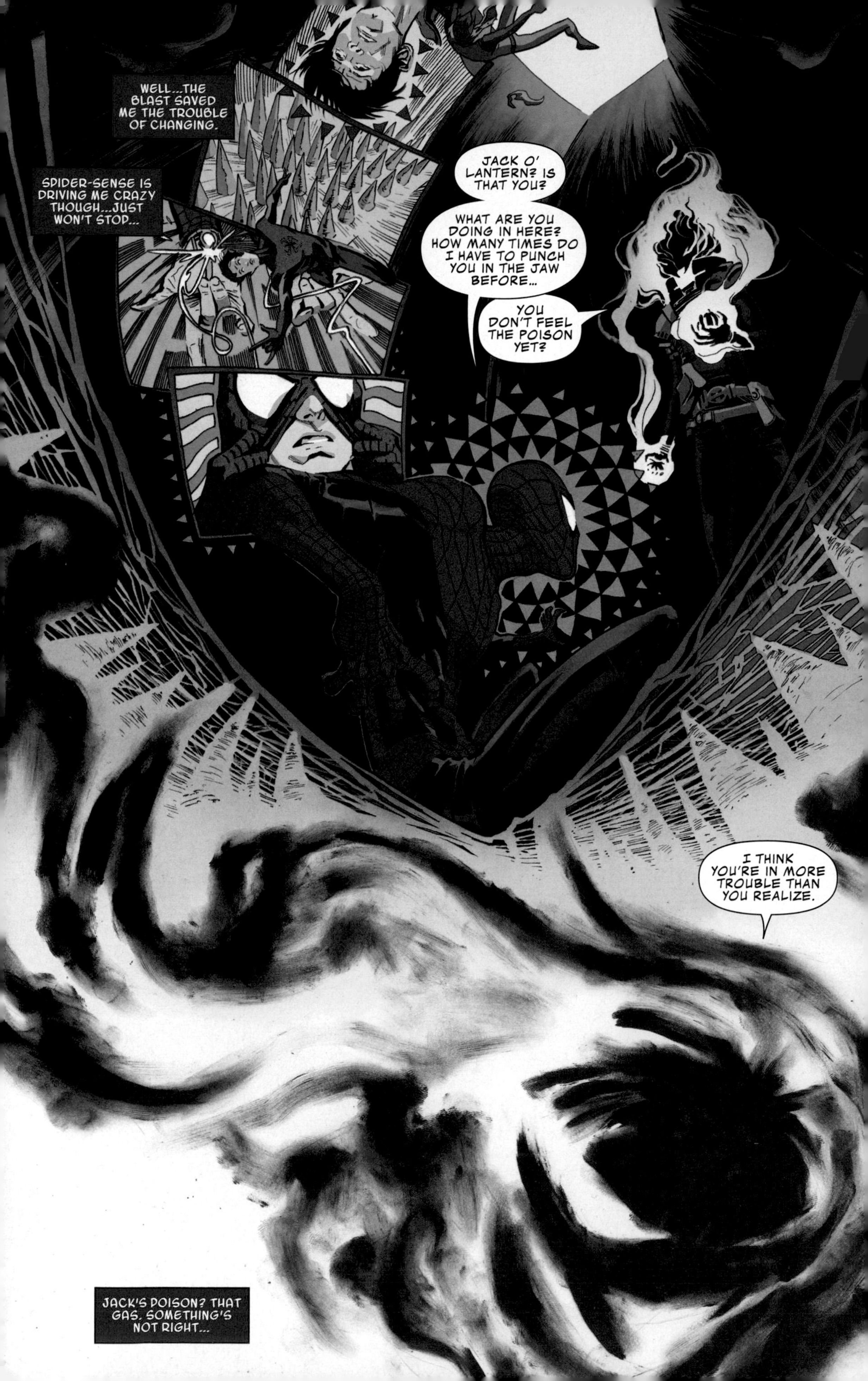
WELL...THE BLAST SAVED ME THE TROUBLE OF CHANGING.
SPIDER-SENSE IS DRIVING ME CRAZY THOUGH...JUST WON'T STOP...
JACK O' LANTERN? IS THAT YOU?
WHAT ARE YOU DOING IN HERE? HOW MANY TIMES DO I HAVE TO PUNCH YOU IN THE JAW BEFORE...
YOU DON'T FEEL THE POISON YET?
I THINK YOU'RE IN MORE TROUBLE THAN YOU REALIZE.
JACK'S POISON? THAT GAS. SOMETHING'S NOT RIGHT...

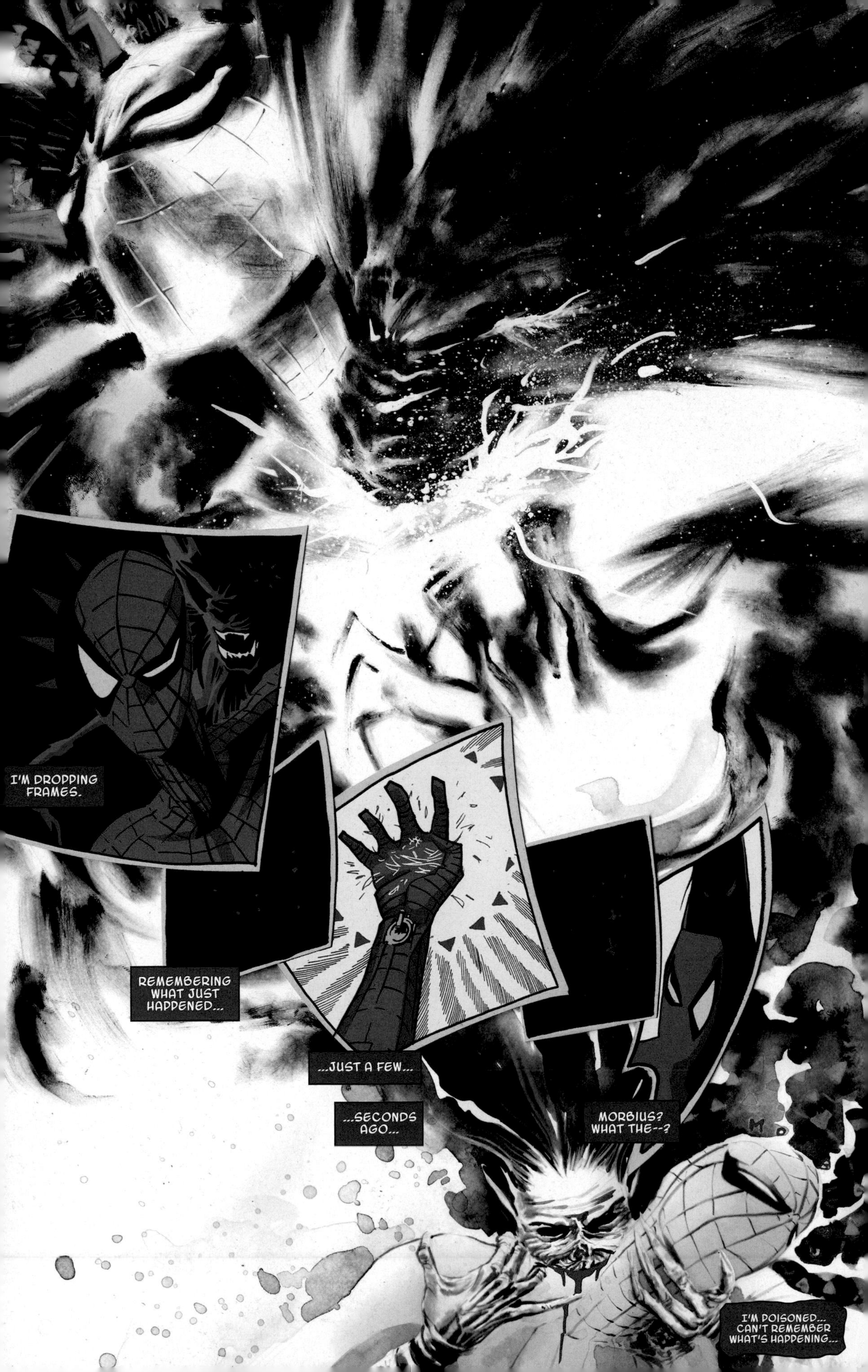
I'M DROPPING FRAMES.
REMEMBERING WHAT JUST HAPPENED...
...JUST A FEW...
...SECONDS AGO...
MORBIUS? WHAT THE--?
I'M POISONED... CAN'T REMEMBER WHAT'S HAPPENING...

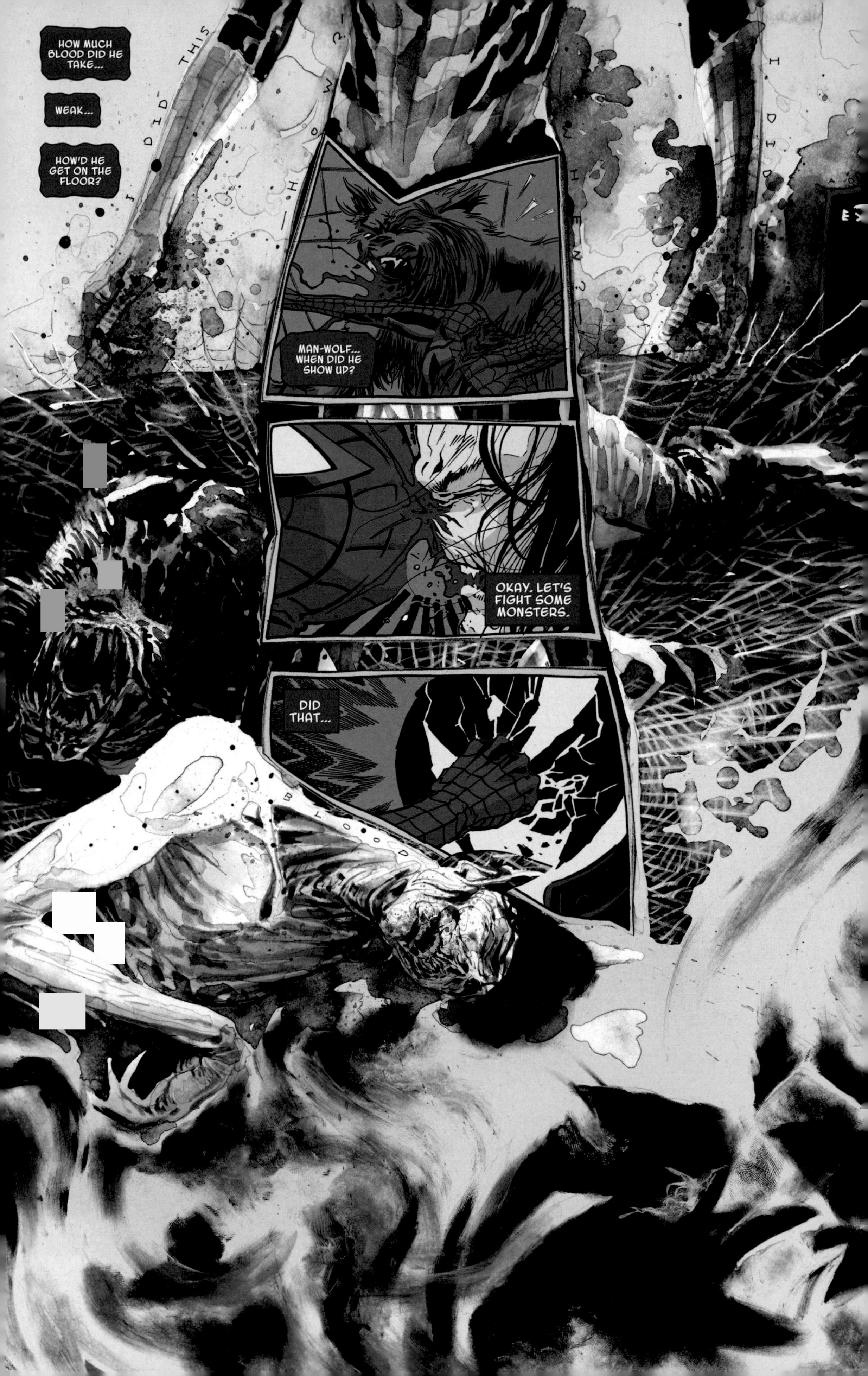
HOW MUCH BLOOD DID HE TAKE...
WEAK...
HOW'D HE GET ON THE FLOOR?
I DID THIS
MAN-WOLF... WHEN DID HE SHOW UP?
OKAY. LET'S FIGHT SOME MONSTERS.
DID THAT...
BLOOD

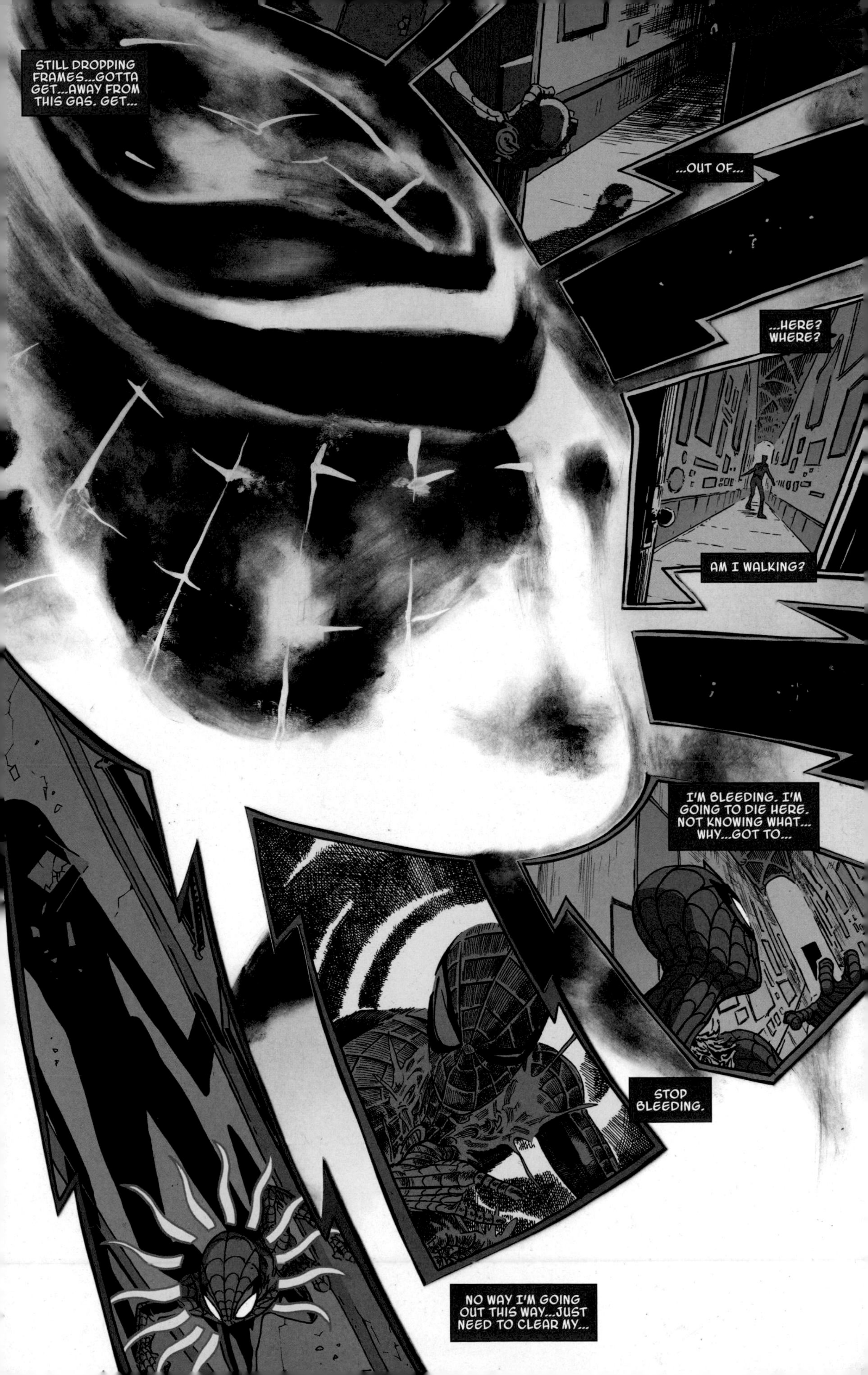
STILL DROPPING FRAMES...GOTTA GET...AWAY FROM THIS GAS. GET...
...OUT OF...
...HERE? WHERE?
AM I WALKING?
I'M BLEEDING. I'M GOING TO DIE HERE. NOT KNOWING WHAT... WHY...GOT TO...
STOP BLEEDING.
NO WAY I'M GOING OUT THIS WAY...JUST NEED TO CLEAR MY...

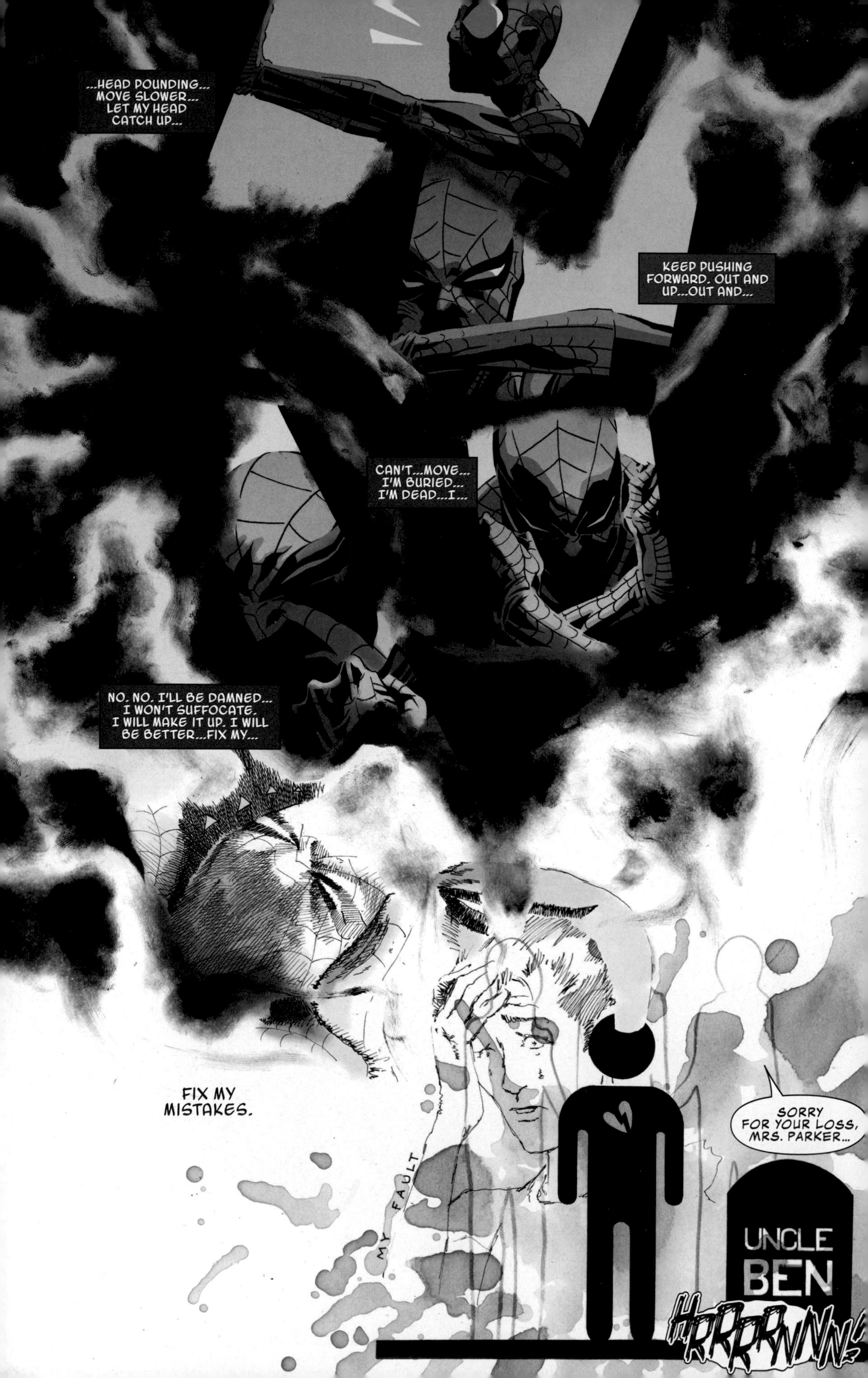
...HEAD POUNDING... MOVE SLOWER... LET MY HEAD CATCH UP...
KEEP PUSHING FORWARD. OUT AND UP...OUT AND...
CAN'T...MOVE... I'M BURIED... I'M DEAD...I...
NO. NO. I'LL BE DAMNED... I WON'T SUFFOCATE. I WILL MAKE IT UP. I WILL BE BETTER...FIX MY...
FIX MY MISTAKES.
MY FAULT
SORRY FOR YOUR LOSS, MRS. PARKER...
UNCLE BEN
HRRRRNNN!

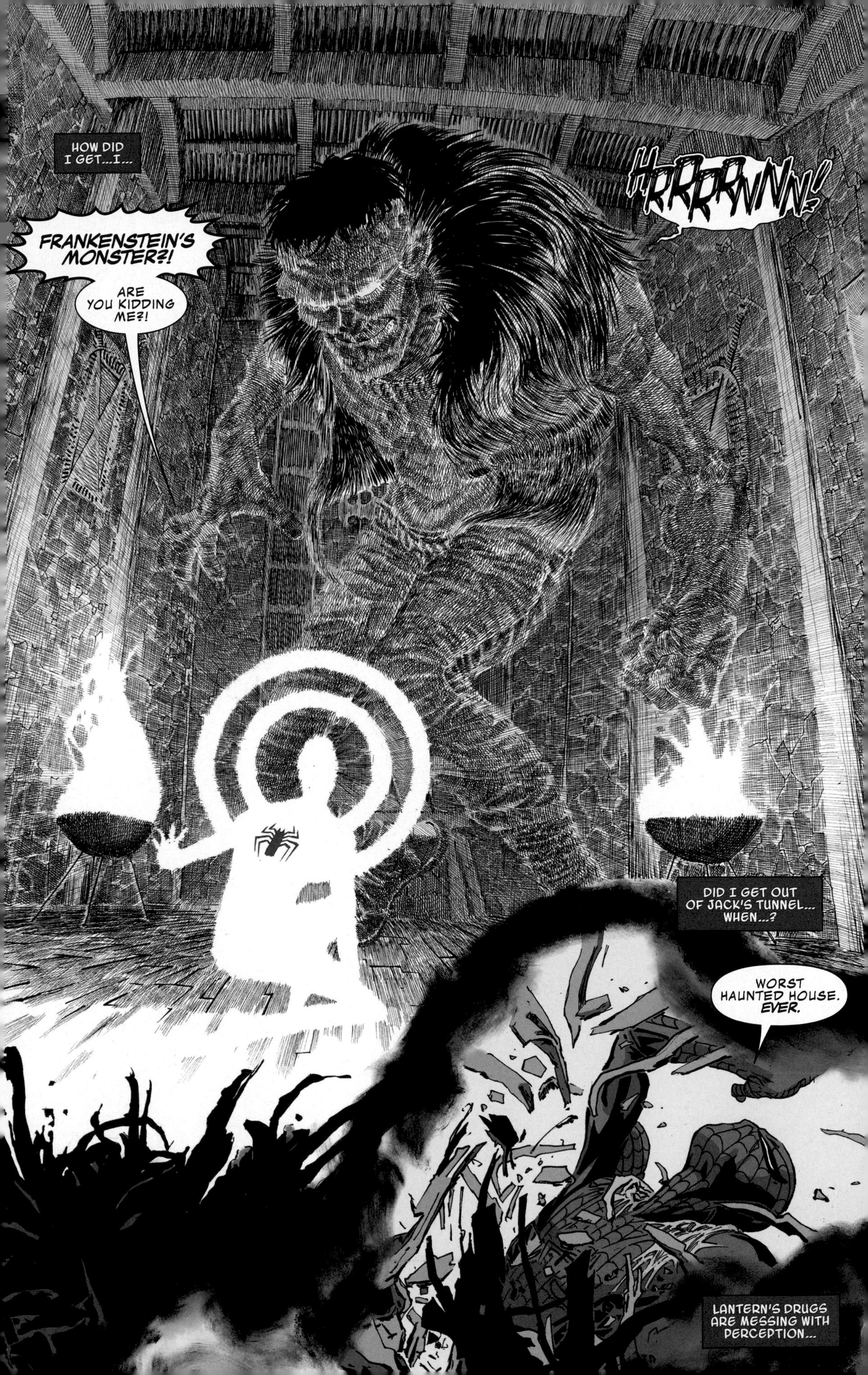
HOW DID I GET...I...
FRANKENSTEIN'S MONSTER?!
ARE YOU KIDDING ME?!
HRRRRNNN!
DID I GET OUT OF JACK'S TUNNEL... WHEN...?
WORST HAUNTED HOUSE. EVER.
LANTERN'S DRUGS ARE MESSING WITH PERCEPTION...

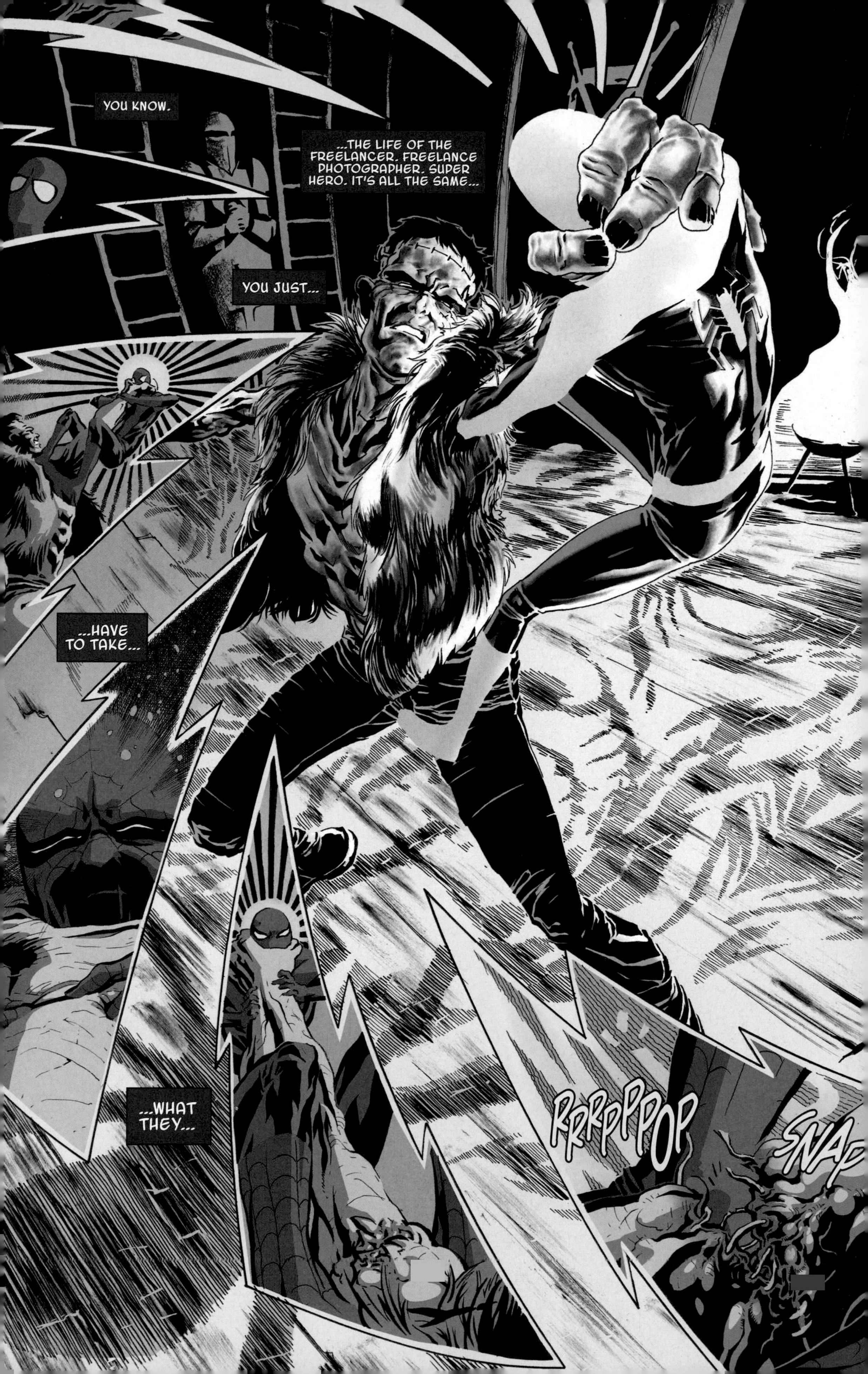
YOU KNOW.
...THE LIFE OF THE FREELANCER. FREELANCE PHOTOGRAPHER. SUPER HERO. IT'S ALL THE SAME...
YOU JUST...
...HAVE TO TAKE...
...WHAT THEY...
RRRPPPOP
SNAP

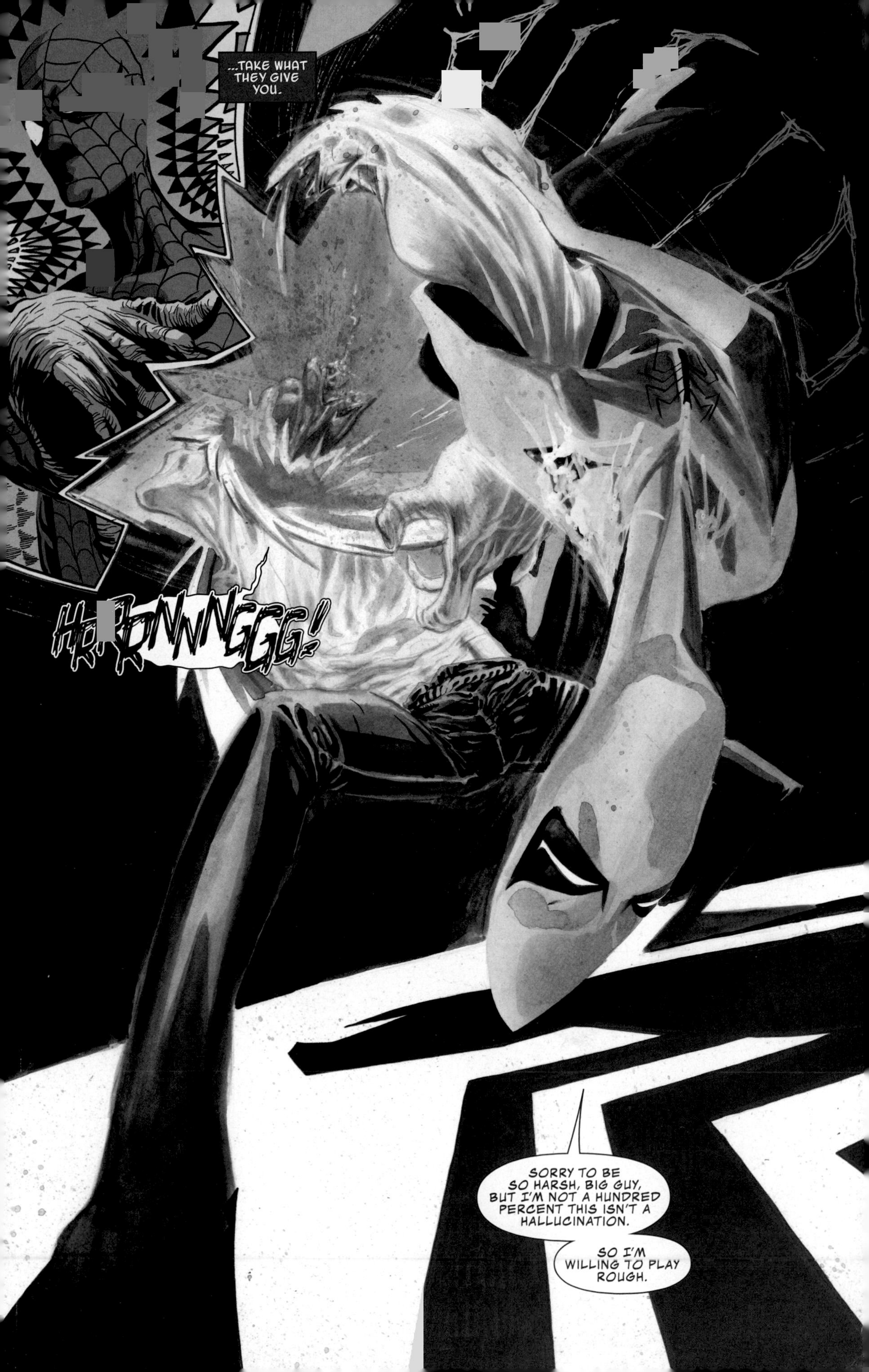
...TAKE WHAT THEY GIVE YOU.
SORRY TO BE SO HARSH, BIG GUY, BUT I'M NOT A HUNDRED PERCENT THIS ISN'T A HALLUCINATION.
SO I'M WILLING TO PLAY ROUGH.

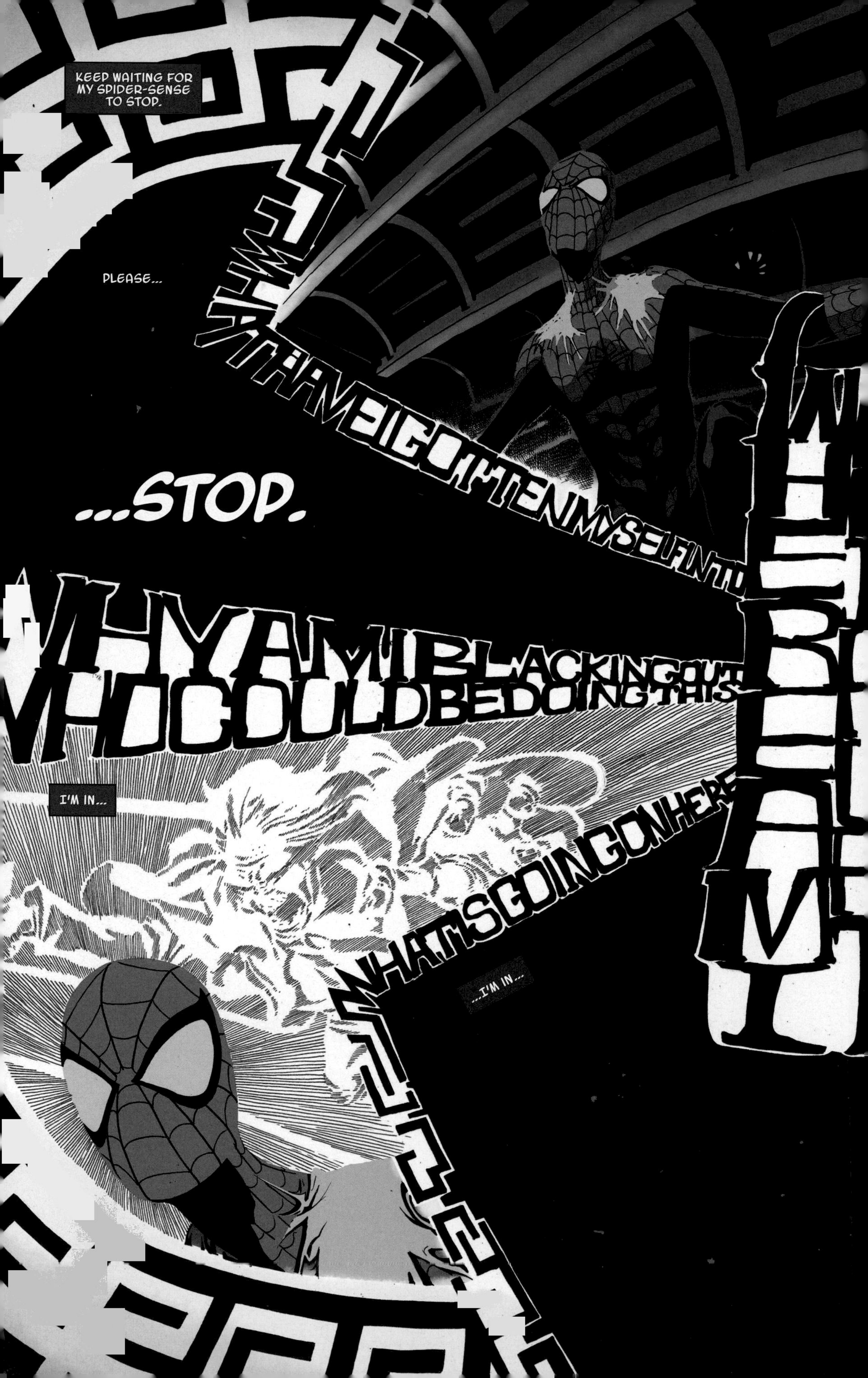
KEEP WAITING FOR MY SPIDER-SENSE TO STOP.
PLEASE...
WHAT HAVE I GOTTEN MYSELF INTO
...STOP.
WHY AM I BLACKING OUT
WHO COULD BE DOING THIS
I'M IN...
WHAT IS GOING ON HERE
...I'M IN...

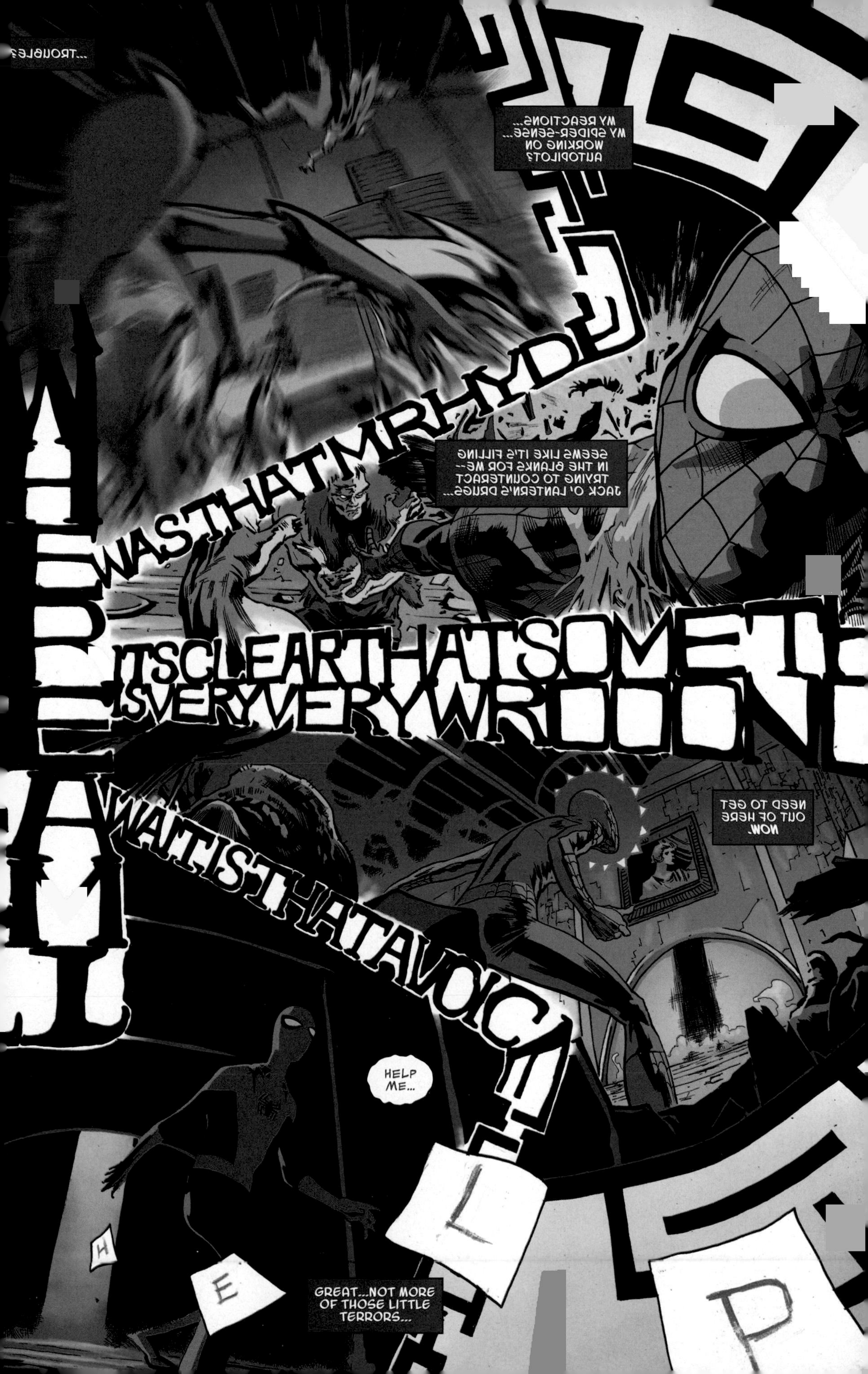
...TROUBLE?
MY REACTIONS... MY SPIDER-SENSE... WORKING ON AUTOPILOT?
WASTHATMRHYDE
SEEMS LIKE IT'S FILLING IN THE BLANKS FOR ME-- TRYING TO COUNTERACT JACK O' LANTERN'S DRUGS...
ITSCLEARTHATSOMET
ISVERYVERYWROOOON
NEED TO GET OUT OF HERE NOW.
WAITISTHATAVOICE
HELP ME...
H
E
L
P
GREAT...NOT MORE OF THOSE LITTLE TERRORS...

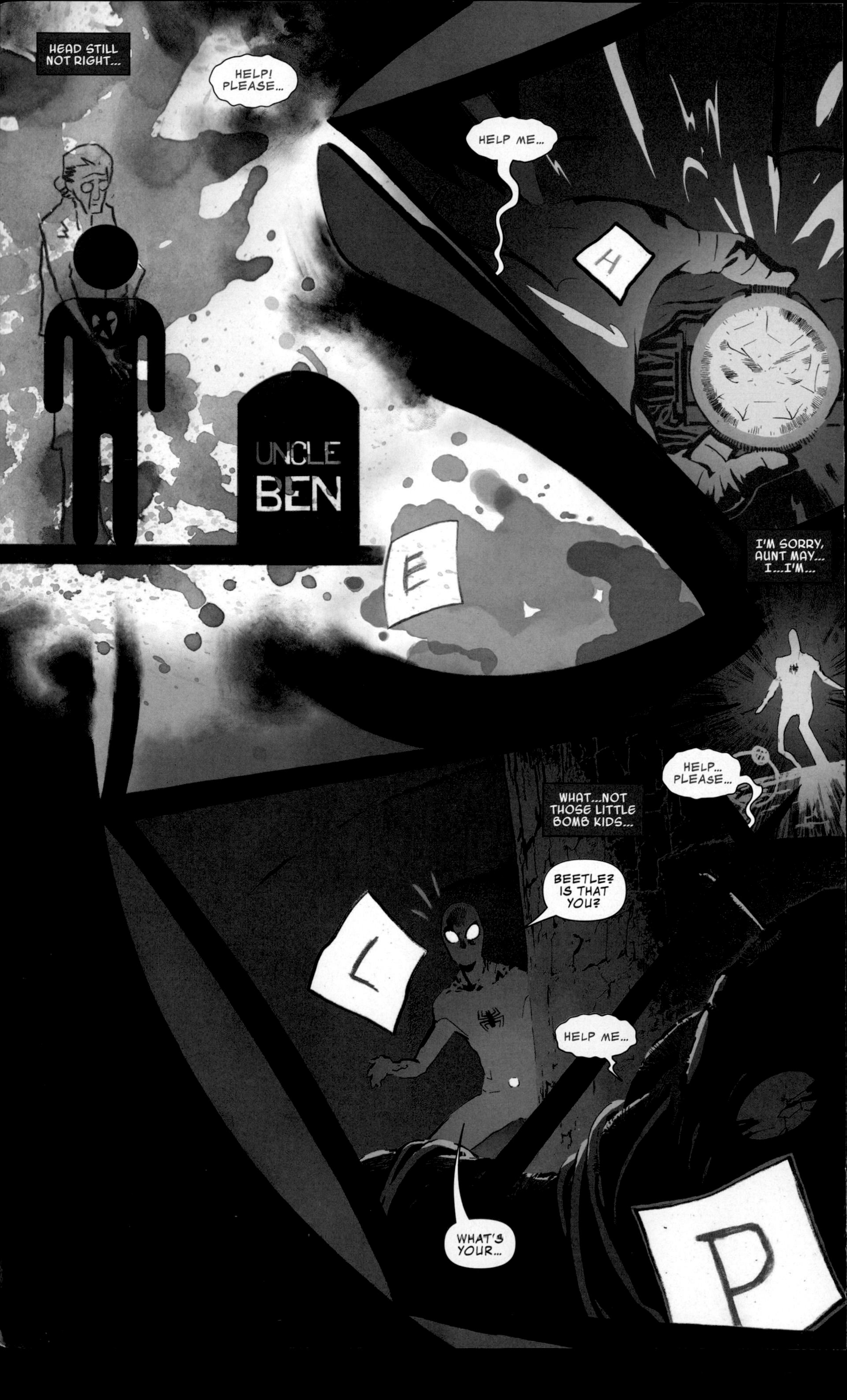
HEAD STILL NOT RIGHT...
HELP! PLEASE...
UNCLE BEN
HELP ME...
H
E
I'M SORRY, AUNT MAY... I...I'M...
HELP... PLEASE...
WHAT...NOT THOSE LITTLE BOMB KIDS...
BEETLE? IS THAT YOU?
L
HELP ME...
WHAT'S YOUR...
P

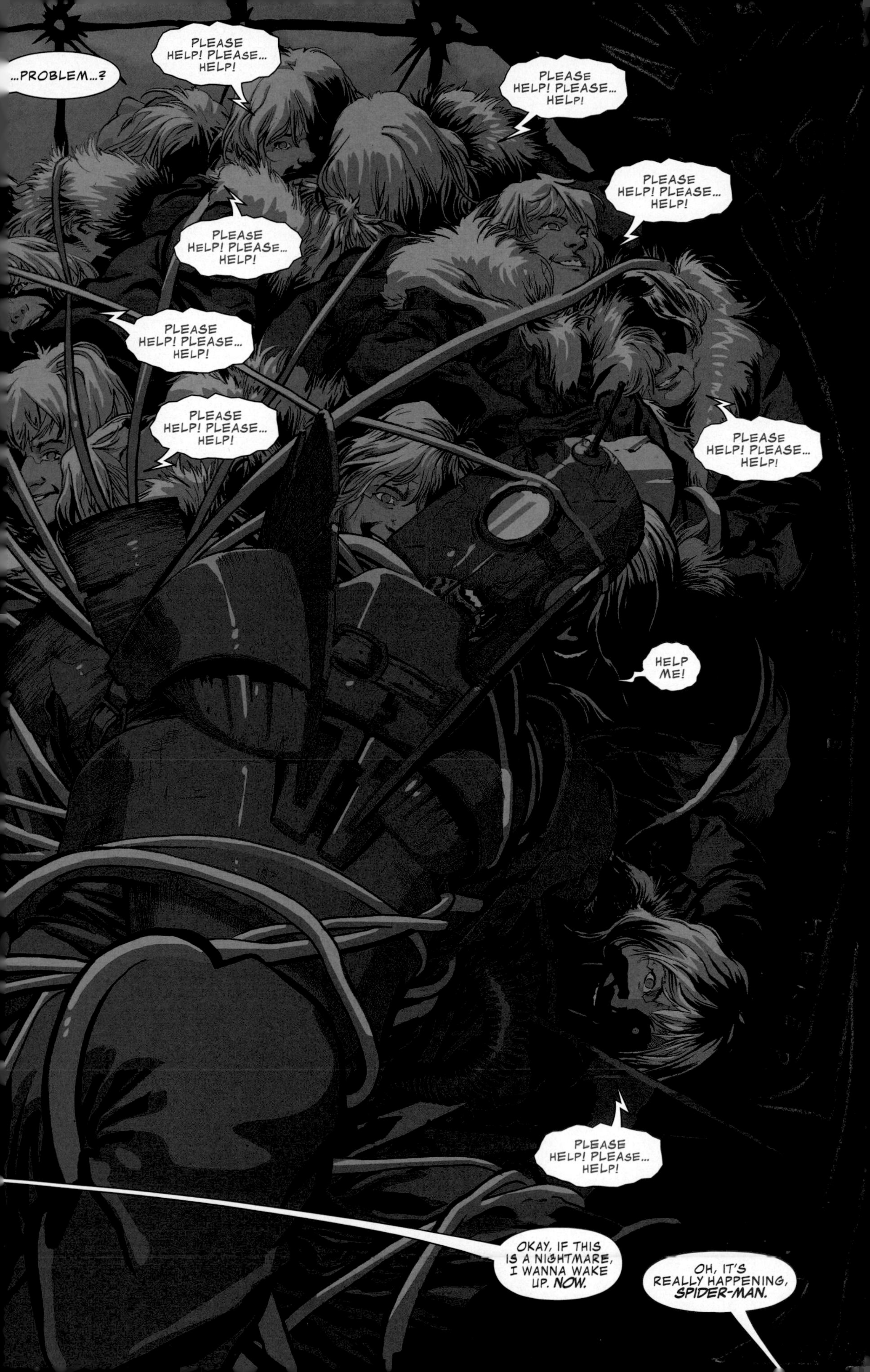
...PROBLEM...?
PLEASE HELP! PLEASE... HELP!
PLEASE HELP! PLEASE... HELP!
PLEASE HELP! PLEASE... HELP!
PLEASE HELP! PLEASE... HELP!
PLEASE HELP! PLEASE... HELP!
PLEASE HELP! PLEASE... HELP!
PLEASE HELP! PLEASE... HELP!
HELP ME!
PLEASE HELP! PLEASE... HELP!
OKAY, IF THIS IS A NIGHTMARE, I WANNA WAKE UP. *NOW.*
OH, IT'S REALLY HAPPENING, *SPIDER-MAN.*

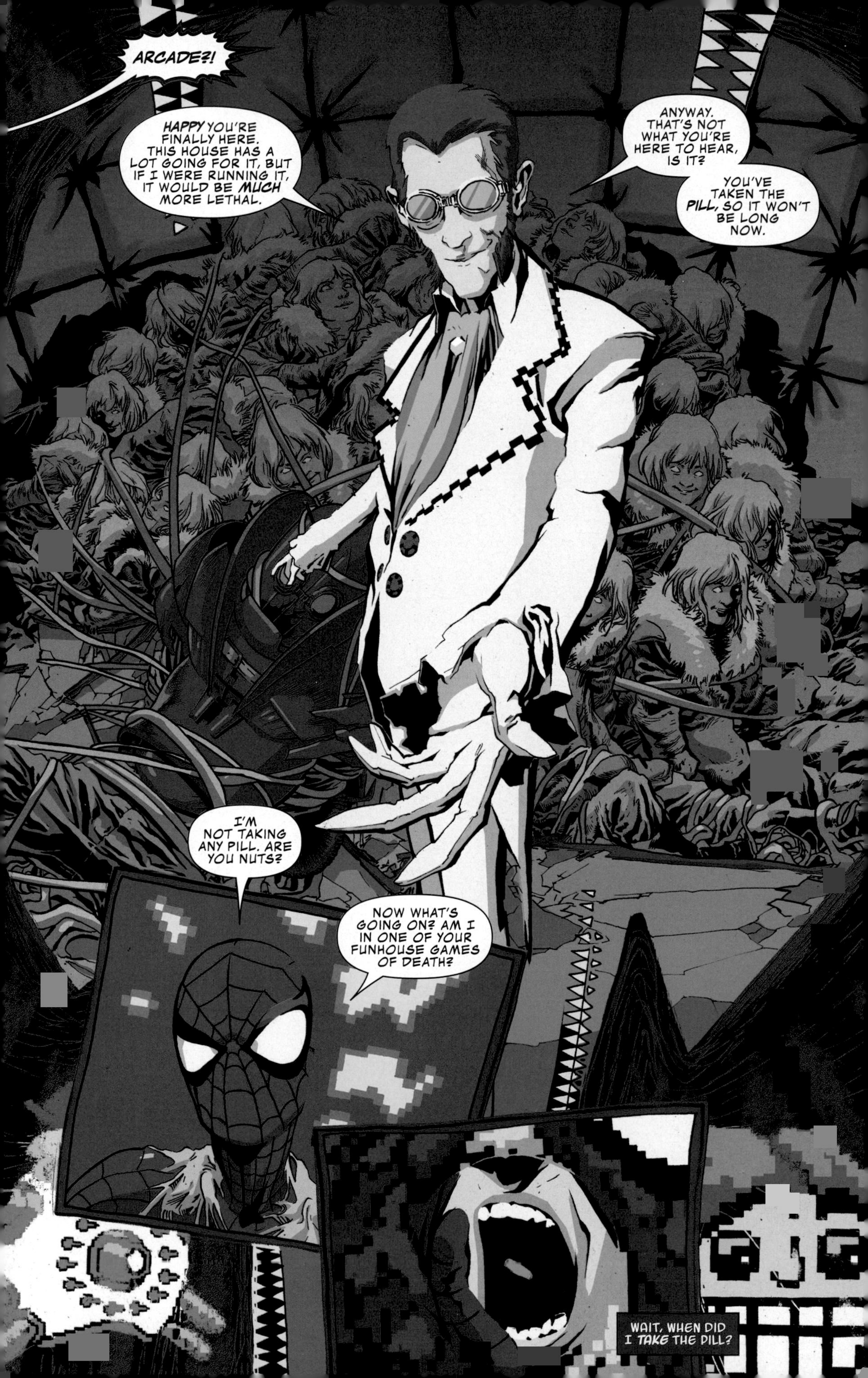
ARCADE?!
HAPPY YOU'RE FINALLY HERE. THIS HOUSE HAS A LOT GOING FOR IT, BUT IF I WERE RUNNING IT, IT WOULD BE MUCH MORE LETHAL.
ANYWAY. THAT'S NOT WHAT YOU'RE HERE TO HEAR, IS IT?
YOU'VE TAKEN THE PILL, SO IT WON'T BE LONG NOW.
I'M NOT TAKING ANY PILL. ARE YOU NUTS?
NOW WHAT'S GOING ON? AM I IN ONE OF YOUR FUNHOUSE GAMES OF DEATH?
WAIT, WHEN DID I TAKE THE PILL?

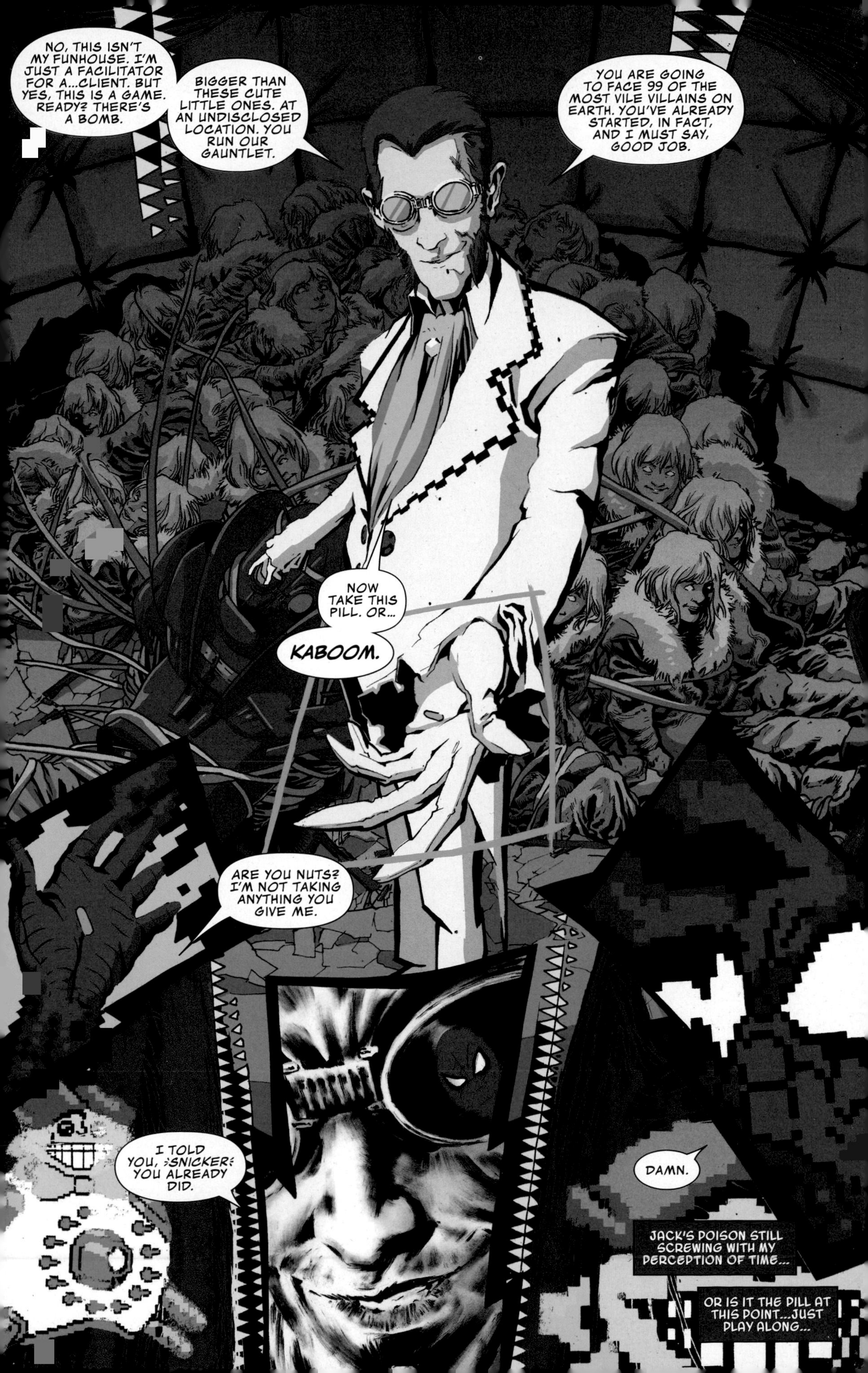
NO, THIS ISN'T MY FUNHOUSE. I'M JUST A FACILITATOR FOR A...CLIENT. BUT YES, THIS IS A GAME. READY? THERE'S A BOMB.
BIGGER THAN THESE CUTE LITTLE ONES. AT AN UNDISCLOSED LOCATION. YOU RUN OUR GAUNTLET.
YOU ARE GOING TO FACE 99 OF THE MOST VILE VILLAINS ON EARTH. YOU'VE ALREADY STARTED, IN FACT, AND I MUST SAY, GOOD JOB.
NOW TAKE THIS PILL. OR...
KABOOM.
ARE YOU NUTS? I'M NOT TAKING ANYTHING YOU GIVE ME.
I TOLD YOU, :SNICKER: YOU ALREADY DID.
DAMN.
JACK'S POISON STILL SCREWING WITH MY PERCEPTION OF TIME...
OR IS IT THE PILL AT THIS POINT...JUST PLAY ALONG...

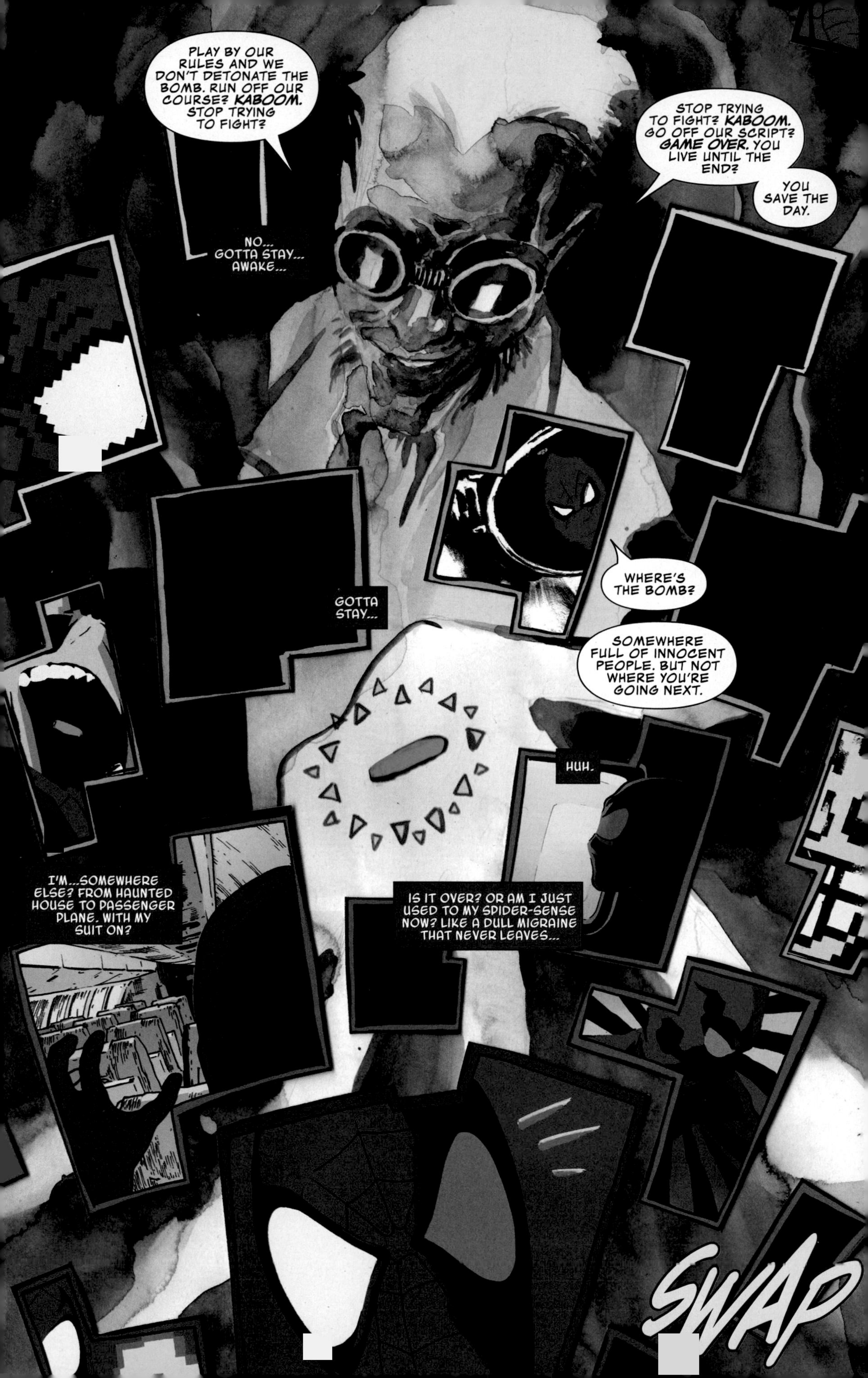
PLAY BY OUR RULES AND WE DON'T DETONATE THE BOMB. RUN OFF OUR COURSE? KABOOM. STOP TRYING TO FIGHT?
STOP TRYING TO FIGHT? KABOOM. GO OFF OUR SCRIPT? GAME OVER. YOU LIVE UNTIL THE END?
YOU SAVE THE DAY.
NO... GOTTA STAY... AWAKE...
GOTTA STAY...
WHERE'S THE BOMB?
SOMEWHERE FULL OF INNOCENT PEOPLE. BUT NOT WHERE YOU'RE GOING NEXT.
HUH.
I'M...SOMEWHERE ELSE? FROM HAUNTED HOUSE TO PASSENGER PLANE. WITH MY SUIT ON?
IS IT OVER? OR AM I JUST USED TO MY SPIDER-SENSE NOW? LIKE A DULL MIGRAINE THAT NEVER LEAVES...
SWAP

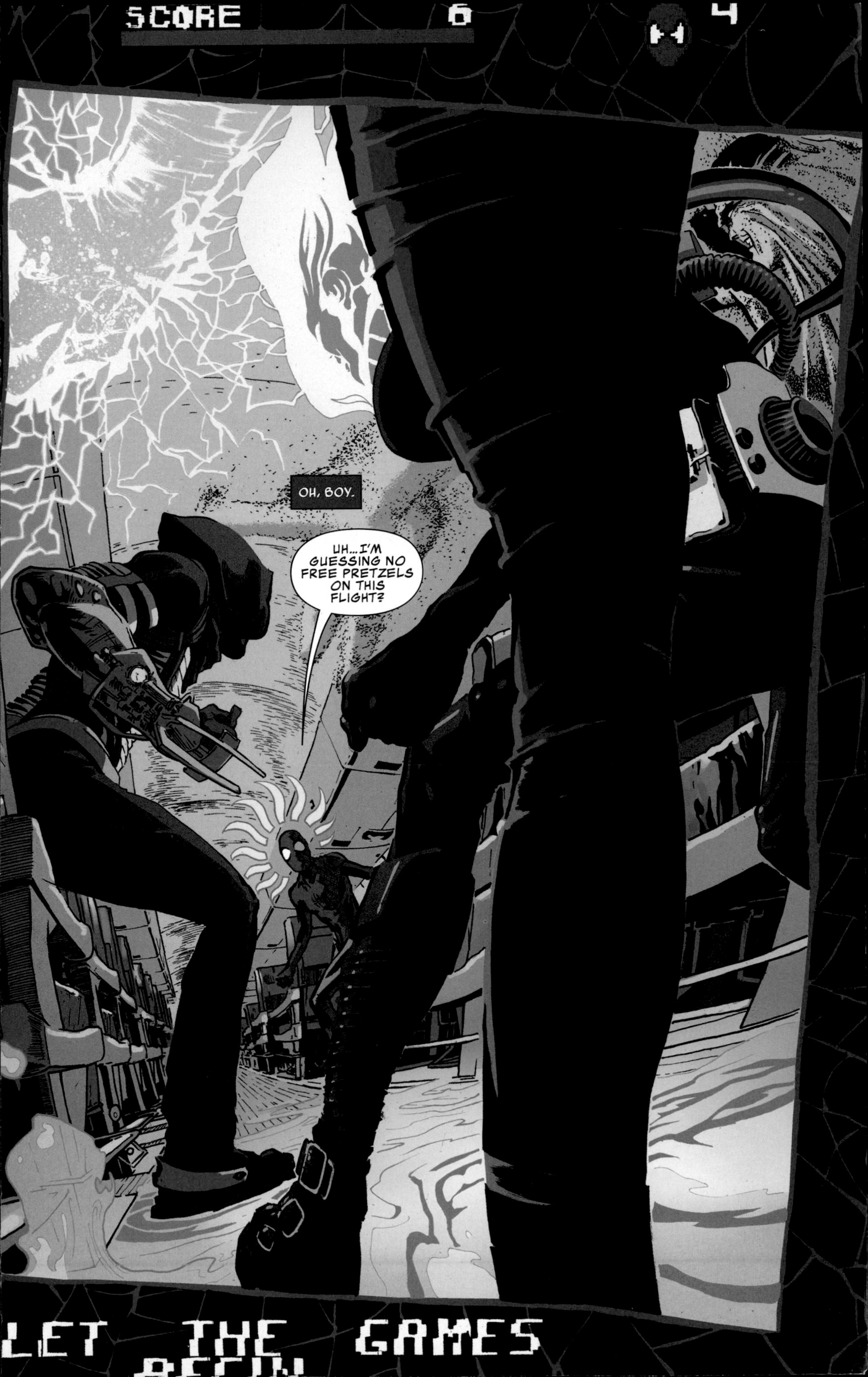
SCORE 6
4
OH, BOY.
UH... I'M GUESSING NO FREE PRETZELS ON THIS FLIGHT?
LET THE GAMES

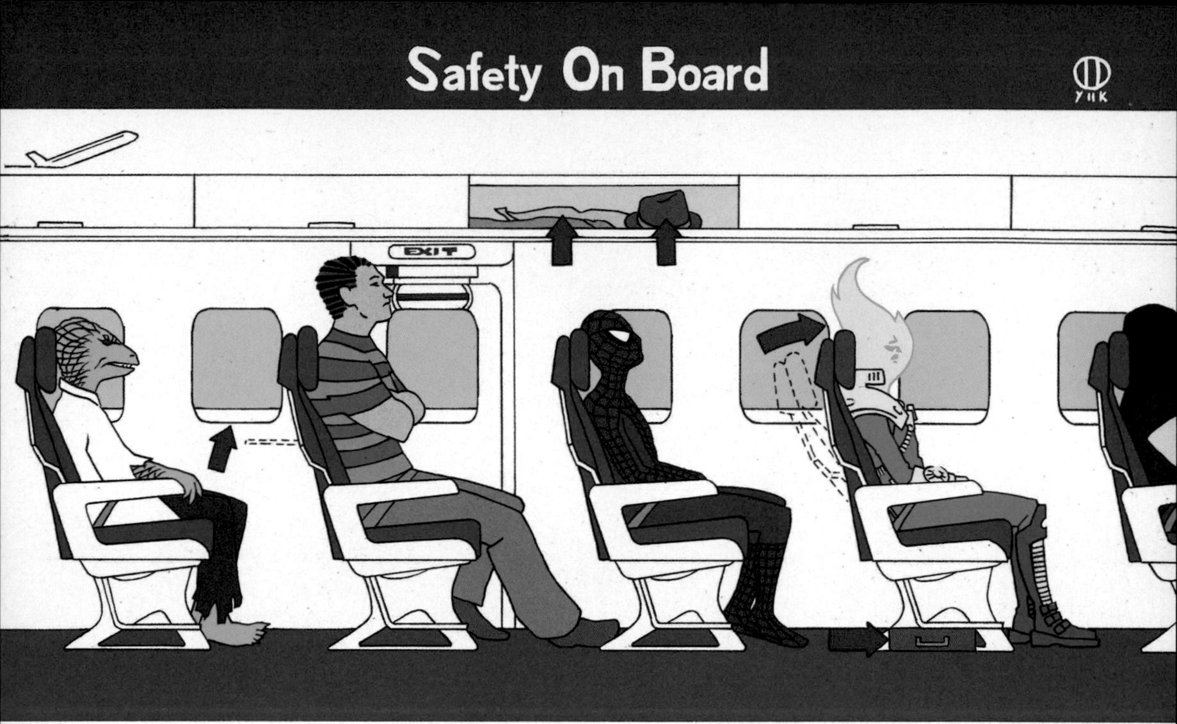
Safety On Board
EXIT

2

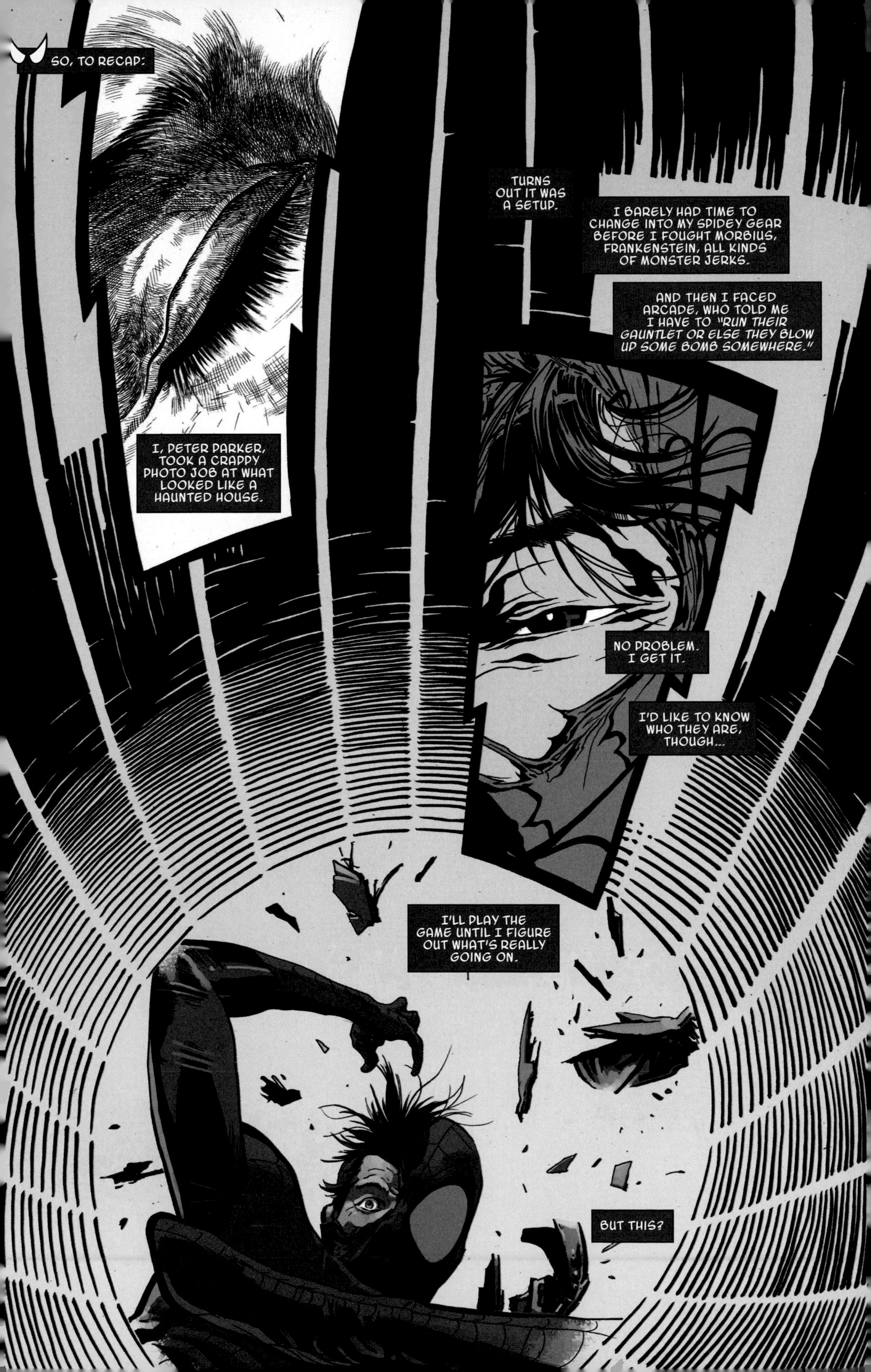
SO, TO RECAP:
I, PETER PARKER, TOOK A CRAPPY PHOTO JOB AT WHAT LOOKED LIKE A HAUNTED HOUSE.
TURNS OUT IT WAS A SETUP.
I BARELY HAD TIME TO CHANGE INTO MY SPIDEY GEAR BEFORE I FOUGHT MORBIUS, FRANKENSTEIN, ALL KINDS OF MONSTER JERKS.
AND THEN I FACED ARCADE, WHO TOLD ME I HAVE TO "RUN THEIR GAUNTLET OR ELSE THEY BLOW UP SOME BOMB SOMEWHERE."
NO PROBLEM. I GET IT.
I'D LIKE TO KNOW WHO THEY ARE, THOUGH...
I'LL PLAY THE GAME UNTIL I FIGURE OUT WHAT'S REALLY GOING ON.
BUT THIS?

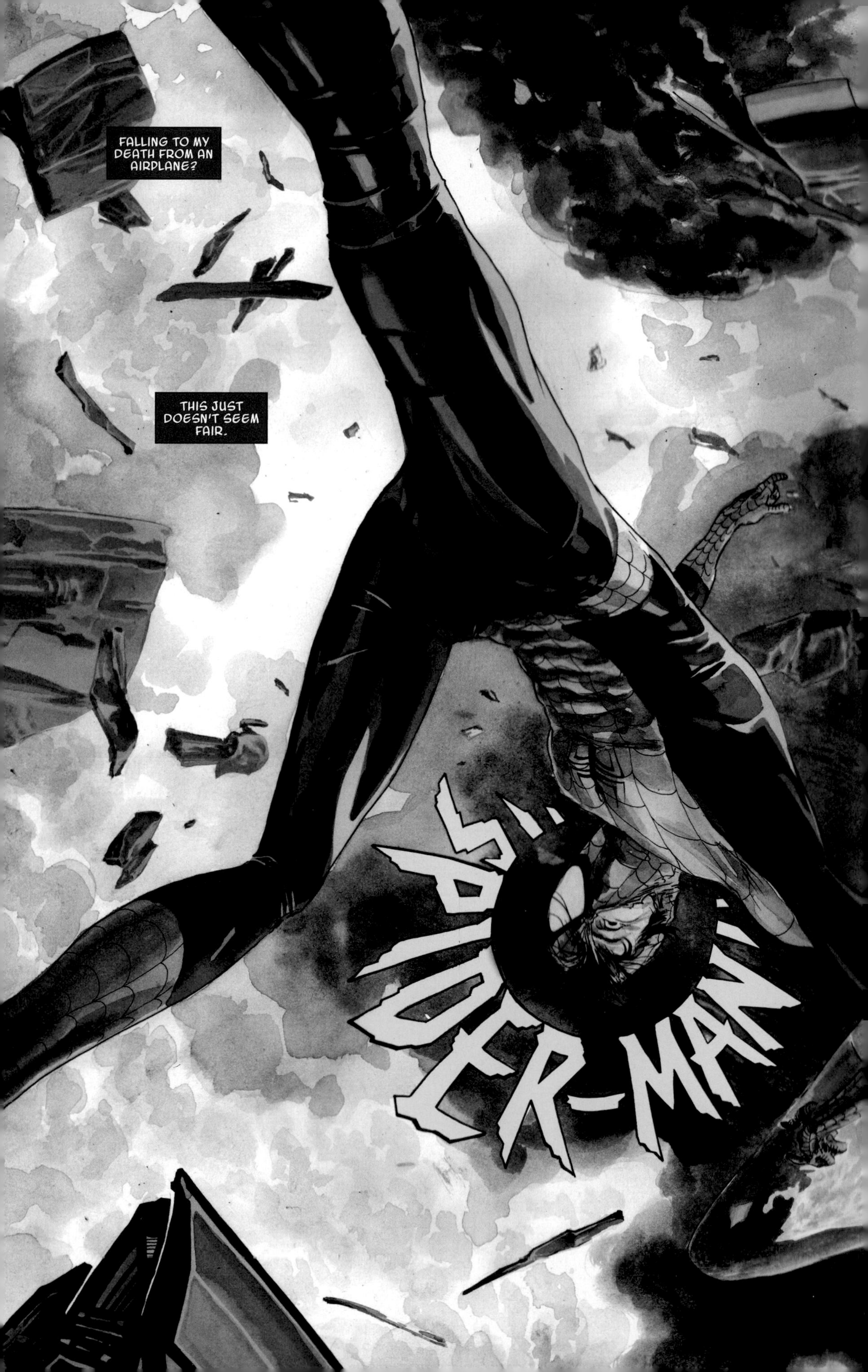
FALLING TO MY DEATH FROM AN AIRPLANE?
THIS JUST DOESN'T SEEM FAIR.

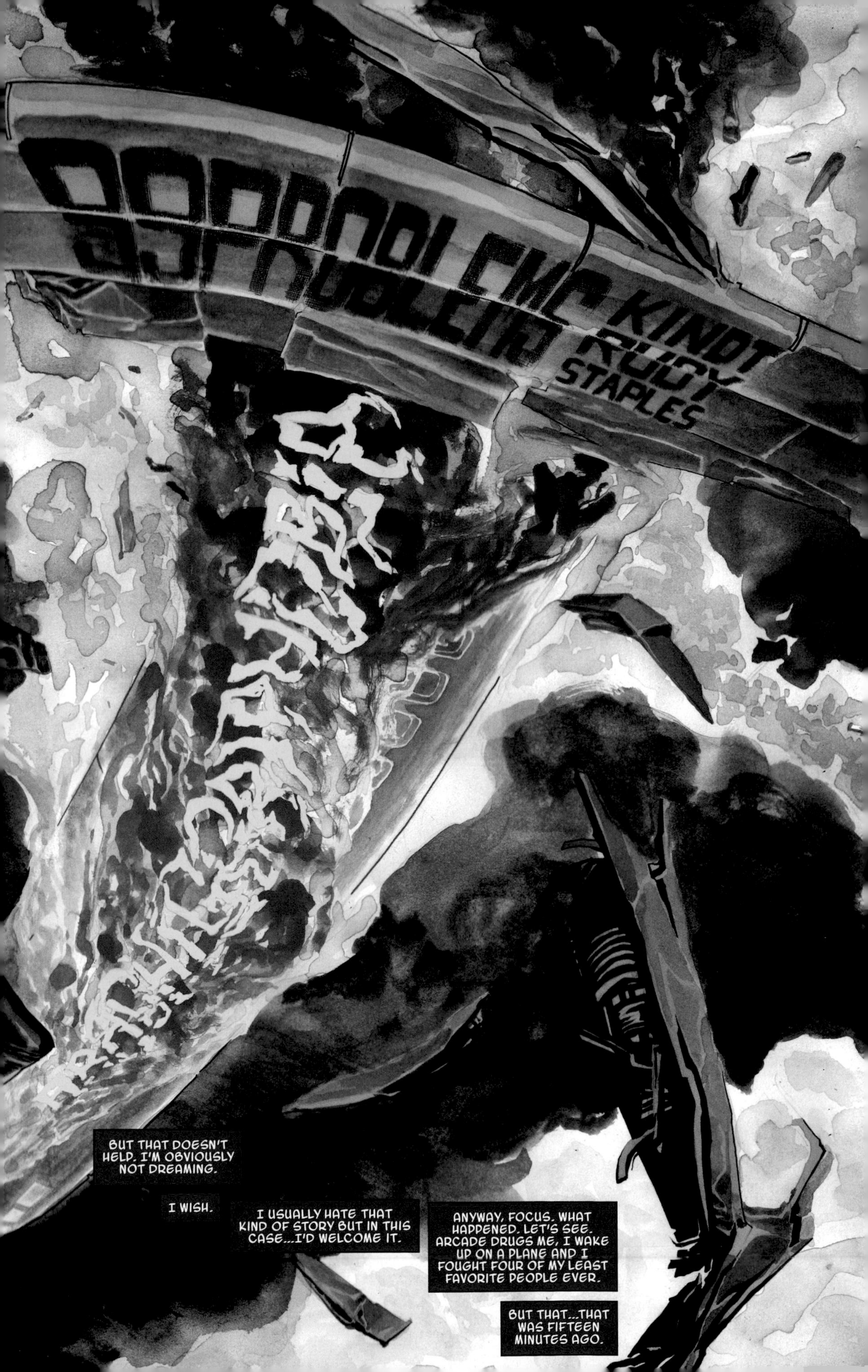
KINDT
RUDY
STAPLES
BUT THAT DOESN'T HELP. I'M OBVIOUSLY NOT DREAMING.
I WISH.
I USUALLY HATE THAT KIND OF STORY BUT IN THIS CASE...I'D WELCOME IT.
ANYWAY, FOCUS. WHAT HAPPENED. LET'S SEE. ARCADE DRUGS ME, I WAKE UP ON A PLANE AND I FOUGHT FOUR OF MY LEAST FAVORITE PEOPLE EVER.
BUT THAT...THAT WAS FIFTEEN MINUTES AGO.

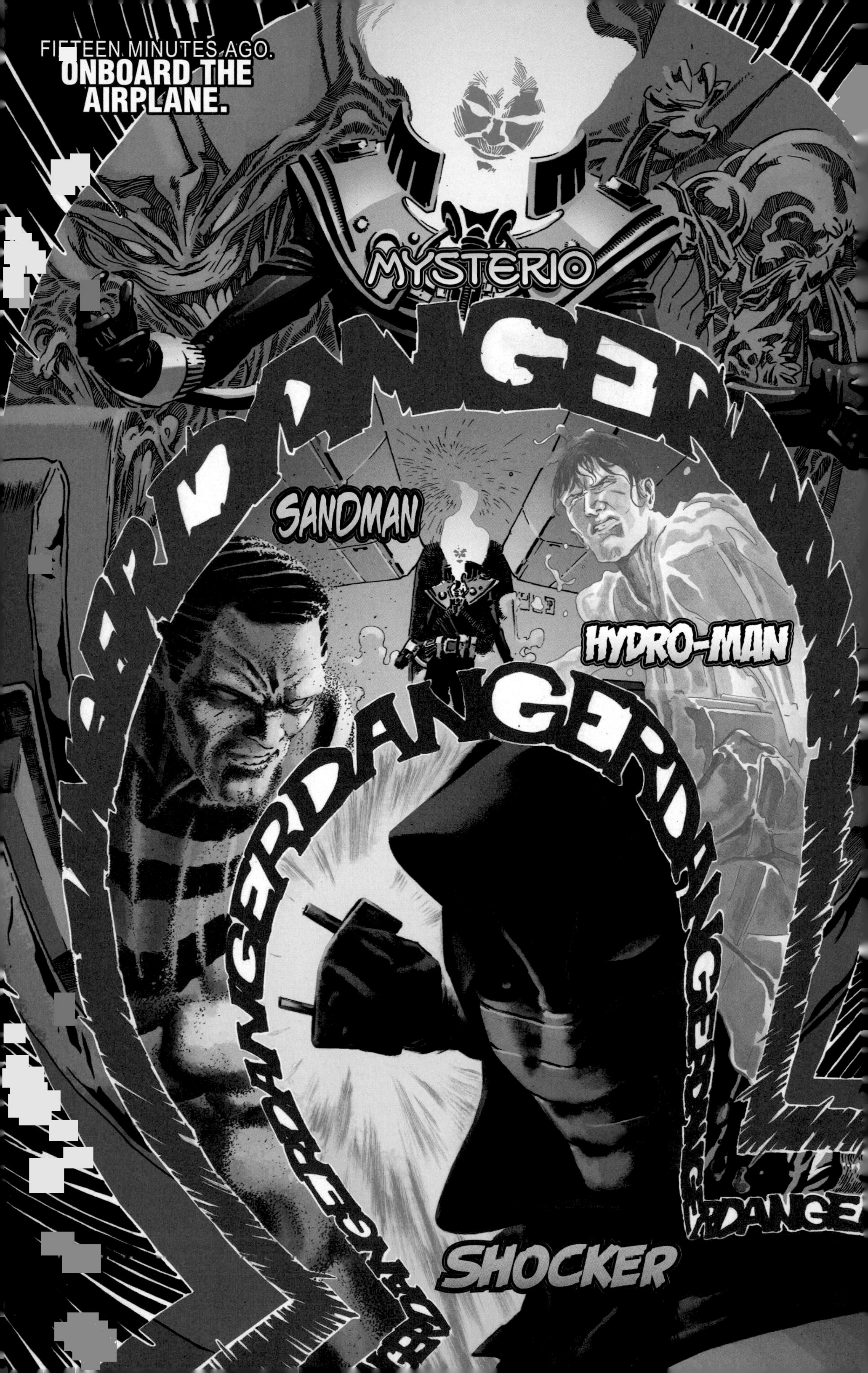
FIFTEEN MINUTES AGO.
ONBOARD THE AIRPLANE.
MYSTERIO
SANDMAN
HYDRO-MAN
SHOCKER

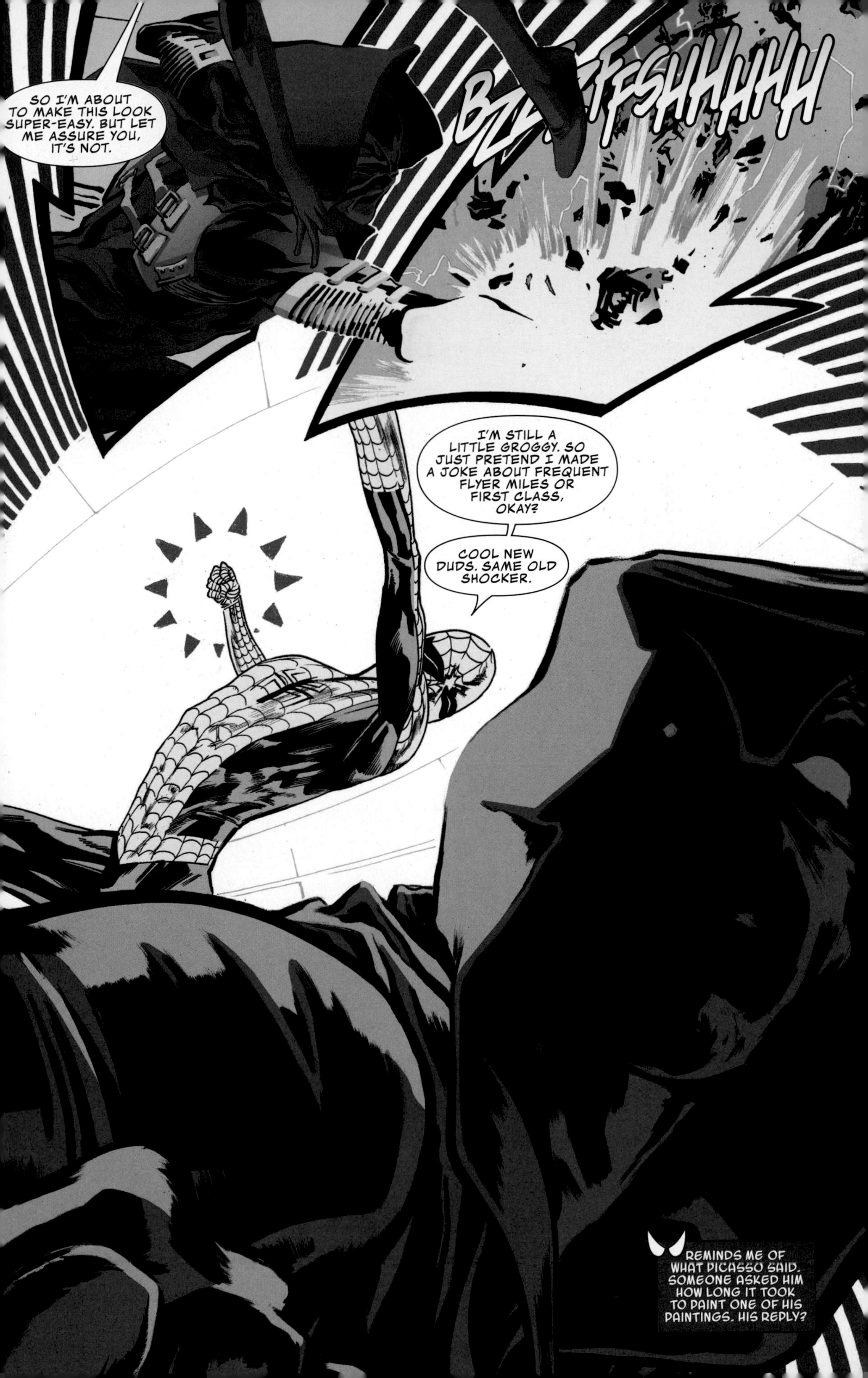
SO I'M ABOUT TO MAKE THIS LOOK SUPER-EASY. BUT LET ME ASSURE YOU, IT'S NOT.
I'M STILL A LITTLE GROGGY. SO JUST PRETEND I MADE A JOKE ABOUT FREQUENT FLYER MILES OR FIRST CLASS, OKAY?
COOL NEW DUDS. SAME OLD SHOCKER.
REMINDS ME OF WHAT PICASSO SAID. SOMEONE ASKED HIM HOW LONG IT TOOK TO PAINT ONE OF HIS PAINTINGS. HIS REPLY?

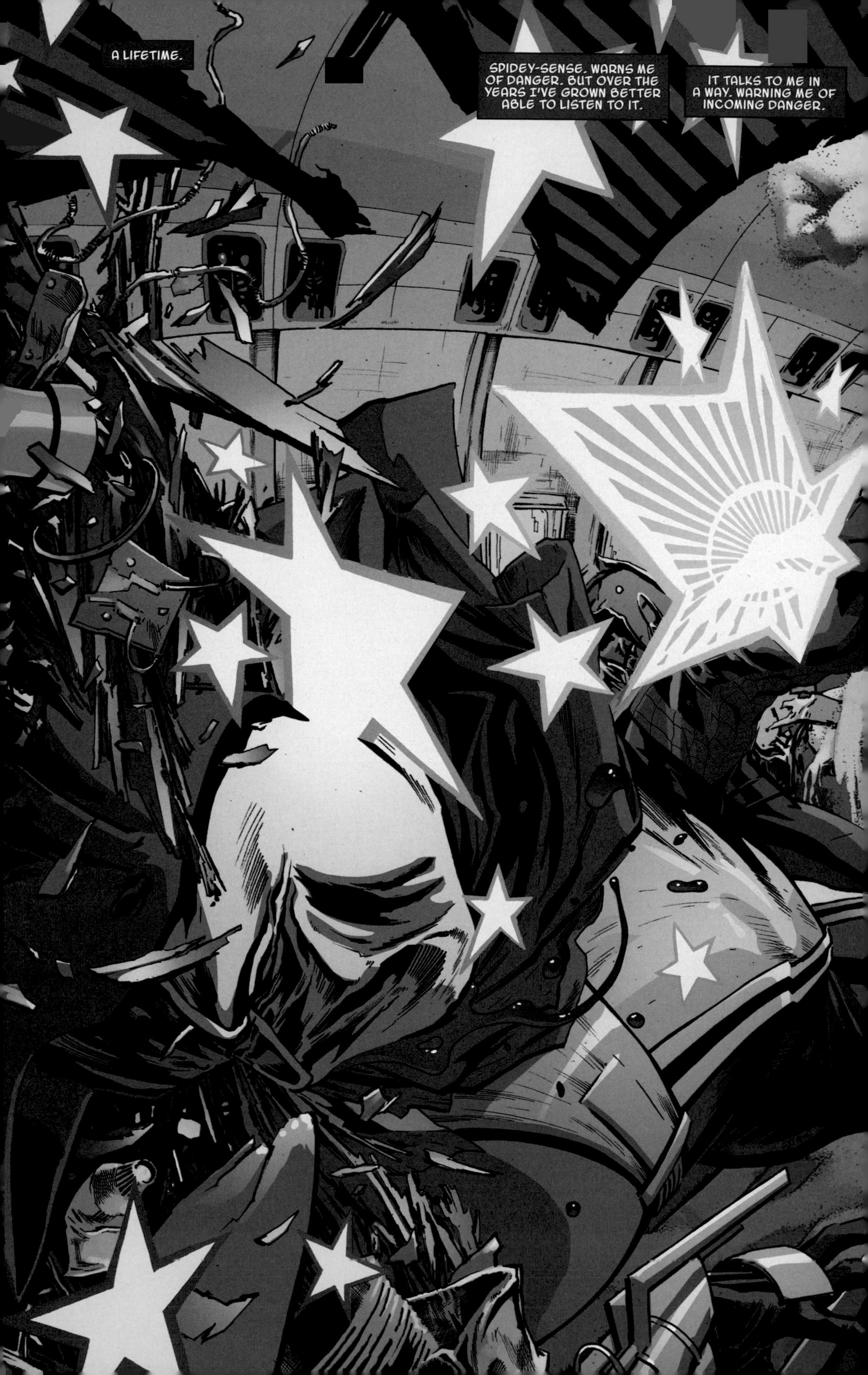
A LIFETIME.
SPIDEY-SENSE. WARNS ME OF DANGER. BUT OVER THE YEARS I'VE GROWN BETTER ABLE TO LISTEN TO IT.
IT TALKS TO ME IN A WAY. WARNING ME OF INCOMING DANGER.

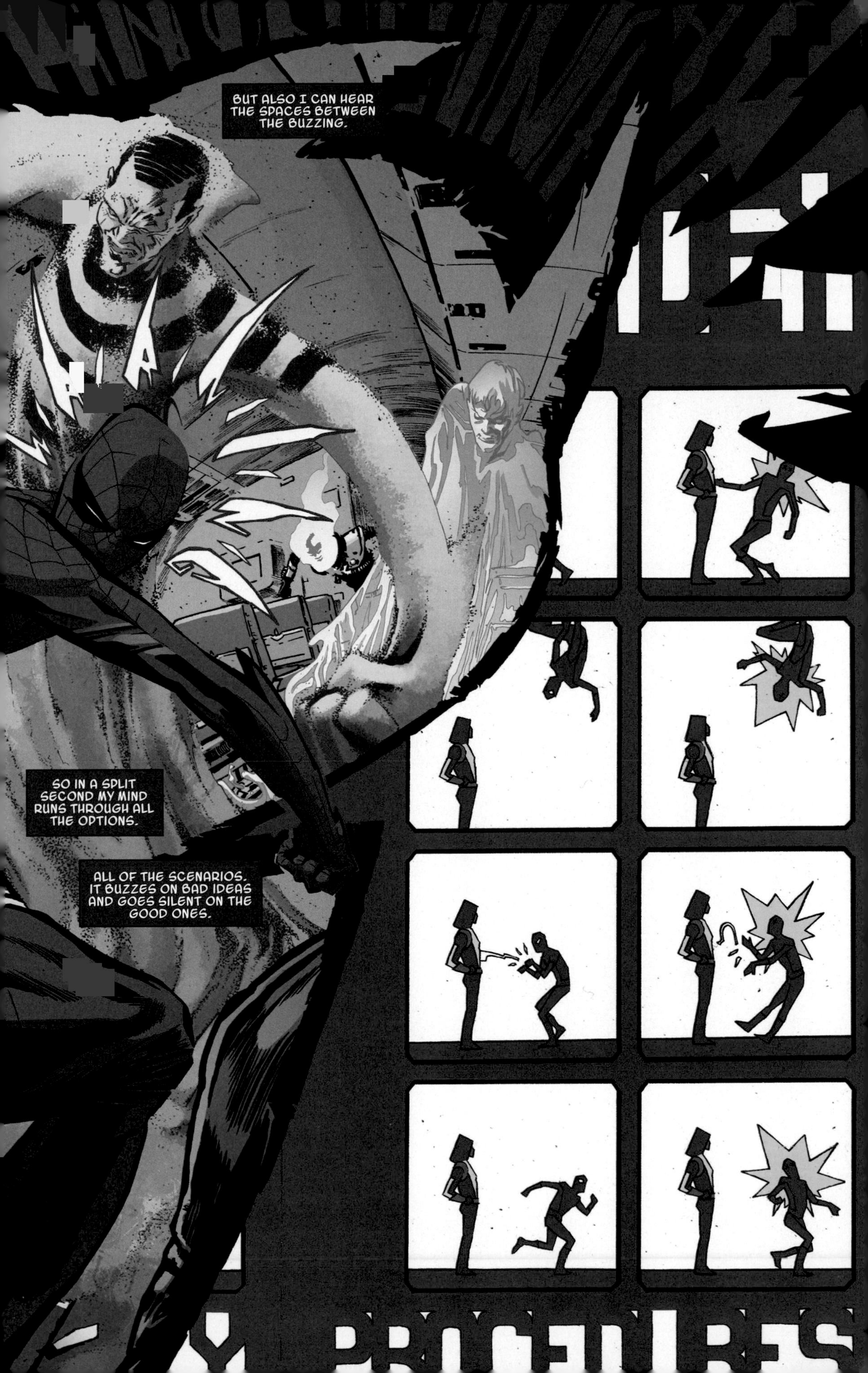
BUT ALSO I CAN HEAR THE SPACES BETWEEN THE BUZZING.
SO IN A SPLIT SECOND MY MIND RUNS THROUGH ALL THE OPTIONS.
ALL OF THE SCENARIOS. IT BUZZES ON BAD IDEAS AND GOES SILENT ON THE GOOD ONES.

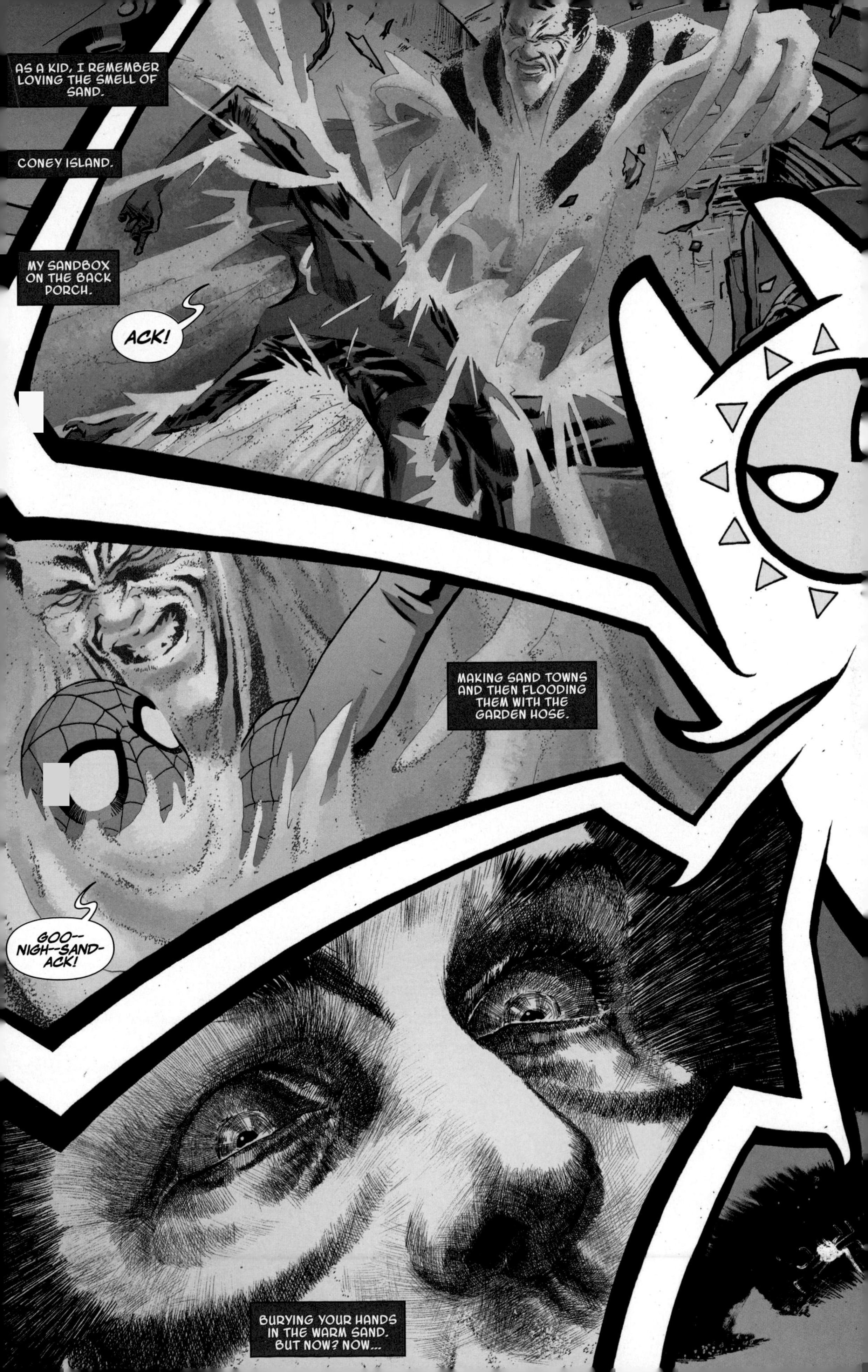
AS A KID, I REMEMBER LOVING THE SMELL OF SAND.
CONEY ISLAND.
MY SANDBOX ON THE BACK PORCH.
ACK!
MAKING SAND TOWNS AND THEN FLOODING THEM WITH THE GARDEN HOSE.
GOO-- NIGH--SAND-ACK!
BURYING YOUR HANDS IN THE WARM SAND. BUT NOW? NOW...

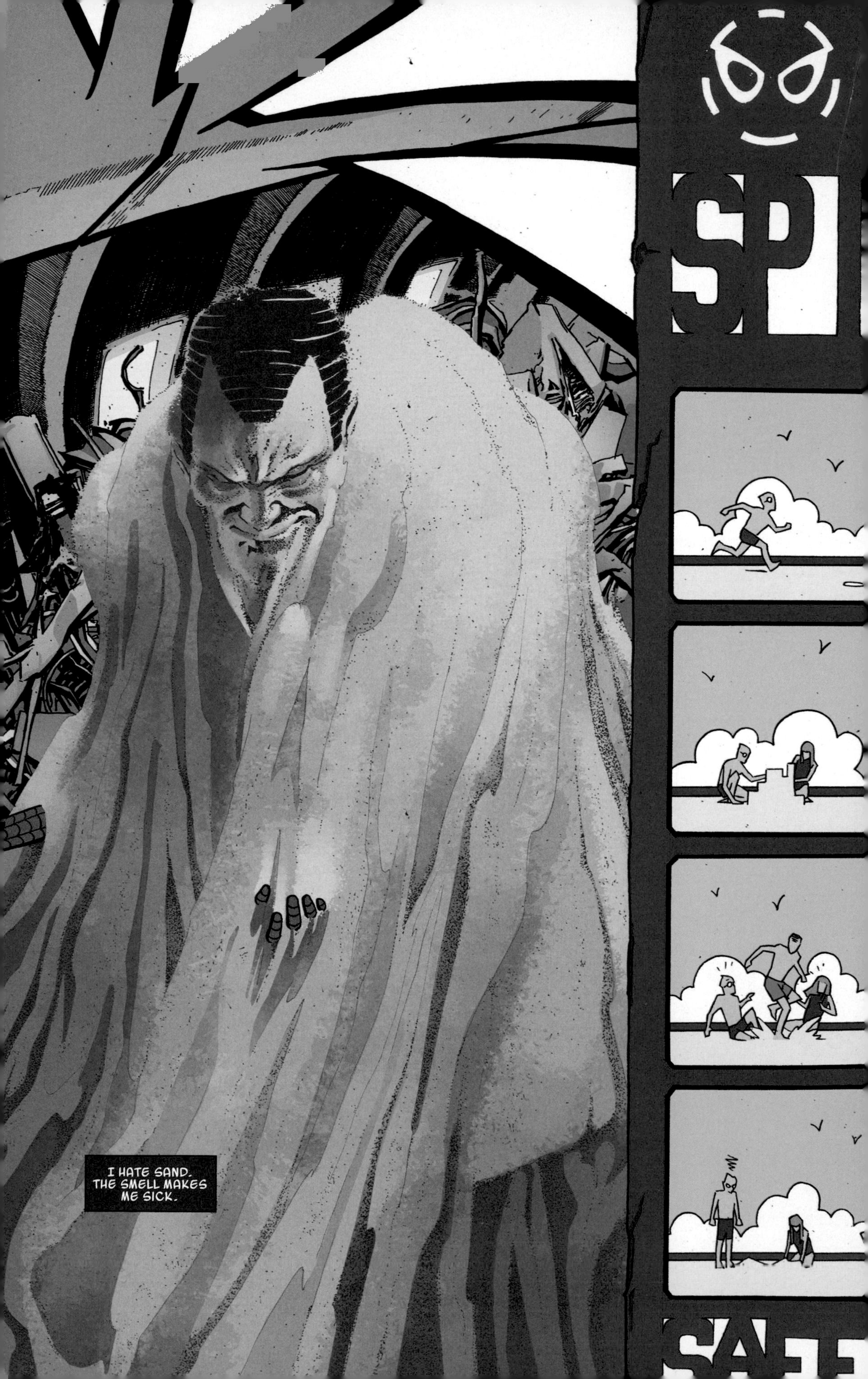
I HATE SAND.
THE SMELL MAKES
ME SICK.

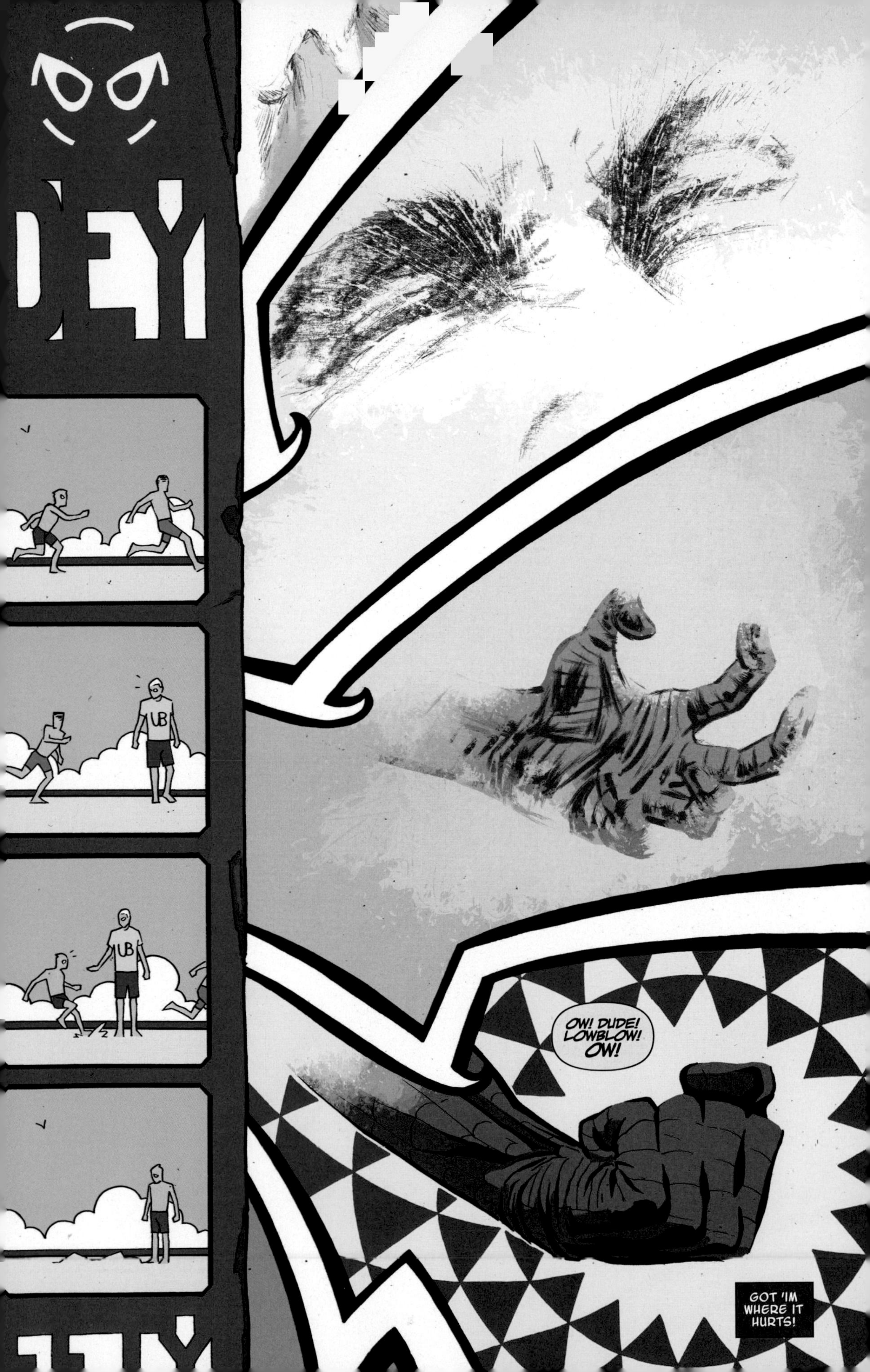
OW! DUDE! LOWBLOW! OW!
GOT 'IM WHERE IT HURTS!

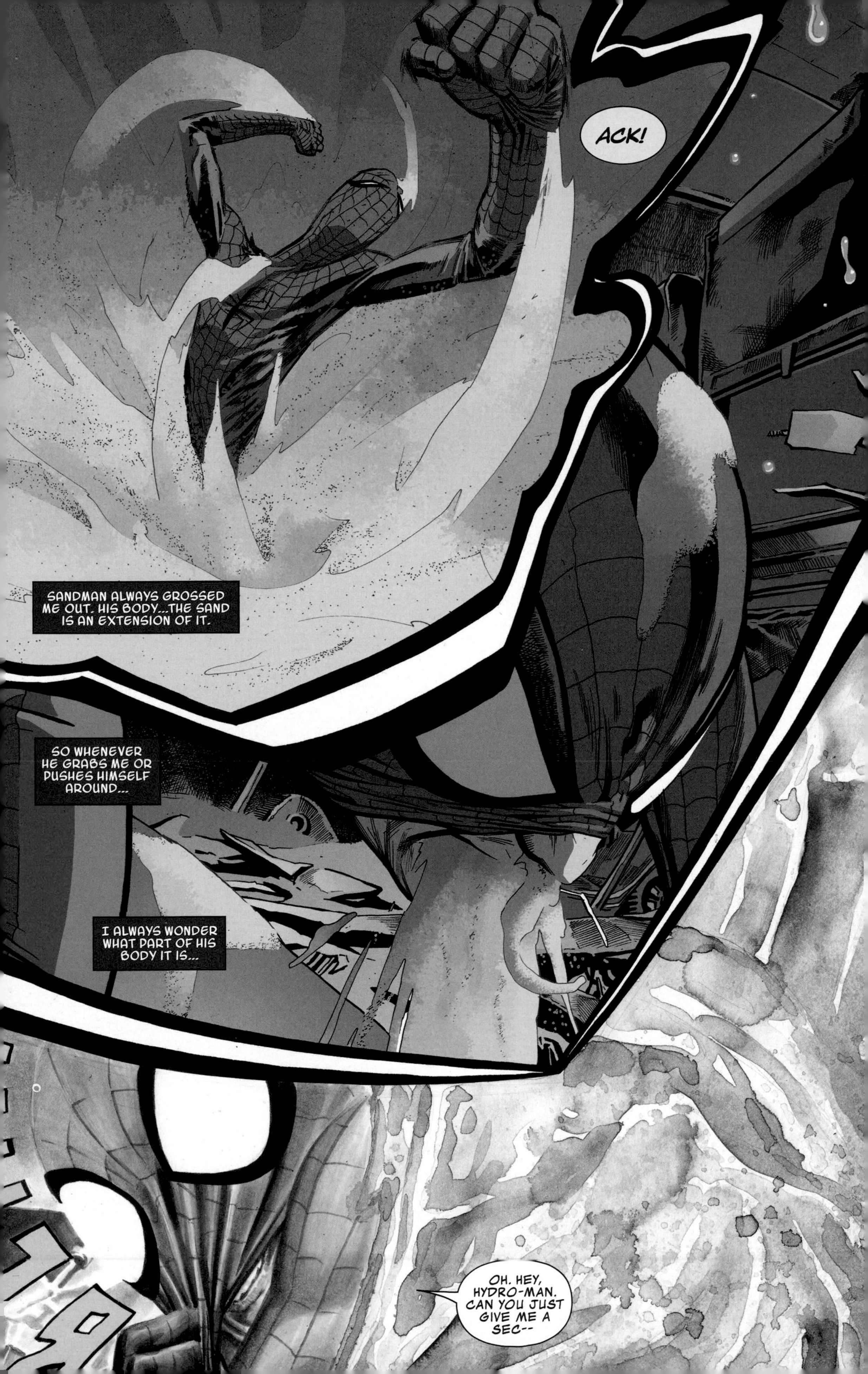

ACK!
SANDMAN ALWAYS GROSSED ME OUT. HIS BODY...THE SAND IS AN EXTENSION OF IT.
SO WHENEVER HE GRABS ME OR PUSHES HIMSELF AROUND...
I ALWAYS WONDER WHAT PART OF HIS BODY IT IS...
OH. HEY, HYDRO-MAN. CAN YOU JUST GIVE ME A SEC--

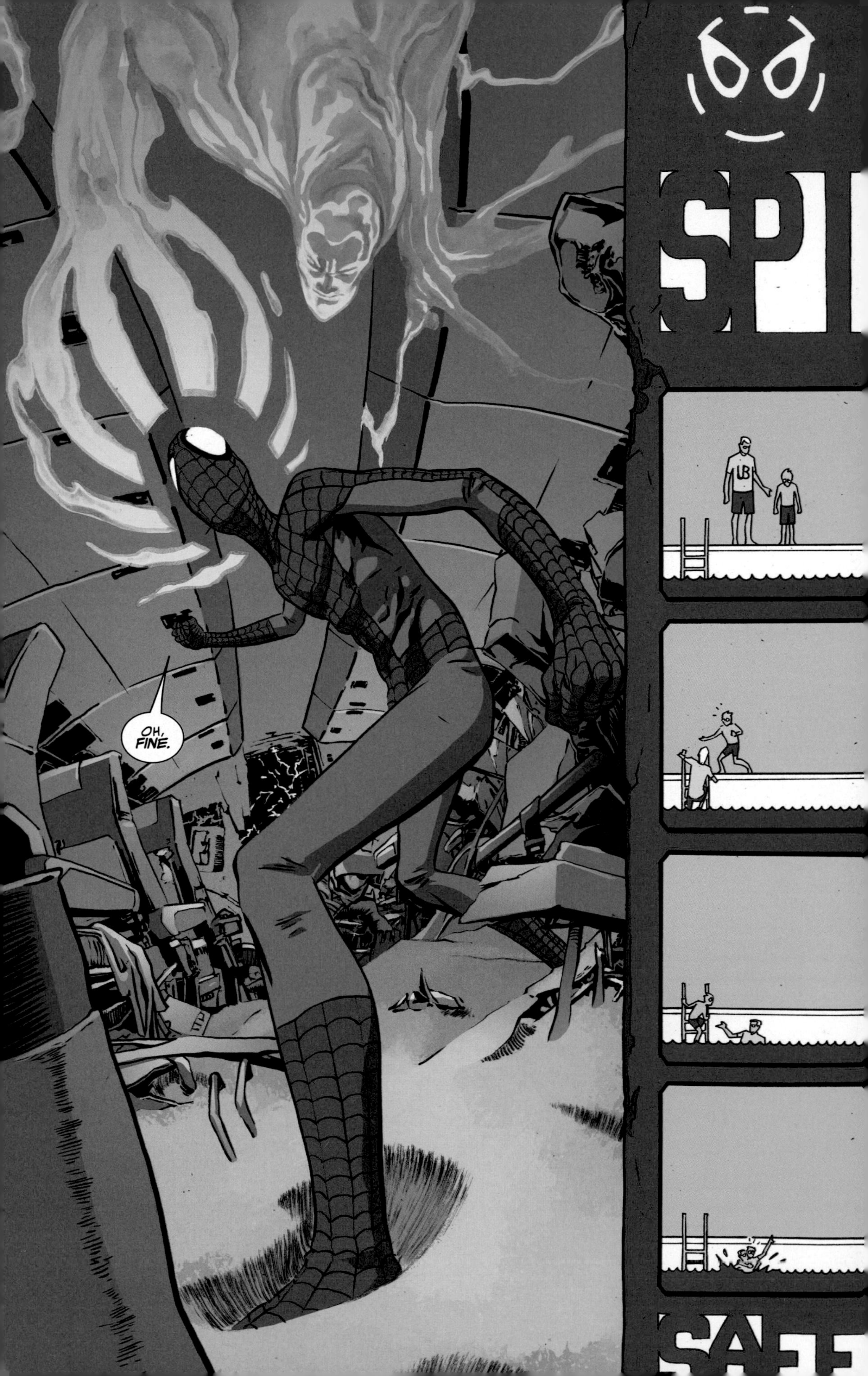
OH, FINE.
SPI
SAF

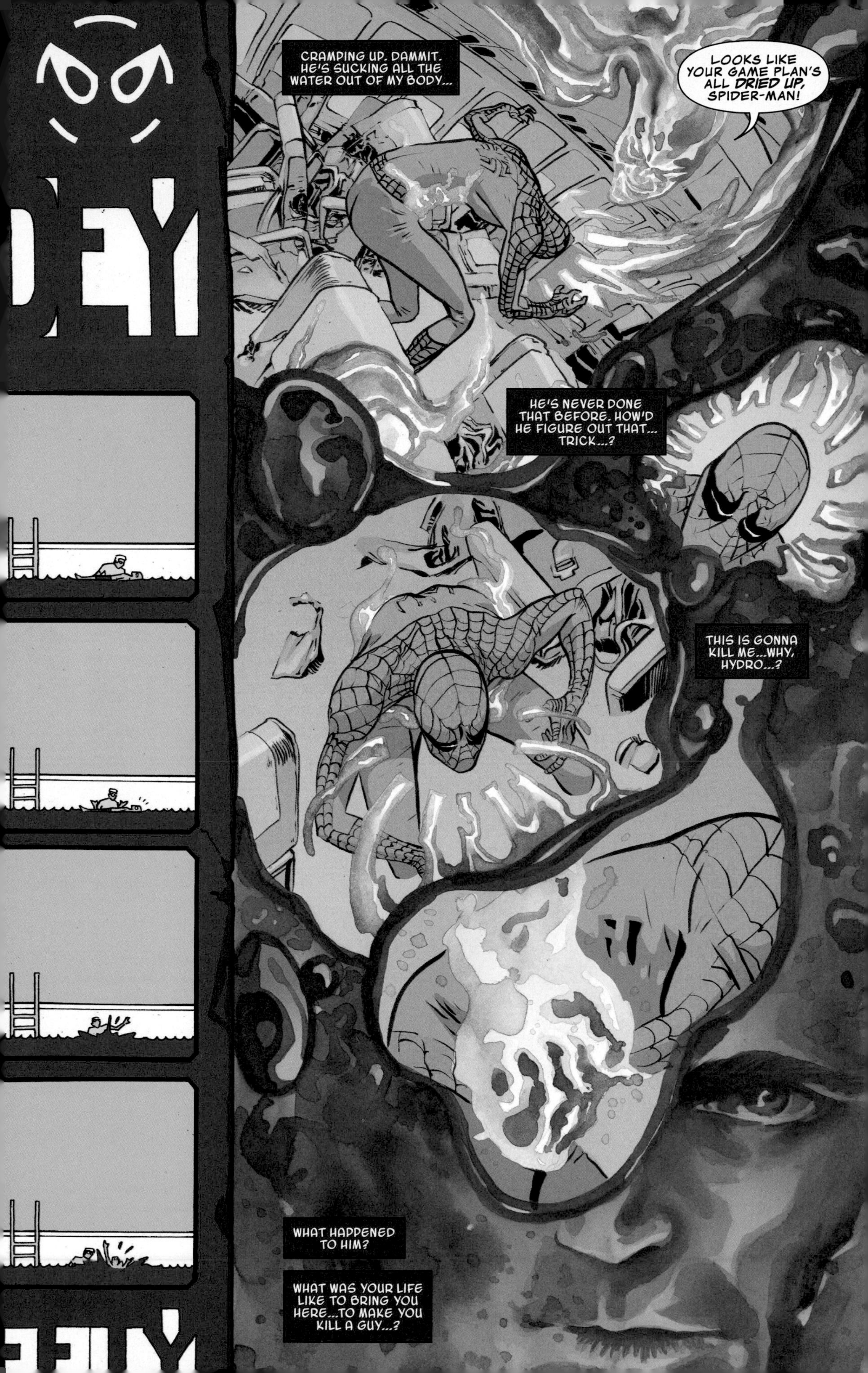
CRAMPING UP. DAMMIT. HE'S SUCKING ALL THE WATER OUT OF MY BODY...
LOOKS LIKE YOUR GAME PLAN'S ALL DRIED UP, SPIDER-MAN!
HE'S NEVER DONE THAT BEFORE. HOW'D HE FIGURE OUT THAT... TRICK...?
THIS IS GONNA KILL ME...WHY, HYDRO...?
WHAT HAPPENED TO HIM?
WHAT WAS YOUR LIFE LIKE TO BRING YOU HERE...TO MAKE YOU KILL A GUY...?

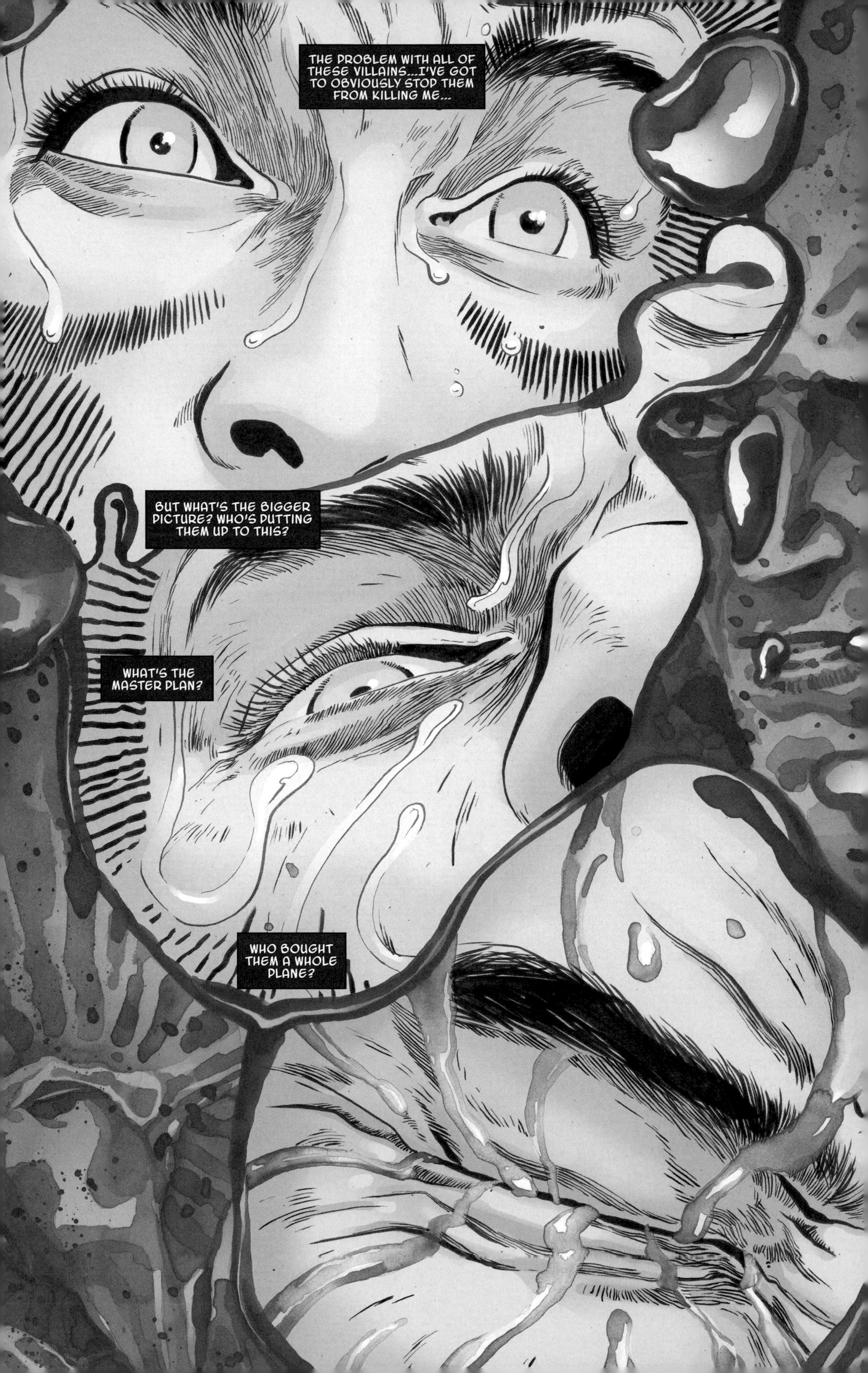
THE PROBLEM WITH ALL OF THESE VILLAINS...I'VE GOT TO OBVIOUSLY STOP THEM FROM KILLING ME...
BUT WHAT'S THE BIGGER PICTURE? WHO'S PUTTING THEM UP TO THIS?
WHAT'S THE MASTER PLAN?
WHO BOUGHT THEM A WHOLE PLANE?

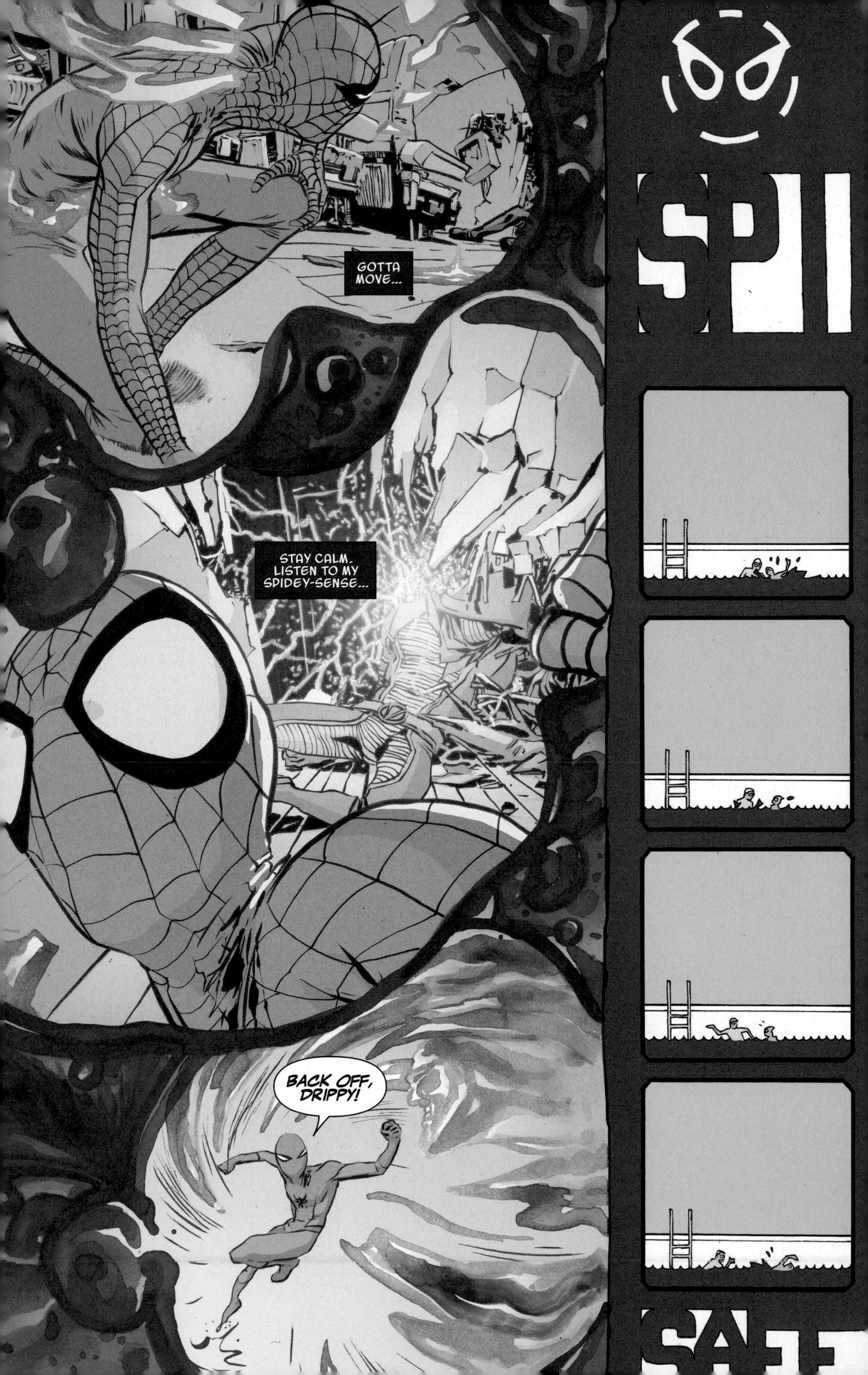
GOTTA MOVE...
STAY CALM. LISTEN TO MY SPIDEY-SENSE...
BACK OFF, DRIPPY!
SPI
SAF

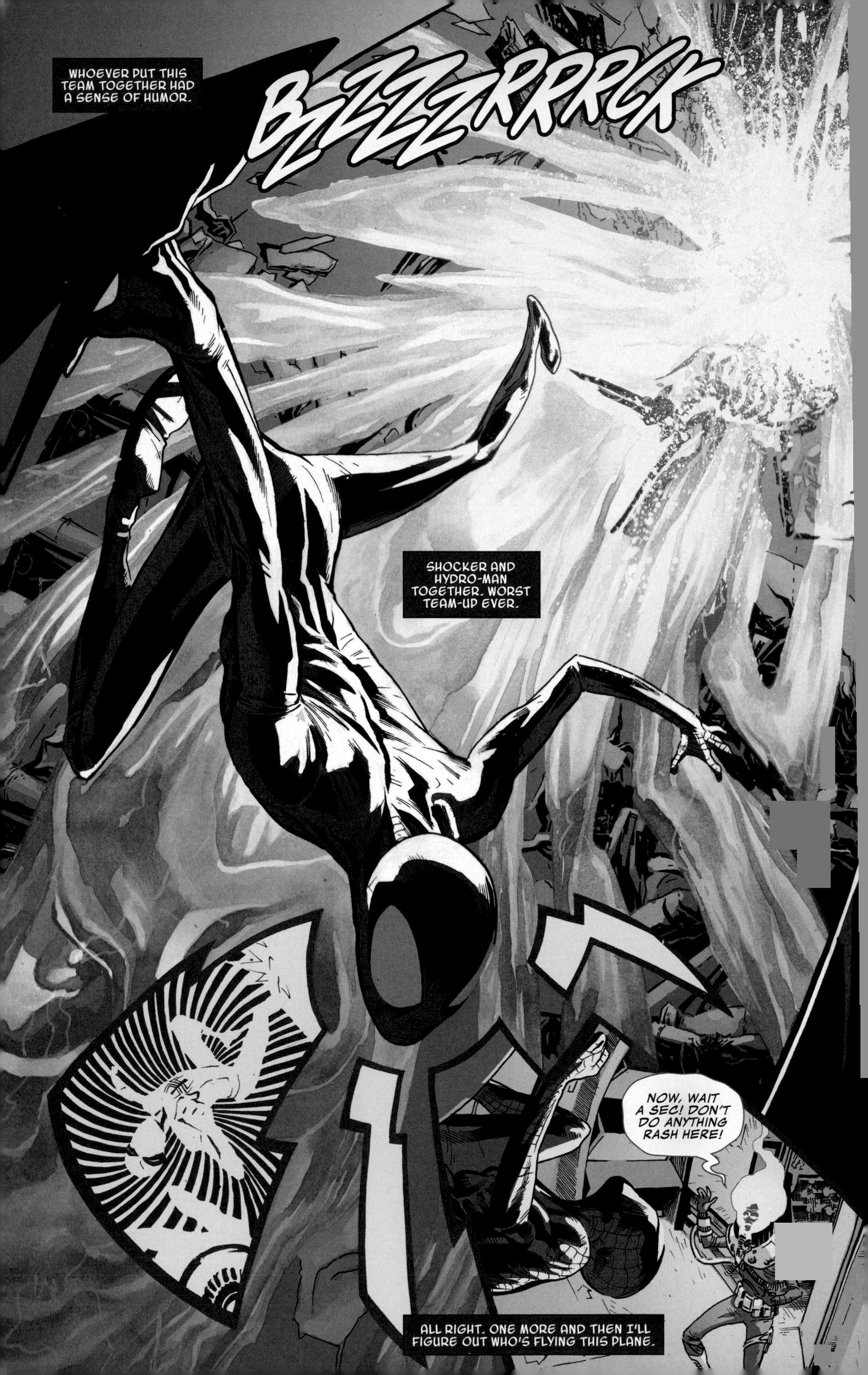
WHOEVER PUT THIS TEAM TOGETHER HAD A SENSE OF HUMOR.
BZZZZRRRRCK
SHOCKER AND HYDRO-MAN TOGETHER. WORST TEAM-UP EVER.
NOW, WAIT A SEC! DON'T DO ANYTHING RASH HERE!
ALL RIGHT. ONE MORE AND THEN I'LL FIGURE OUT WHO'S FLYING THIS PLANE.

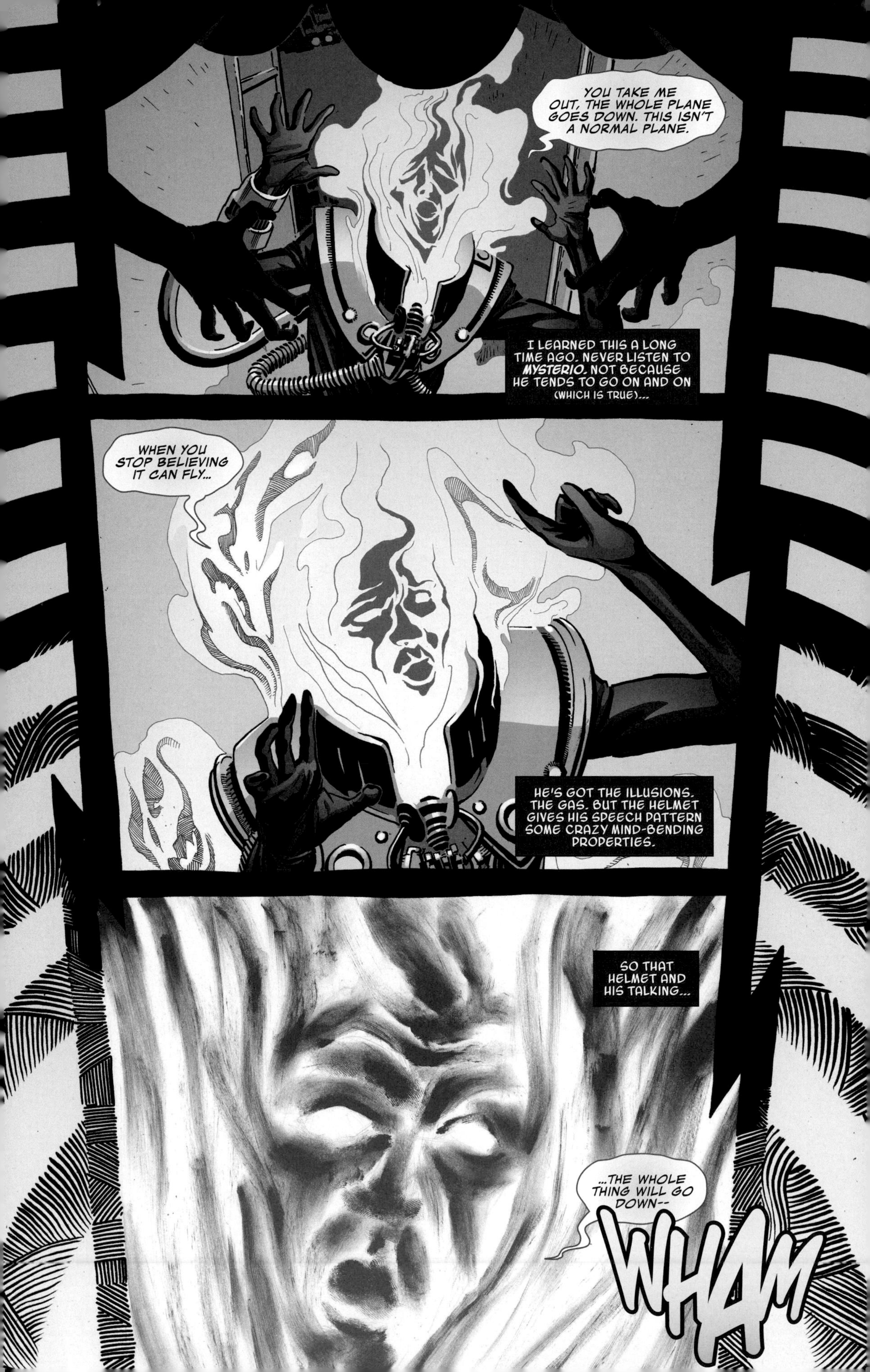
YOU TAKE ME OUT, THE WHOLE PLANE GOES DOWN. THIS ISN'T A NORMAL PLANE.
I LEARNED THIS A LONG TIME AGO. NEVER LISTEN TO MYSTERIO. NOT BECAUSE HE TENDS TO GO ON AND ON (WHICH IS TRUE)...
WHEN YOU STOP BELIEVING IT CAN FLY...
HE'S GOT THE ILLUSIONS. THE GAS. BUT THE HELMET GIVES HIS SPEECH PATTERN SOME CRAZY MIND-BENDING PROPERTIES.
SO THAT HELMET AND HIS TALKING...
...THE WHOLE THING WILL GO DOWN--
WHAM

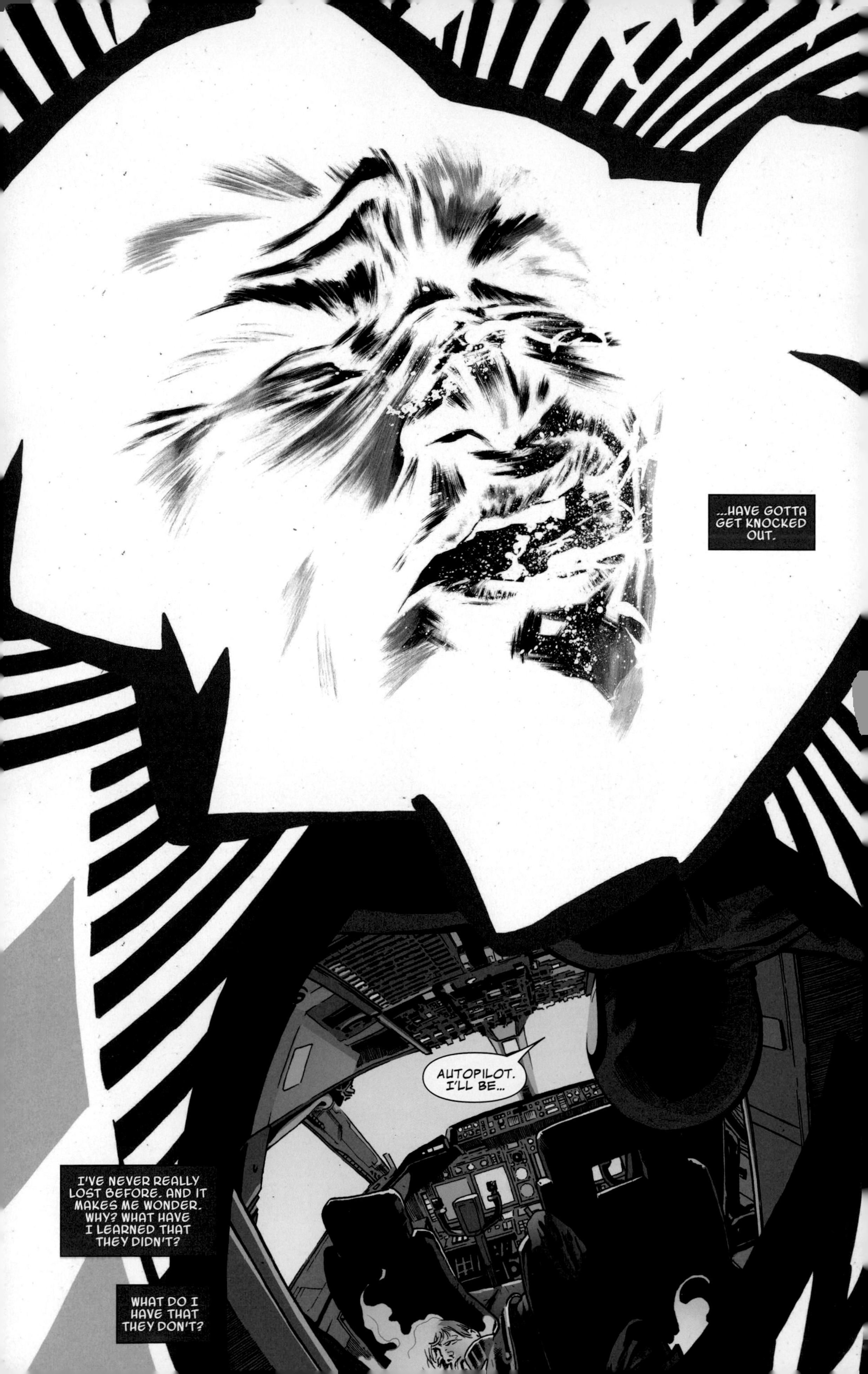
...HAVE GOTTA GET KNOCKED OUT.
AUTOPILOT. I'LL BE...
I'VE NEVER REALLY LOST BEFORE. AND IT MAKES ME WONDER. WHY? WHAT HAVE I LEARNED THAT THEY DIDN'T?
WHAT DO I HAVE THAT THEY DON'T?

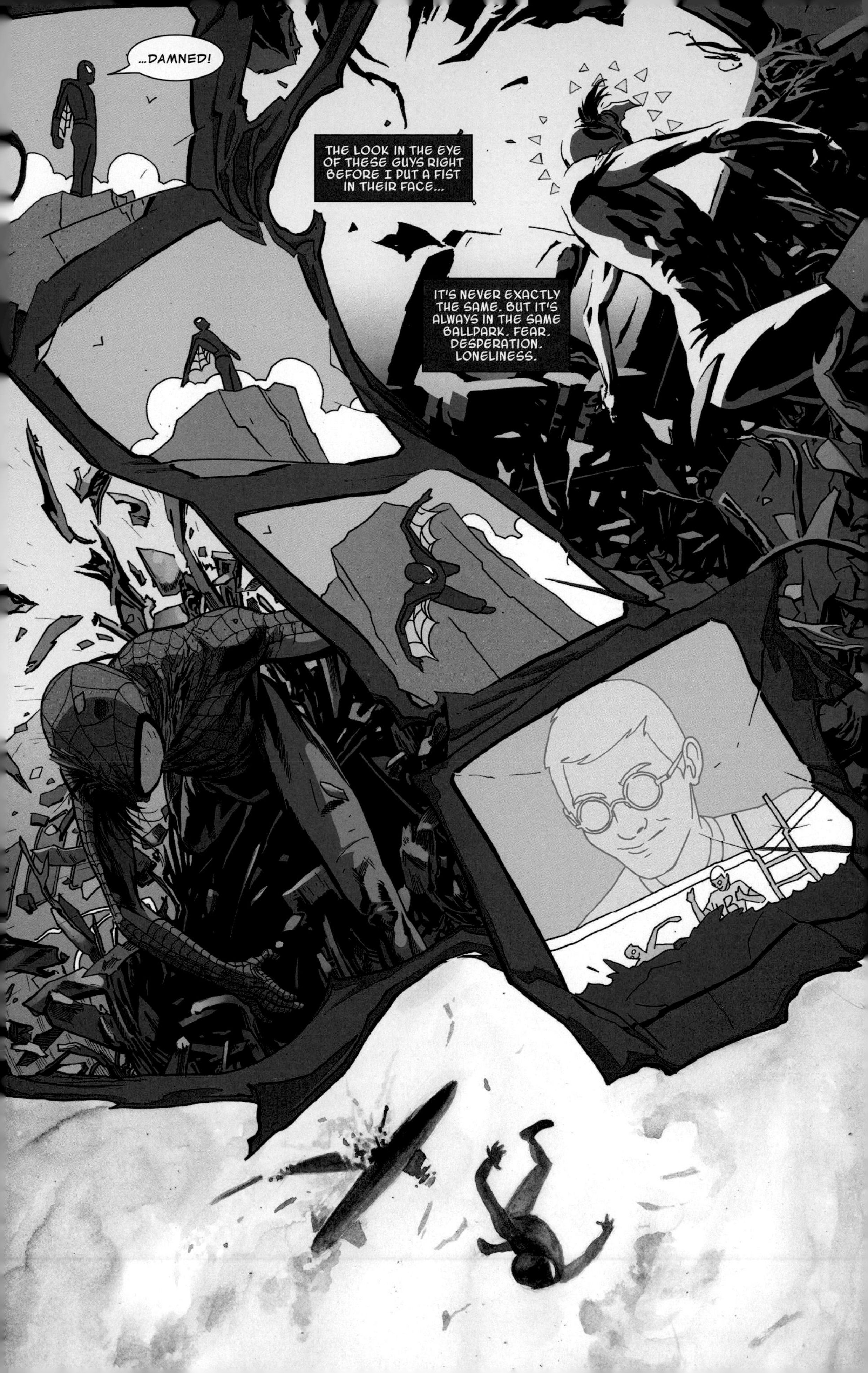
...DAMNED!
THE LOOK IN THE EYE OF THESE GUYS RIGHT BEFORE I PUT A FIST IN THEIR FACE...
IT'S NEVER EXACTLY THE SAME. BUT IT'S ALWAYS IN THE SAME BALLPARK. FEAR. DESPERATION. LONELINESS.

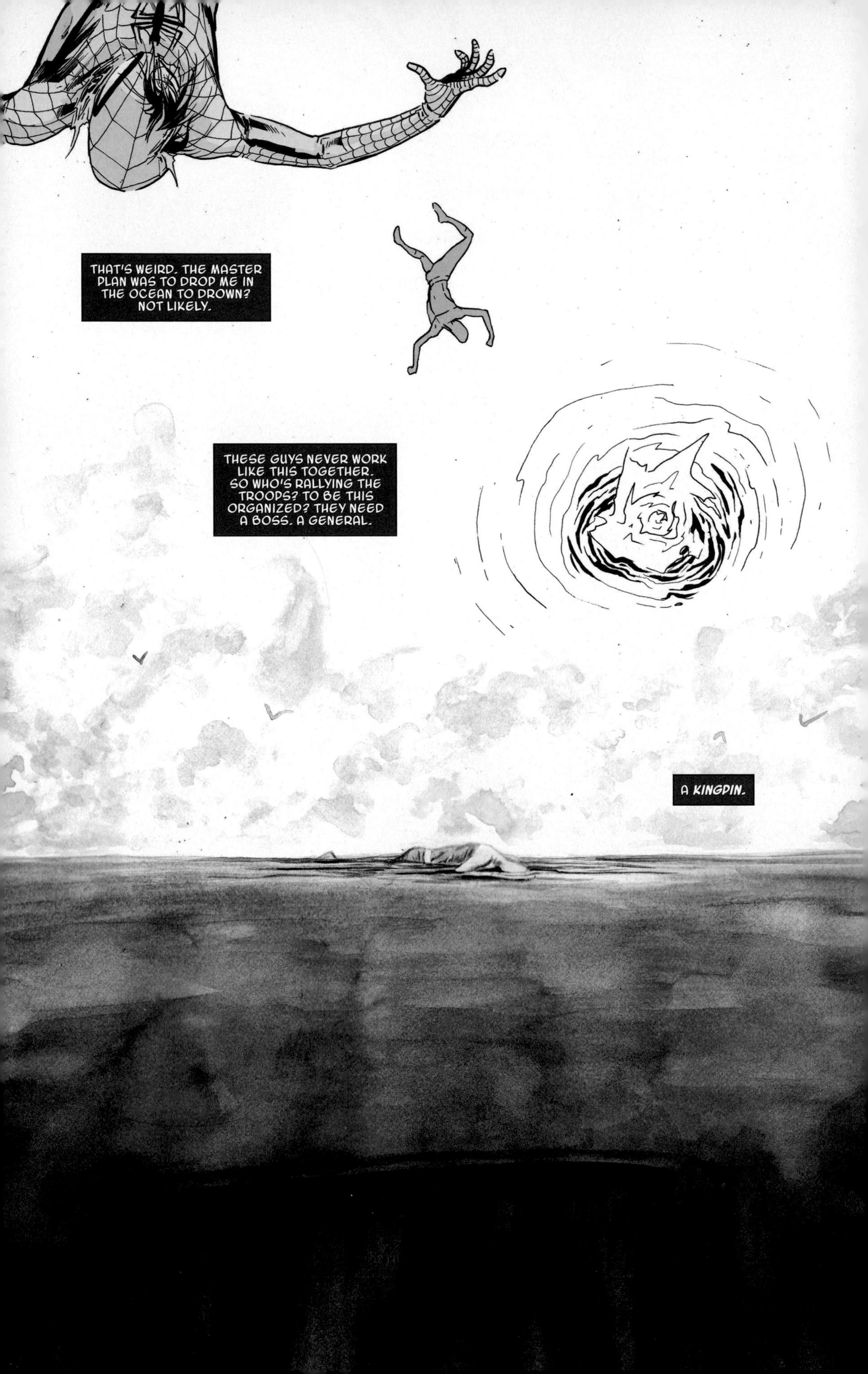
THAT'S WEIRD. THE MASTER PLAN WAS TO DROP ME IN THE OCEAN TO DROWN? NOT LIKELY.
THESE GUYS NEVER WORK LIKE THIS TOGETHER. SO WHO'S RALLYING THE TROOPS? TO BE THIS ORGANIZED? THEY NEED A BOSS. A GENERAL.
A KINGPIN.

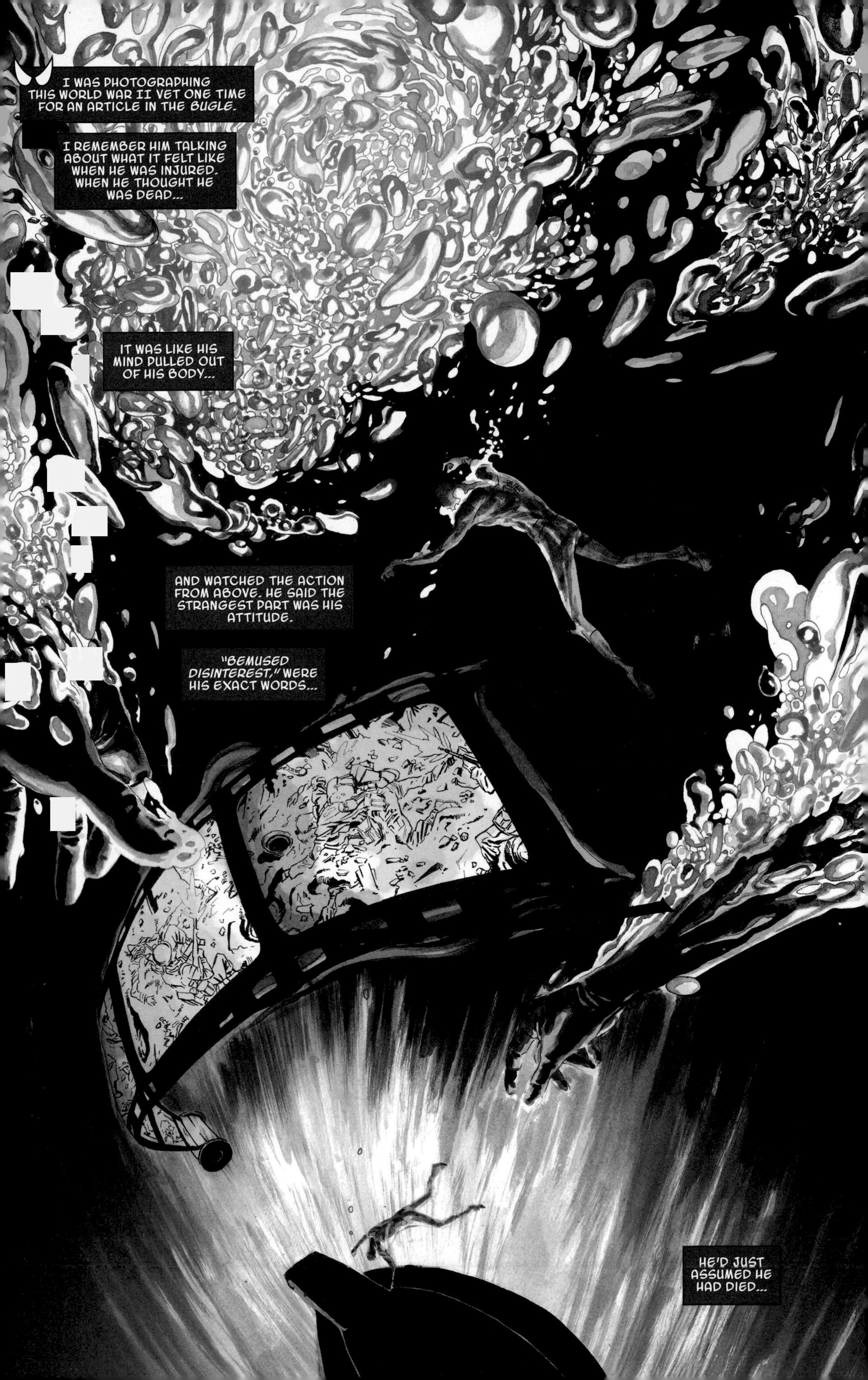
I WAS PHOTOGRAPHING THIS WORLD WAR II VET ONE TIME FOR AN ARTICLE IN THE BUGLE.
I REMEMBER HIM TALKING ABOUT WHAT IT FELT LIKE WHEN HE WAS INJURED. WHEN HE THOUGHT HE WAS DEAD...
IT WAS LIKE HIS MIND PULLED OUT OF HIS BODY...
AND WATCHED THE ACTION FROM ABOVE. HE SAID THE STRANGEST PART WAS HIS ATTITUDE.
"BEMUSED DISINTEREST," WERE HIS EXACT WORDS...
HE'D JUST ASSUMED HE HAD DIED...

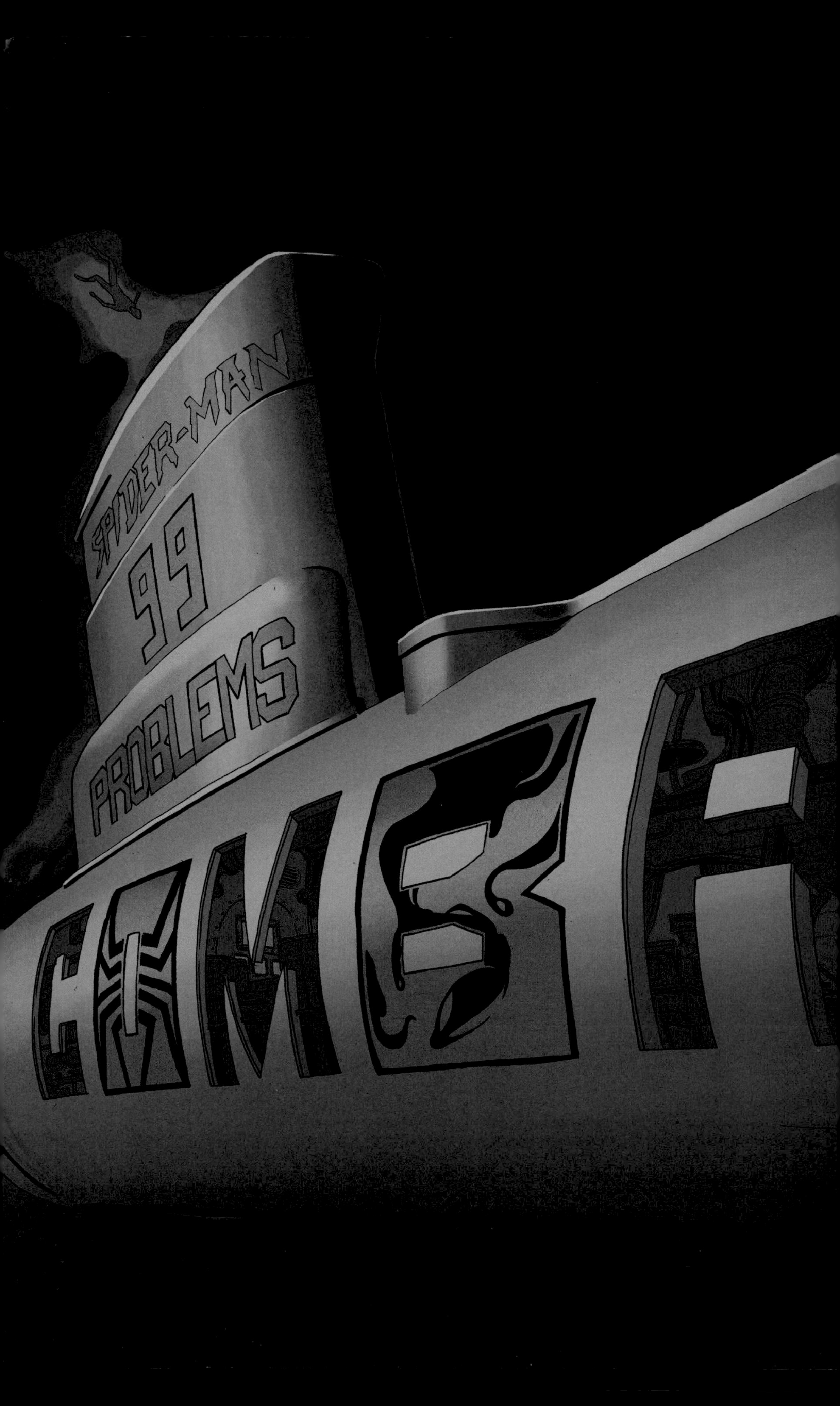
SPIDER-MAN
99
PROBLEMS

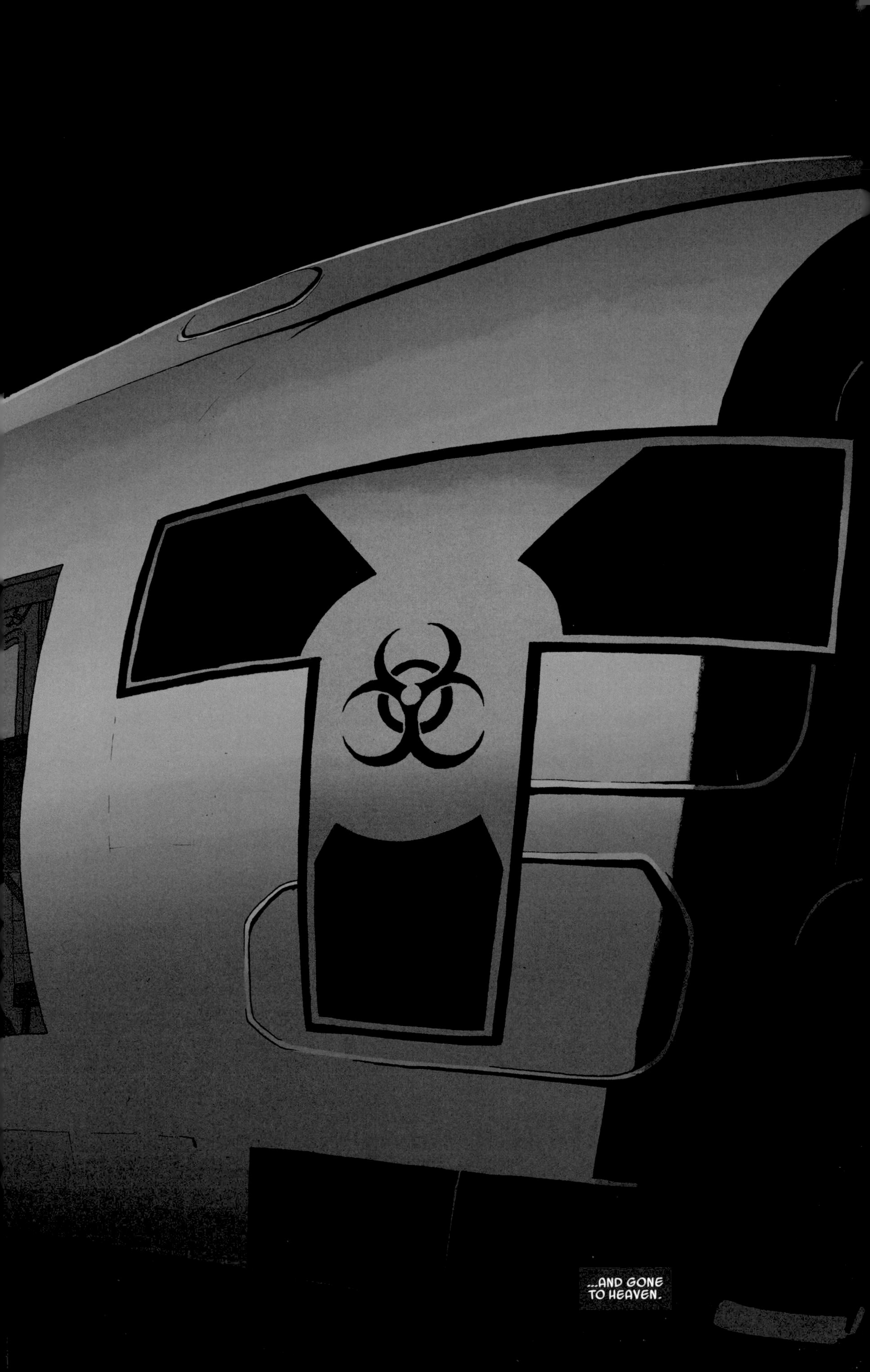
...AND GONE TO HEAVEN.

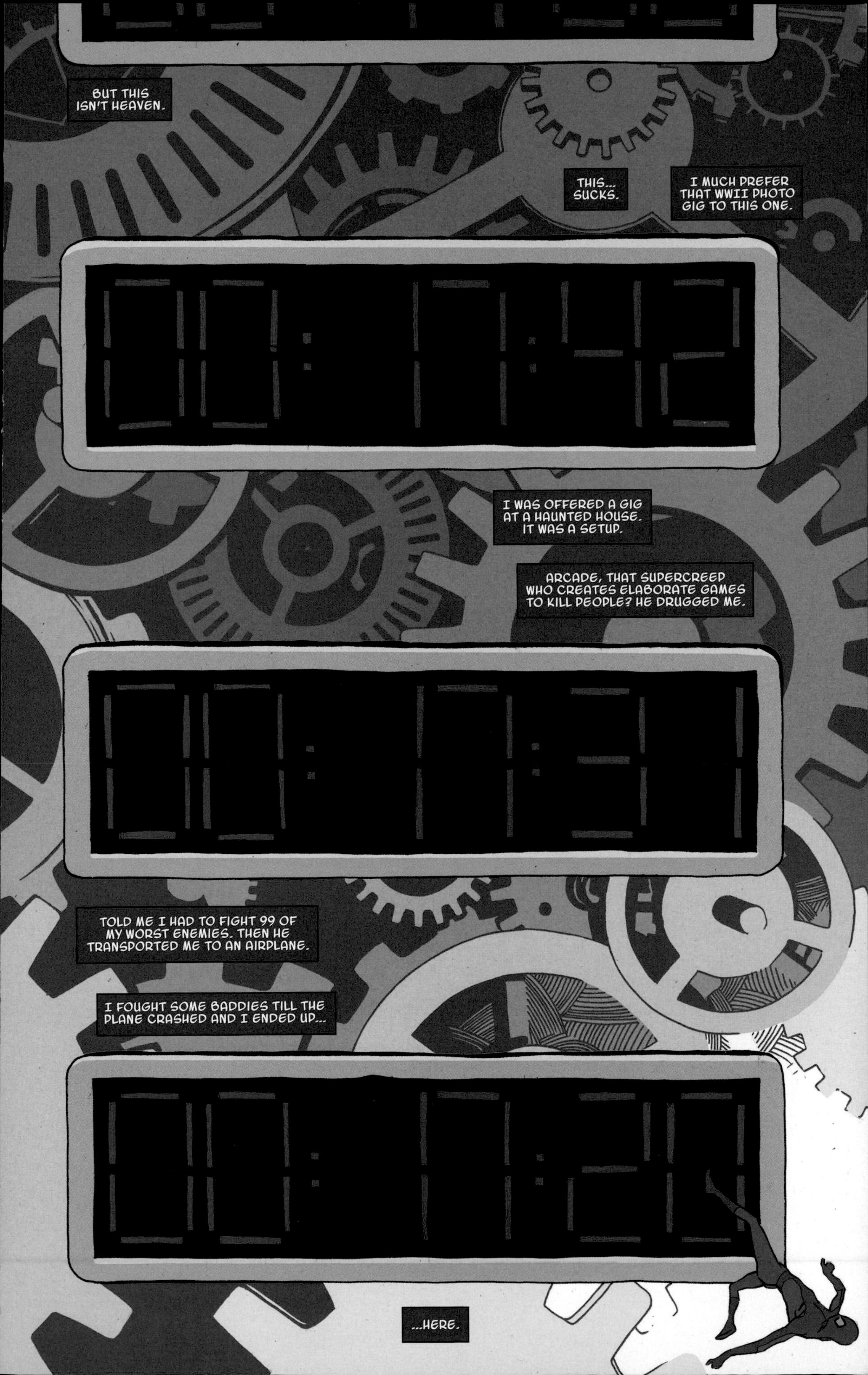
BUT THIS ISN'T HEAVEN.
THIS... SUCKS.
I MUCH PREFER THAT WWII PHOTO GIG TO THIS ONE.
I WAS OFFERED A GIG AT A HAUNTED HOUSE. IT WAS A SETUP.
ARCADE, THAT SUPERCREEP WHO CREATES ELABORATE GAMES TO KILL PEOPLE? HE DRUGGED ME.
TOLD ME I HAD TO FIGHT 99 OF MY WORST ENEMIES. THEN HE TRANSPORTED ME TO AN AIRPLANE.
I FOUGHT SOME BADDIES TILL THE PLANE CRASHED AND I ENDED UP...
...HERE.

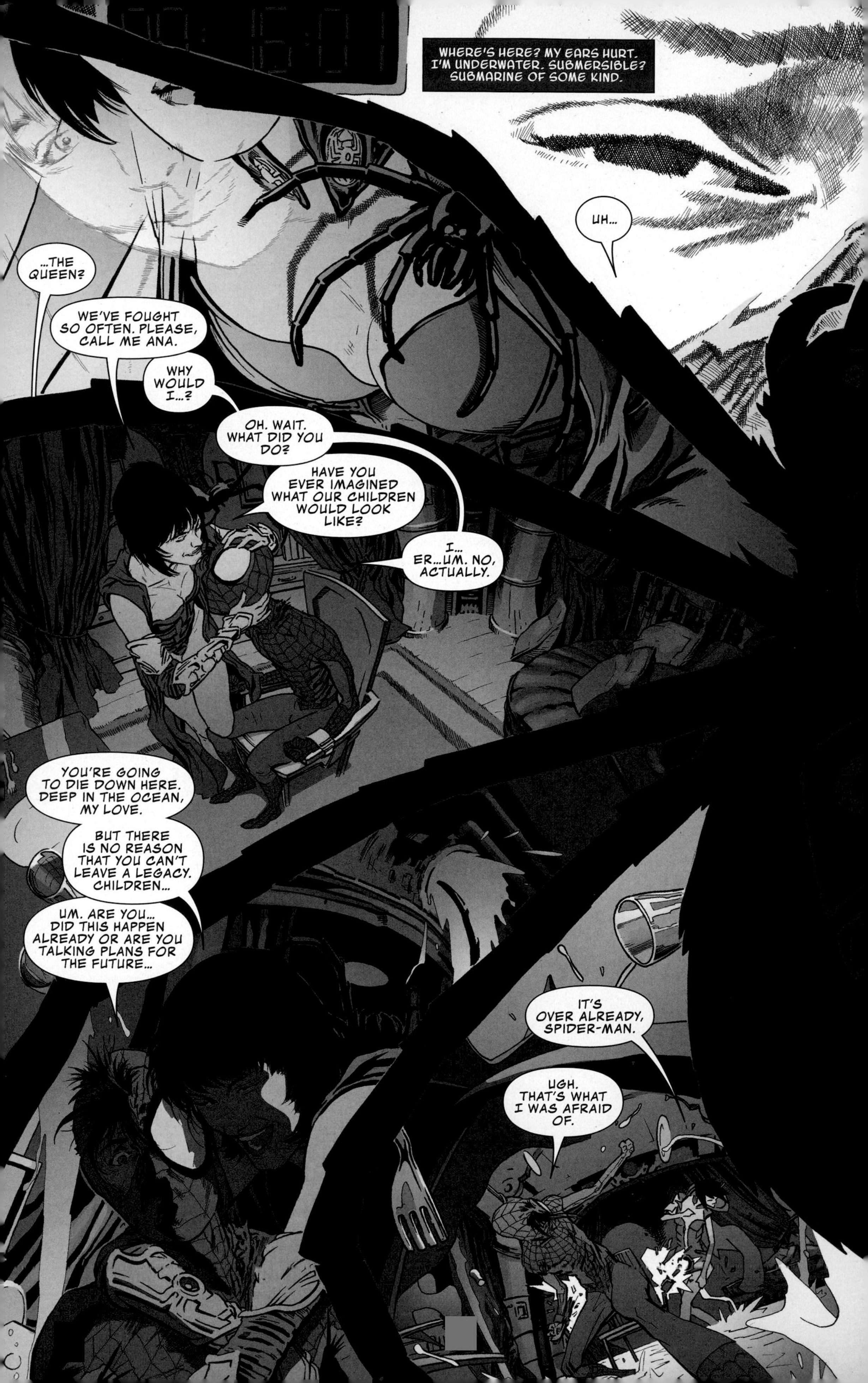
WHERE'S HERE? MY EARS HURT. I'M UNDERWATER. SUBMERSIBLE? SUBMARINE OF SOME KIND.
UH...
...THE QUEEN?
WE'VE FOUGHT SO OFTEN. PLEASE, CALL ME ANA.
WHY WOULD I...?
OH. WAIT. WHAT DID YOU DO?
HAVE YOU EVER IMAGINED WHAT OUR CHILDREN WOULD LOOK LIKE?
I... ER...UM. NO, ACTUALLY.
YOU'RE GOING TO DIE DOWN HERE. DEEP IN THE OCEAN, MY LOVE.
BUT THERE IS NO REASON THAT YOU CAN'T LEAVE A LEGACY. CHILDREN...
UM. ARE YOU... DID THIS HAPPEN ALREADY OR ARE YOU TALKING PLANS FOR THE FUTURE...
IT'S OVER ALREADY, SPIDER-MAN.
UGH. THAT'S WHAT I WAS AFRAID OF.

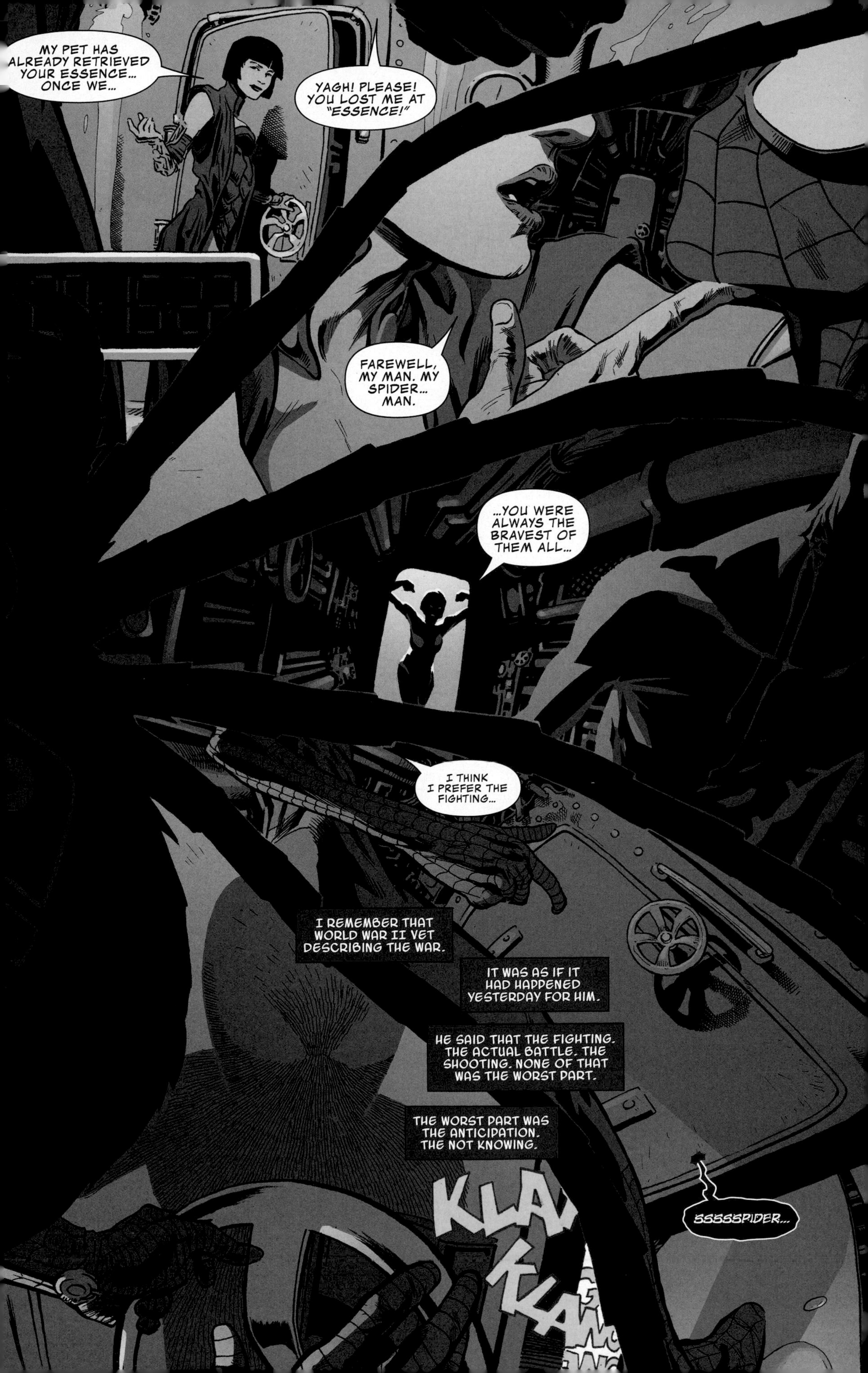
MY PET HAS ALREADY RETRIEVED YOUR ESSENCE... ONCE WE...
YAGH! PLEASE! YOU LOST ME AT "ESSENCE!"
FAREWELL, MY MAN. MY SPIDER... MAN.
...YOU WERE ALWAYS THE BRAVEST OF THEM ALL...
I THINK I PREFER THE FIGHTING...
I REMEMBER THAT WORLD WAR II VET DESCRIBING THE WAR.
IT WAS AS IF IT HAD HAPPENED YESTERDAY FOR HIM.
HE SAID THAT THE FIGHTING. THE ACTUAL BATTLE. THE SHOOTING. NONE OF THAT WAS THE WORST PART.
THE WORST PART WAS THE ANTICIPATION. THE NOT KNOWING.
SSSSSPIDER...
KLA
KLA

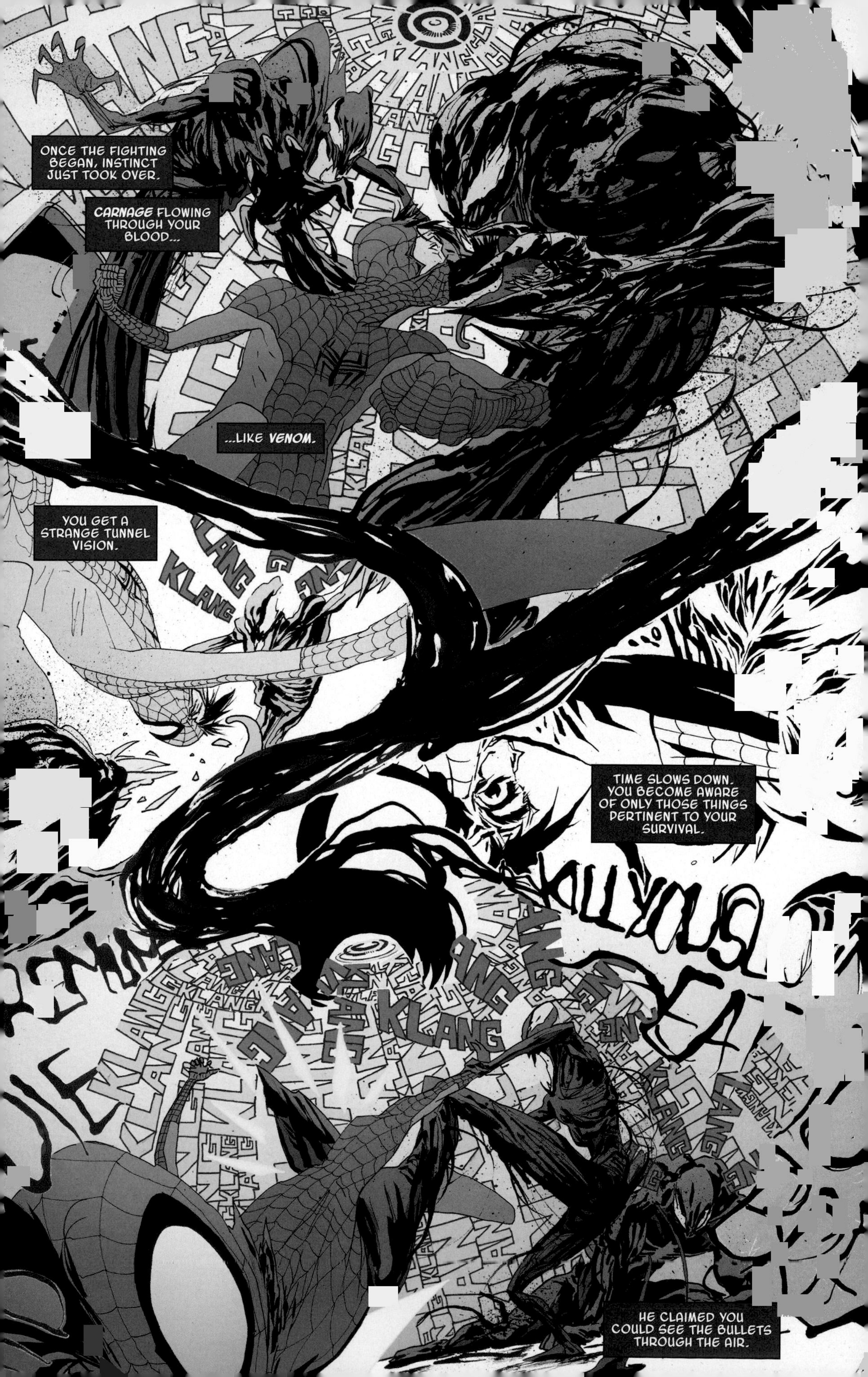
ONCE THE FIGHTING BEGAN, INSTINCT JUST TOOK OVER.
CARNAGE FLOWING THROUGH YOUR BLOOD...
...LIKE VENOM.
YOU GET A STRANGE TUNNEL VISION.
TIME SLOWS DOWN. YOU BECOME AWARE OF ONLY THOSE THINGS PERTINENT TO YOUR SURVIVAL.
HE CLAIMED YOU COULD SEE THE BULLETS THROUGH THE AIR.

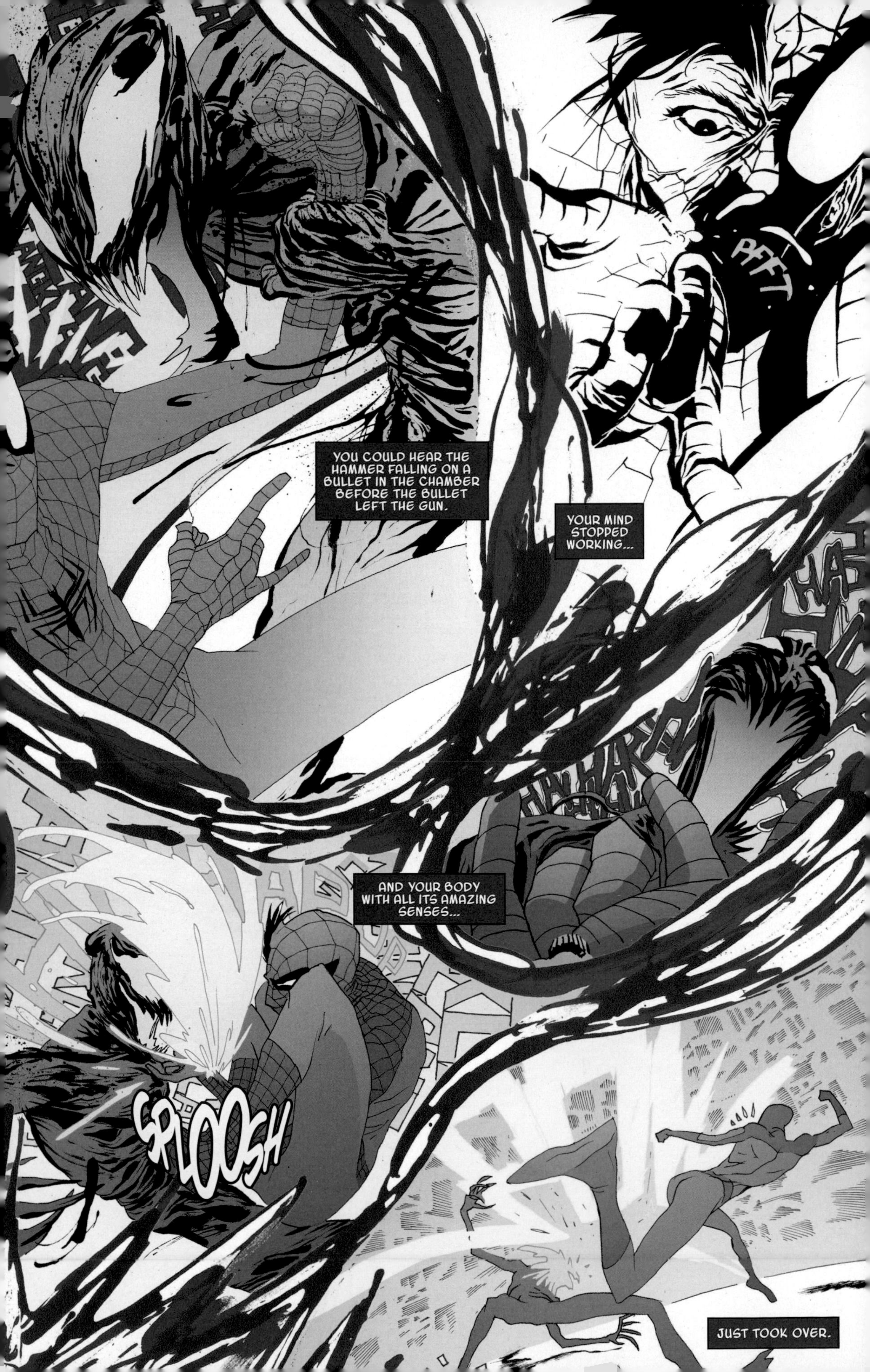

PFFT
YOU COULD HEAR THE HAMMER FALLING ON A BULLET IN THE CHAMBER BEFORE THE BULLET LEFT THE GUN.
YOUR MIND STOPPED WORKING...
AND YOUR BODY WITH ALL ITS AMAZING SENSES...
SPLOOSH
JUST TOOK OVER.

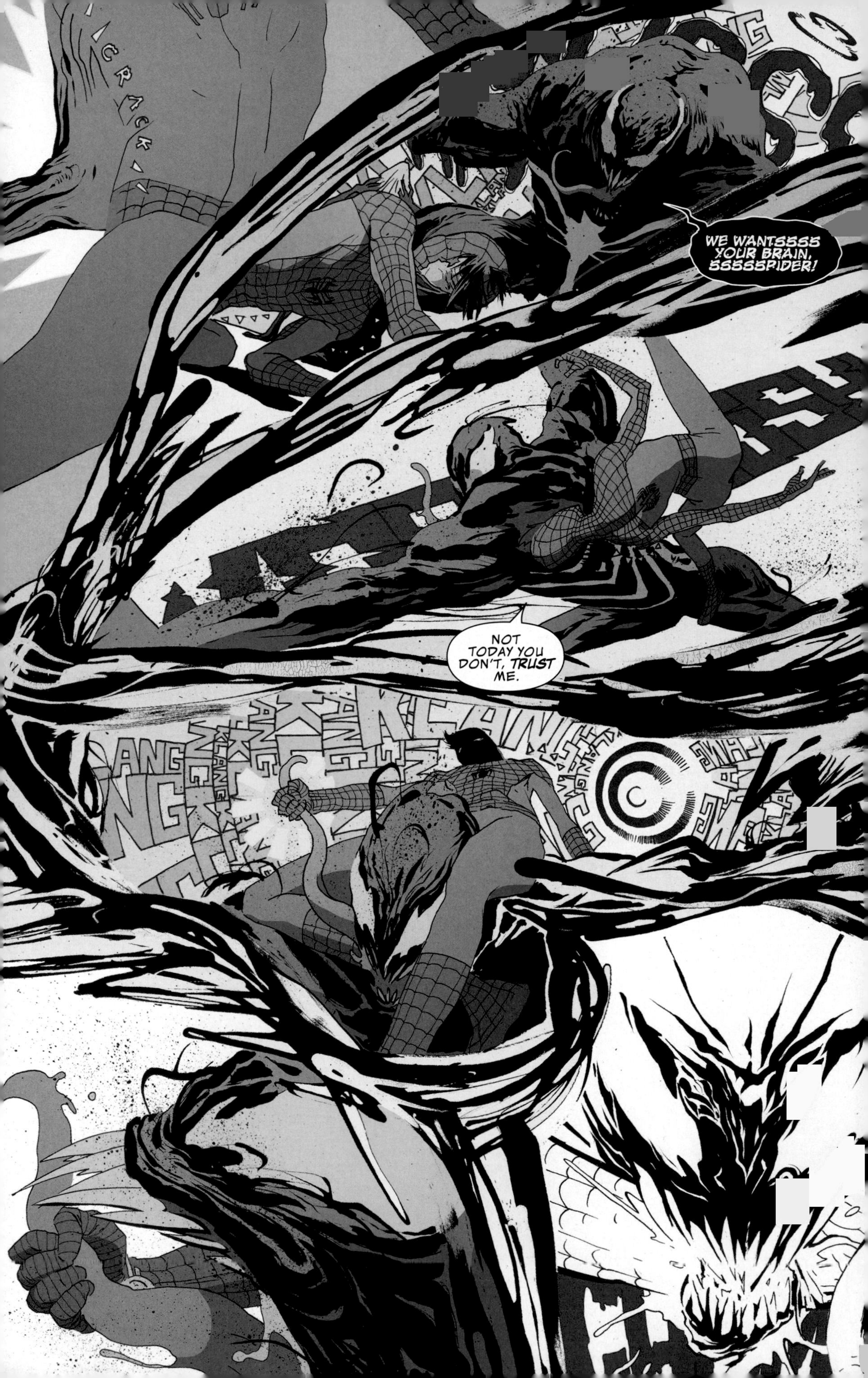
CRACK!
WE WANTSSSS YOUR BRAIN, SSSSSPIDER!
NOT TODAY YOU DON'T, TRUST ME.

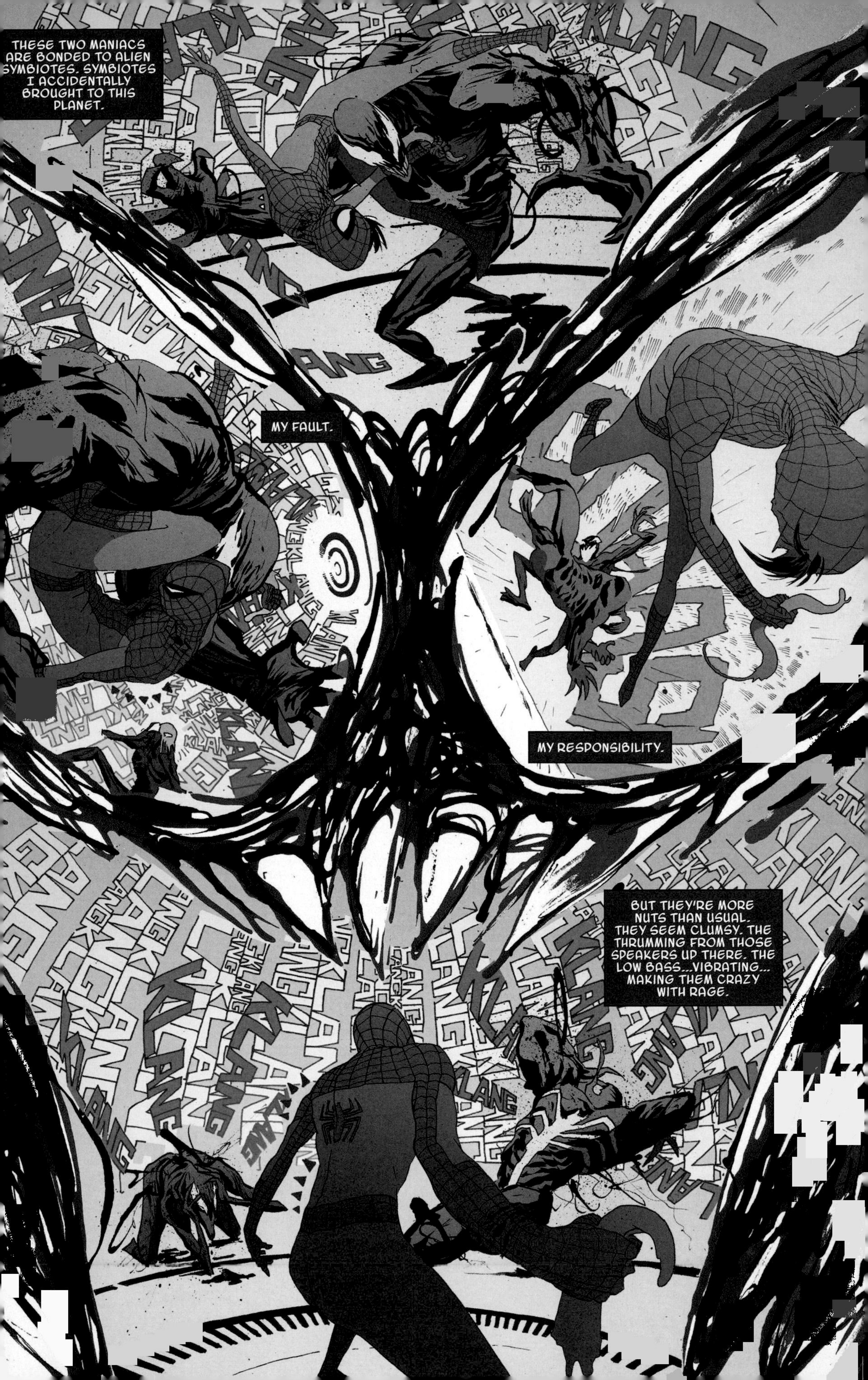
THESE TWO MANIACS ARE BONDED TO ALIEN SYMBIOTES. SYMBIOTES I ACCIDENTALLY BROUGHT TO THIS PLANET.
MY FAULT.
MY RESPONSIBILITY.
BUT THEY'RE MORE NUTS THAN USUAL. THEY SEEM CLUMSY. THE THRUMMING FROM THOSE SPEAKERS UP THERE. THE LOW BASS...VIBRATING... MAKING THEM CRAZY WITH RAGE.
KLANG

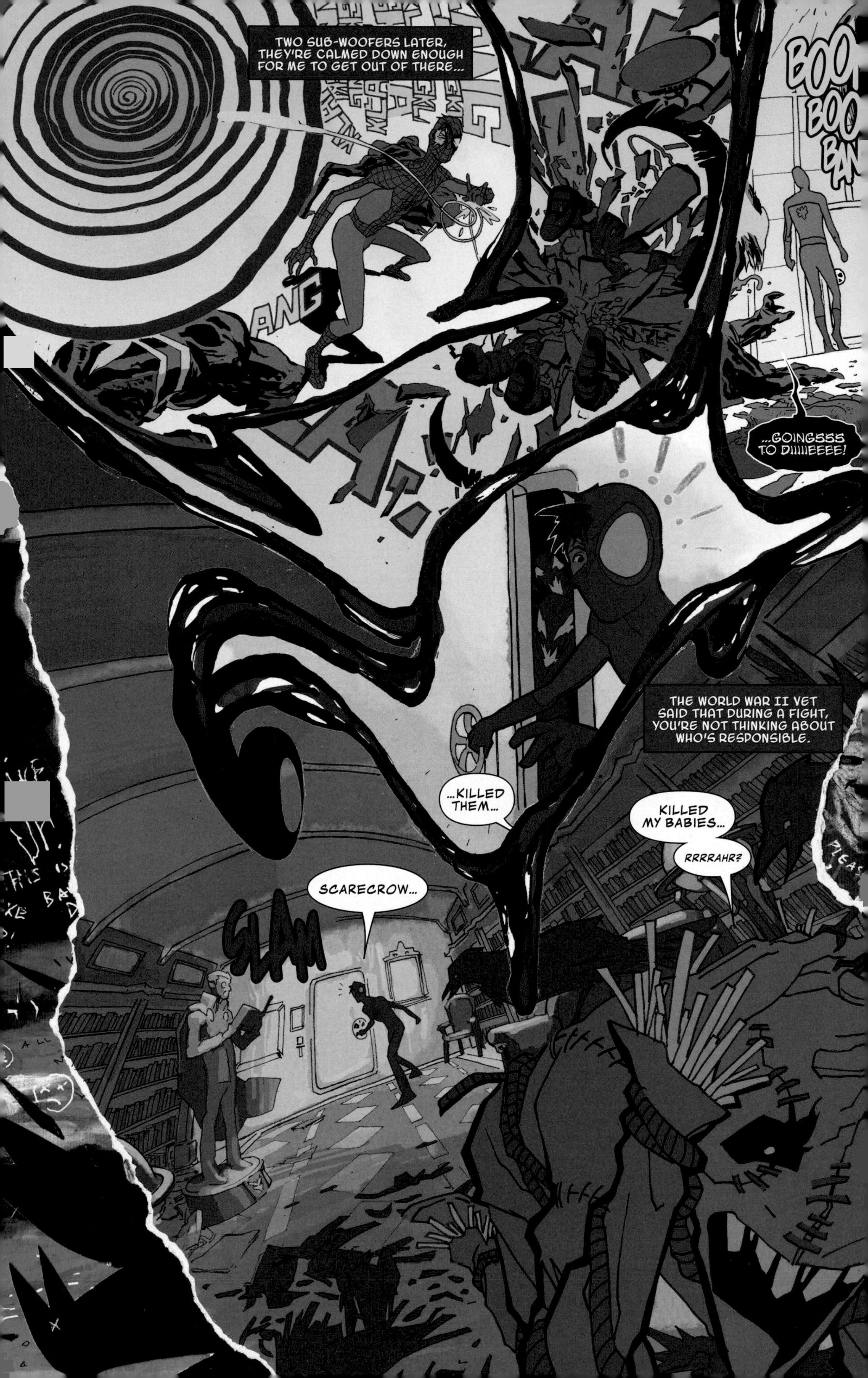
TWO SUB-WOOFERS LATER, THEY'RE CALMED DOWN ENOUGH FOR ME TO GET OUT OF THERE...
BOO
BOO
BAN
ANG
...GOINGSSS TO DIIIIEEEE!
THE WORLD WAR II VET SAID THAT DURING A FIGHT, YOU'RE NOT THINKING ABOUT WHO'S RESPONSIBLE.
...KILLED THEM...
KILLED MY BABIES...
RRRRAHR?
SCARECROW...
SLAM

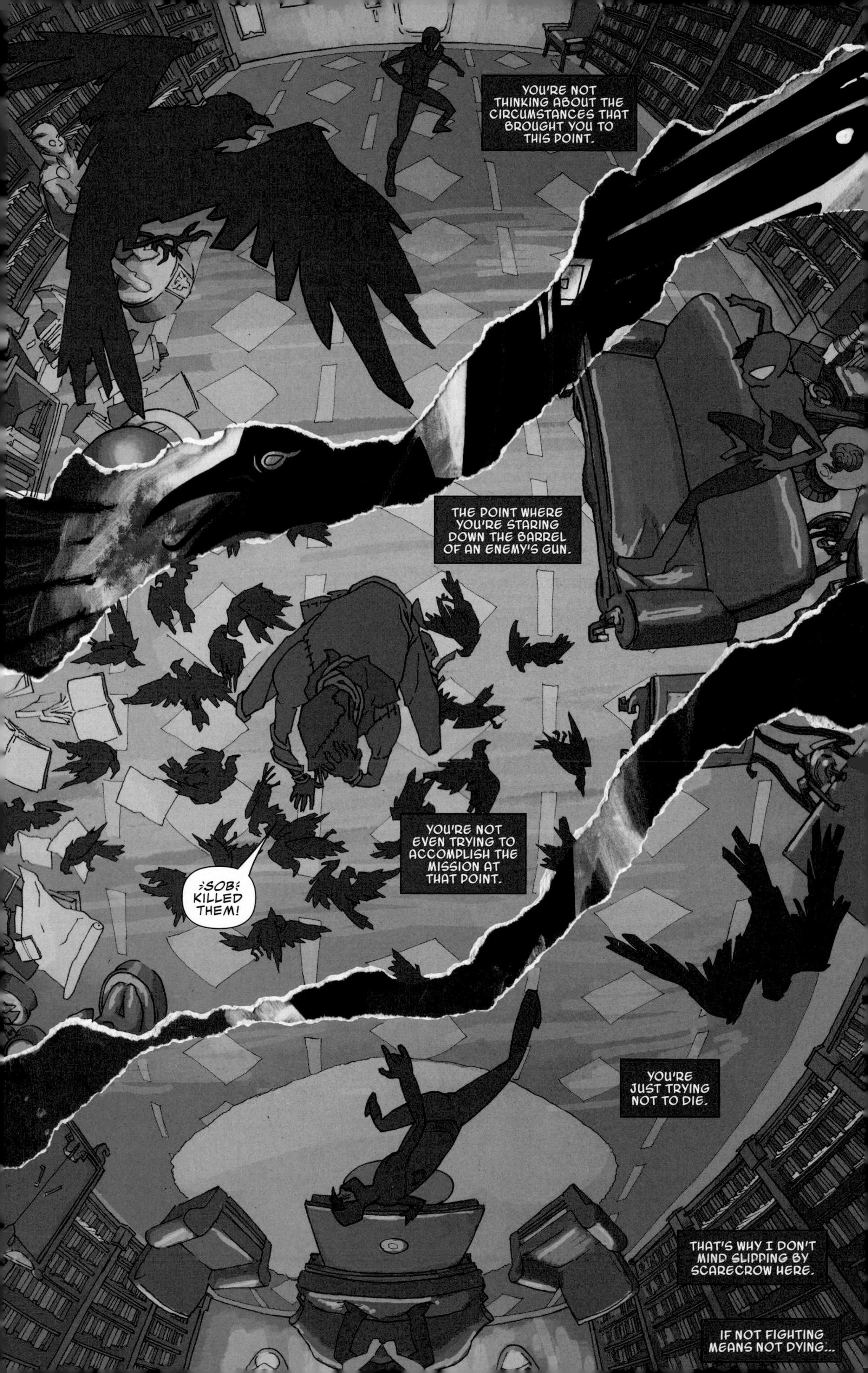
YOU'RE NOT THINKING ABOUT THE CIRCUMSTANCES THAT BROUGHT YOU TO THIS POINT.
THE POINT WHERE YOU'RE STARING DOWN THE BARREL OF AN ENEMY'S GUN.
YOU'RE NOT EVEN TRYING TO ACCOMPLISH THE MISSION AT THAT POINT.
SOB KILLED THEM!
YOU'RE JUST TRYING NOT TO DIE.
THAT'S WHY I DON'T MIND SLIPPING BY SCARECROW HERE.
IF NOT FIGHTING MEANS NOT DYING...

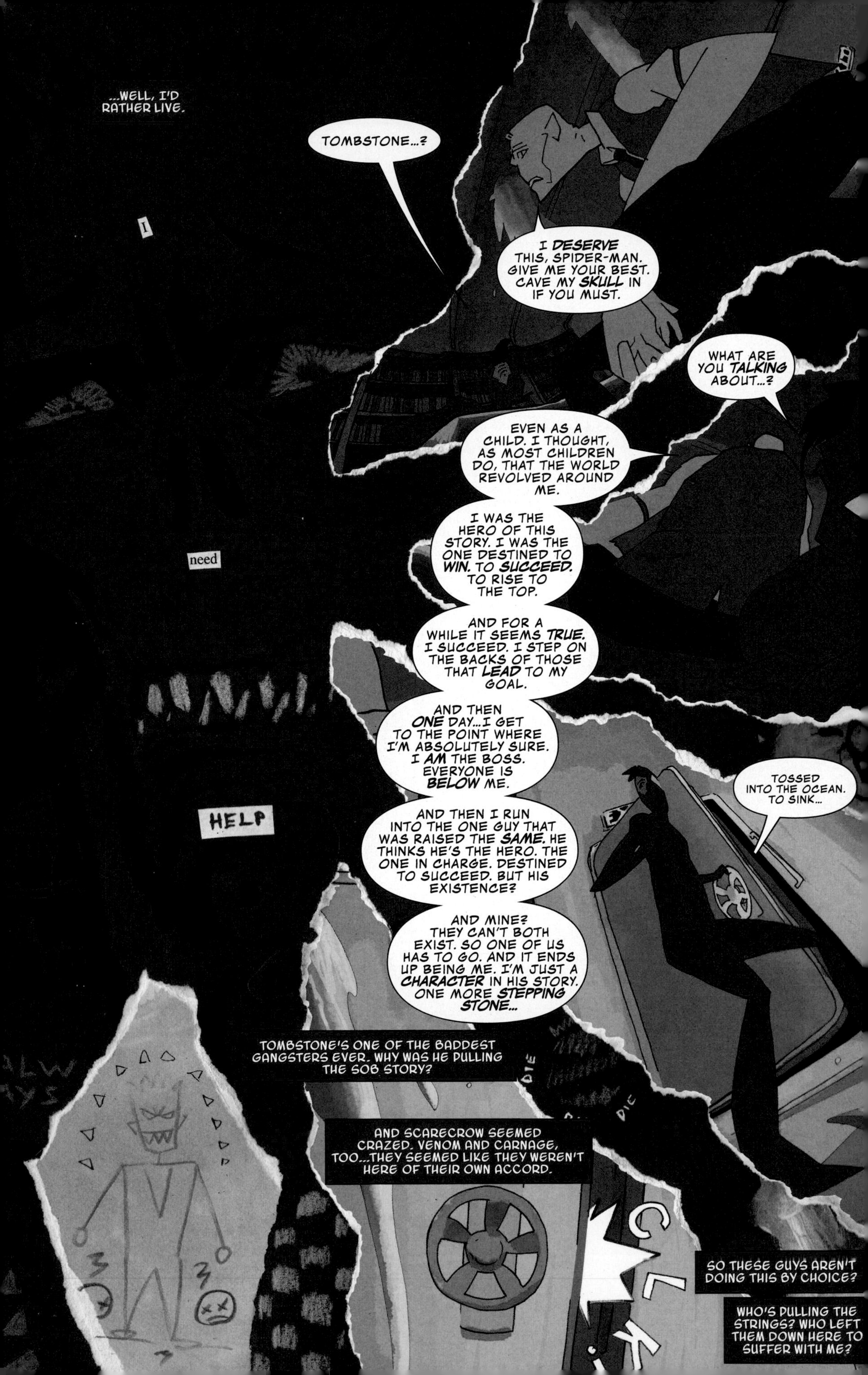
...WELL, I'D RATHER LIVE.
TOMBSTONE...?
I
I DESERVE THIS, SPIDER-MAN. GIVE ME YOUR BEST. CAVE MY SKULL IN IF YOU MUST.
WHAT ARE YOU TALKING ABOUT...?
EVEN AS A CHILD. I THOUGHT, AS MOST CHILDREN DO, THAT THE WORLD REVOLVED AROUND ME.
I WAS THE HERO OF THIS STORY. I WAS THE ONE DESTINED TO WIN. TO SUCCEED. TO RISE TO THE TOP.
need
AND FOR A WHILE IT SEEMS TRUE. I SUCCEED. I STEP ON THE BACKS OF THOSE THAT LEAD TO MY GOAL.
AND THEN ONE DAY...I GET TO THE POINT WHERE I'M ABSOLUTELY SURE. I AM THE BOSS. EVERYONE IS BELOW ME.
HELP
TOSSED INTO THE OCEAN. TO SINK...
AND THEN I RUN INTO THE ONE GUY THAT WAS RAISED THE SAME. HE THINKS HE'S THE HERO. THE ONE IN CHARGE. DESTINED TO SUCCEED. BUT HIS EXISTENCE?
AND MINE? THEY CAN'T BOTH EXIST. SO ONE OF US HAS TO GO. AND IT ENDS UP BEING ME. I'M JUST A CHARACTER IN HIS STORY. ONE MORE STEPPING STONE...
TOMBSTONE'S ONE OF THE BADDEST GANGSTERS EVER. WHY WAS HE PULLING THE SOB STORY?
DIE
DIE
AND SCARECROW SEEMED CRAZED. VENOM AND CARNAGE, TOO...THEY SEEMED LIKE THEY WEREN'T HERE OF THEIR OWN ACCORD.
CLK
SO THESE GUYS AREN'T DOING THIS BY CHOICE?
WHO'S PULLING THE STRINGS? WHO LEFT THEM DOWN HERE TO SUFFER WITH ME?

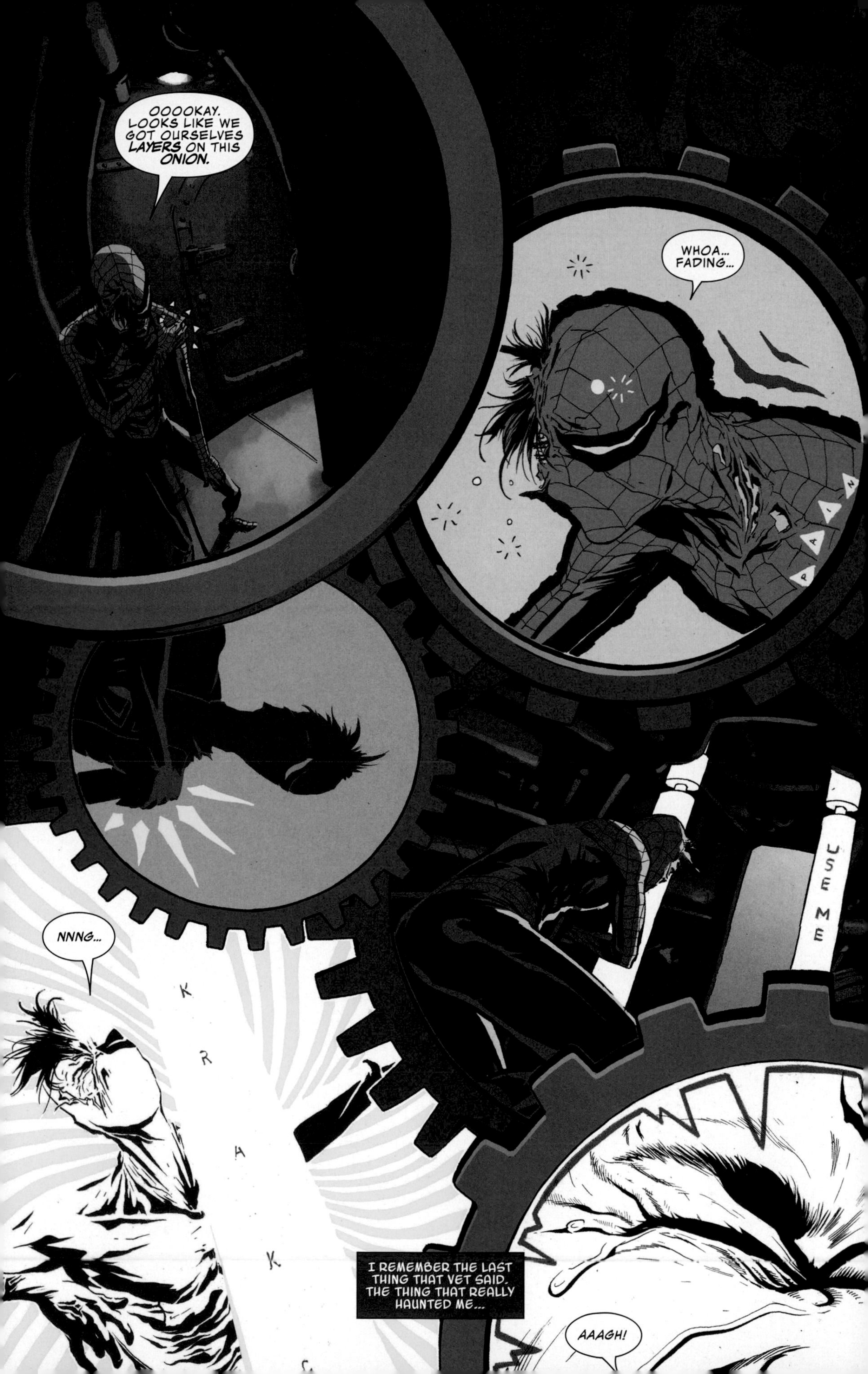
OOOOKAY. LOOKS LIKE WE GOT OURSELVES LAYERS ON THIS ONION.
WHOA... FADING...
PAIN
USE ME
NNNG...
KRAK
I REMEMBER THE LAST THING THAT VET SAID. THE THING THAT REALLY HAUNTED ME...
AAAGH!

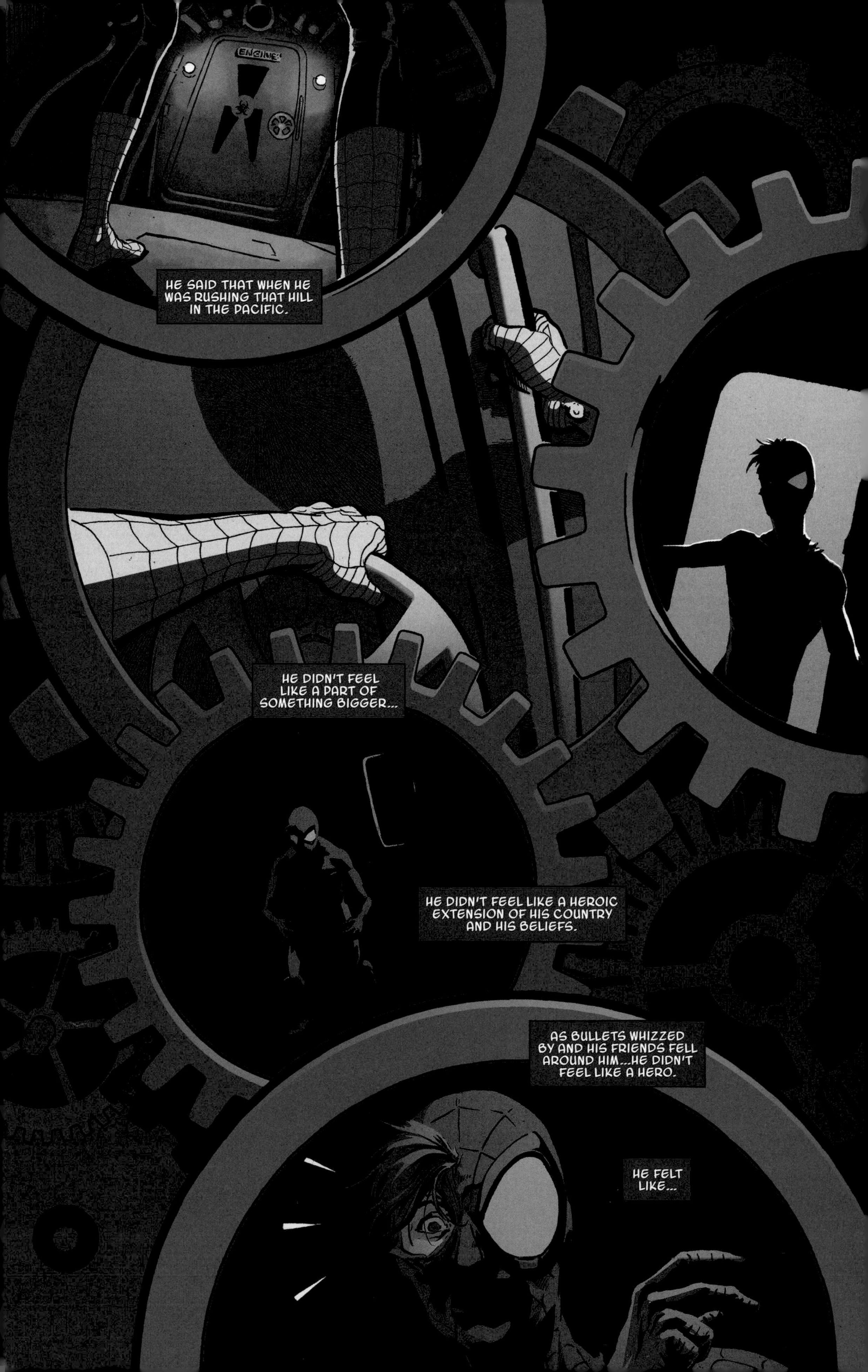

ENGINE
HE SAID THAT WHEN HE WAS RUSHING THAT HILL IN THE PACIFIC.
HE DIDN'T FEEL LIKE A PART OF SOMETHING BIGGER...
HE DIDN'T FEEL LIKE A HEROIC EXTENSION OF HIS COUNTRY AND HIS BELIEFS.
AS BULLETS WHIZZED BY AND HIS FRIENDS FELL AROUND HIM...HE DIDN'T FEEL LIKE A HERO.
HE FELT LIKE...

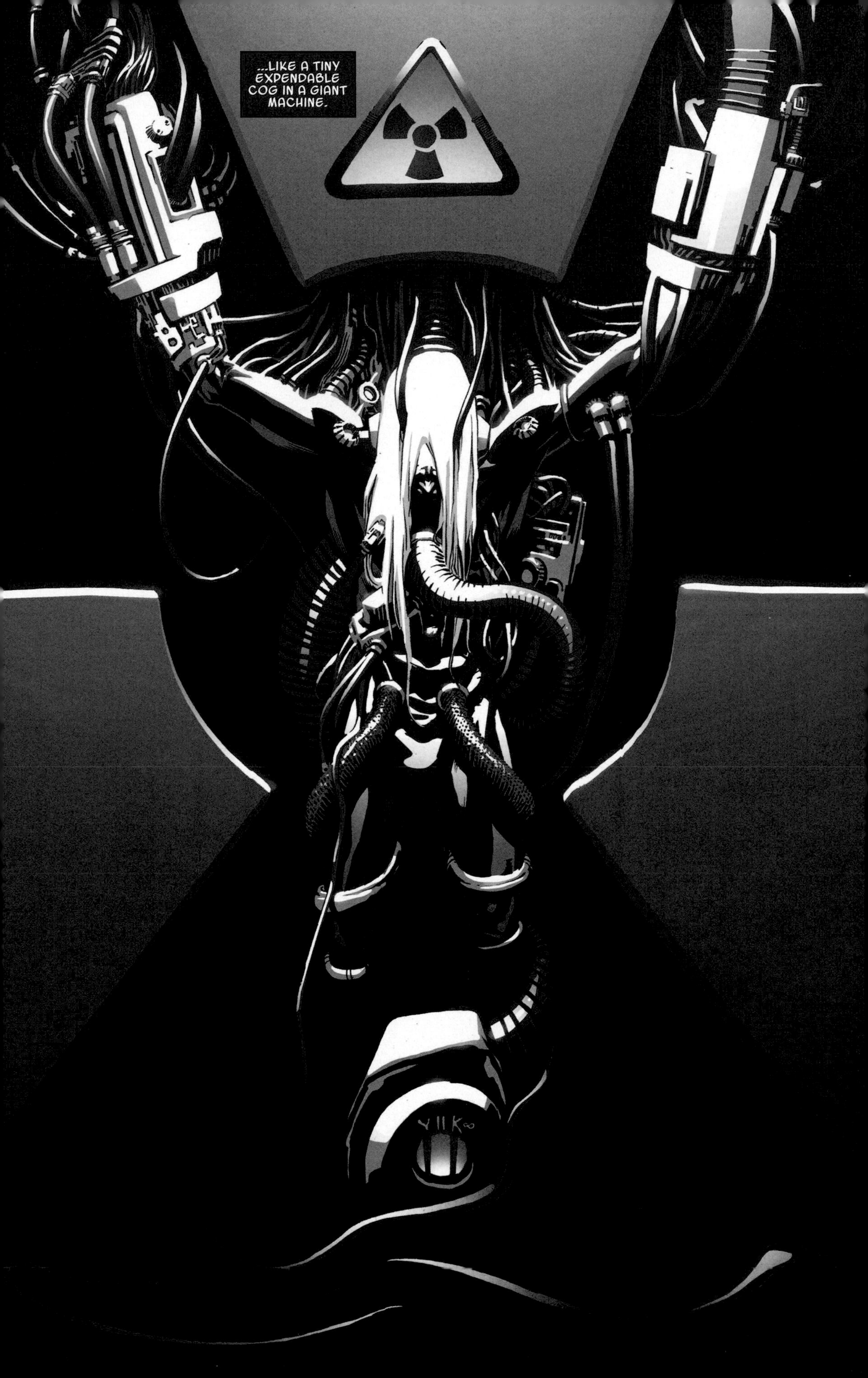
...LIKE A TINY EXPENDABLE COG IN A GIANT MACHINE.

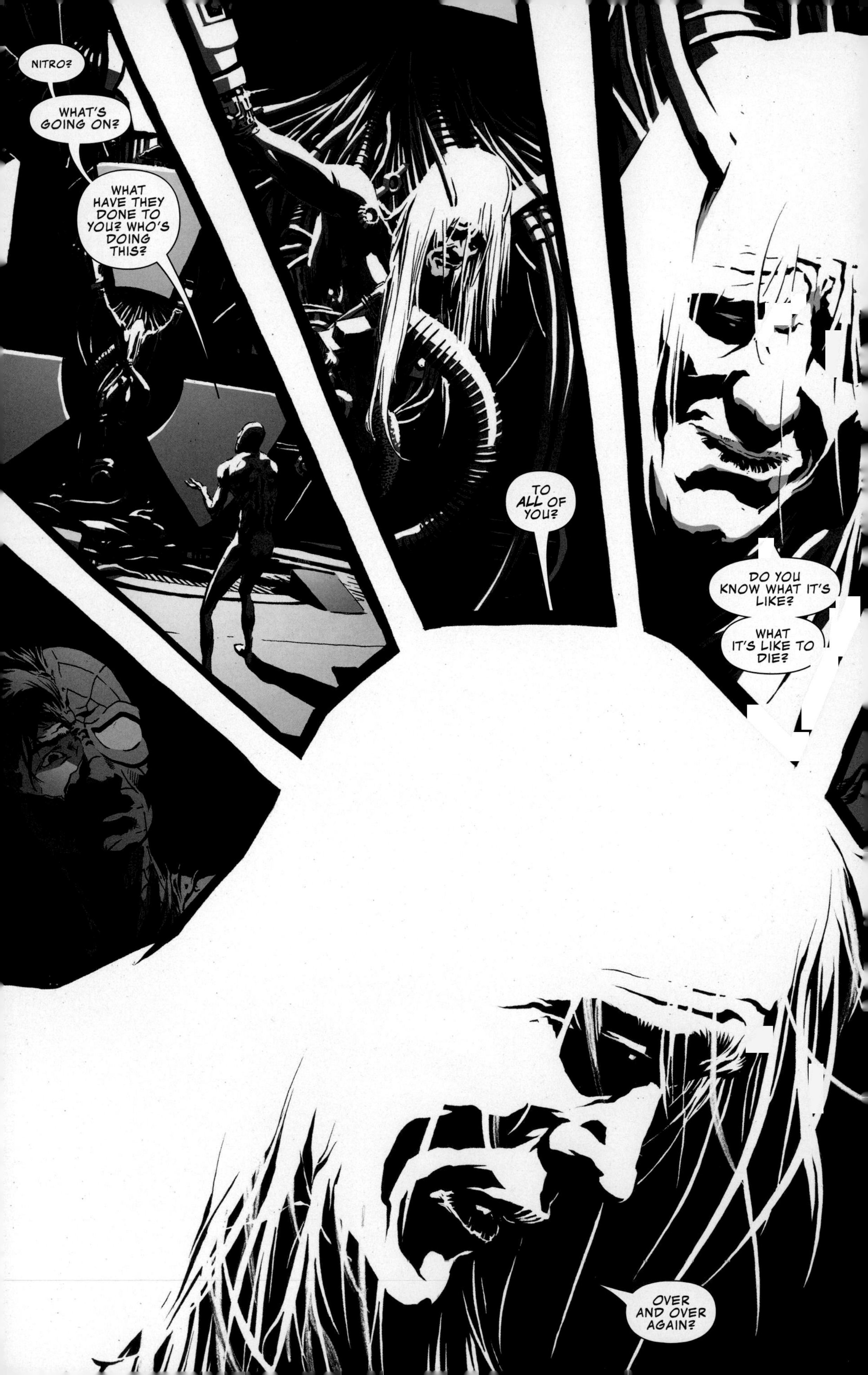
NITRO?
WHAT'S GOING ON?
WHAT HAVE THEY DONE TO YOU? WHO'S DOING THIS?
TO ALL OF YOU?
DO YOU KNOW WHAT IT'S LIKE?
WHAT IT'S LIKE TO DIE?
OVER AND OVER AGAIN?

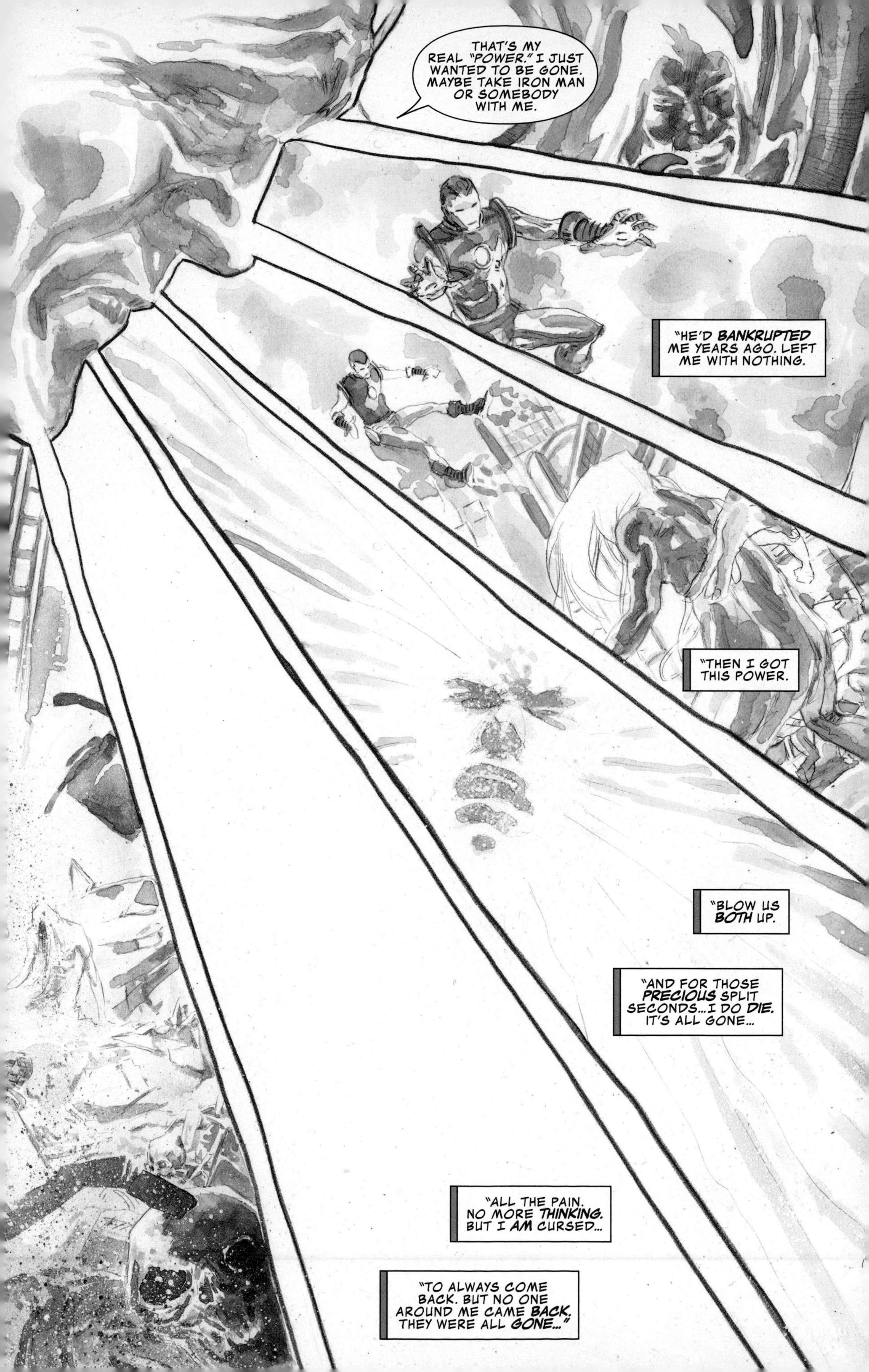
THAT'S MY REAL "POWER." I JUST WANTED TO BE GONE. MAYBE TAKE IRON MAN OR SOMEBODY WITH ME.
"HE'D BANKRUPTED ME YEARS AGO. LEFT ME WITH NOTHING.
"THEN I GOT THIS POWER.
"BLOW US BOTH UP.
"AND FOR THOSE PRECIOUS SPLIT SECONDS...I DO DIE. IT'S ALL GONE...
"ALL THE PAIN. NO MORE THINKING. BUT I AM CURSED...
"TO ALWAYS COME BACK. BUT NO ONE AROUND ME CAME BACK. THEY WERE ALL GONE..."

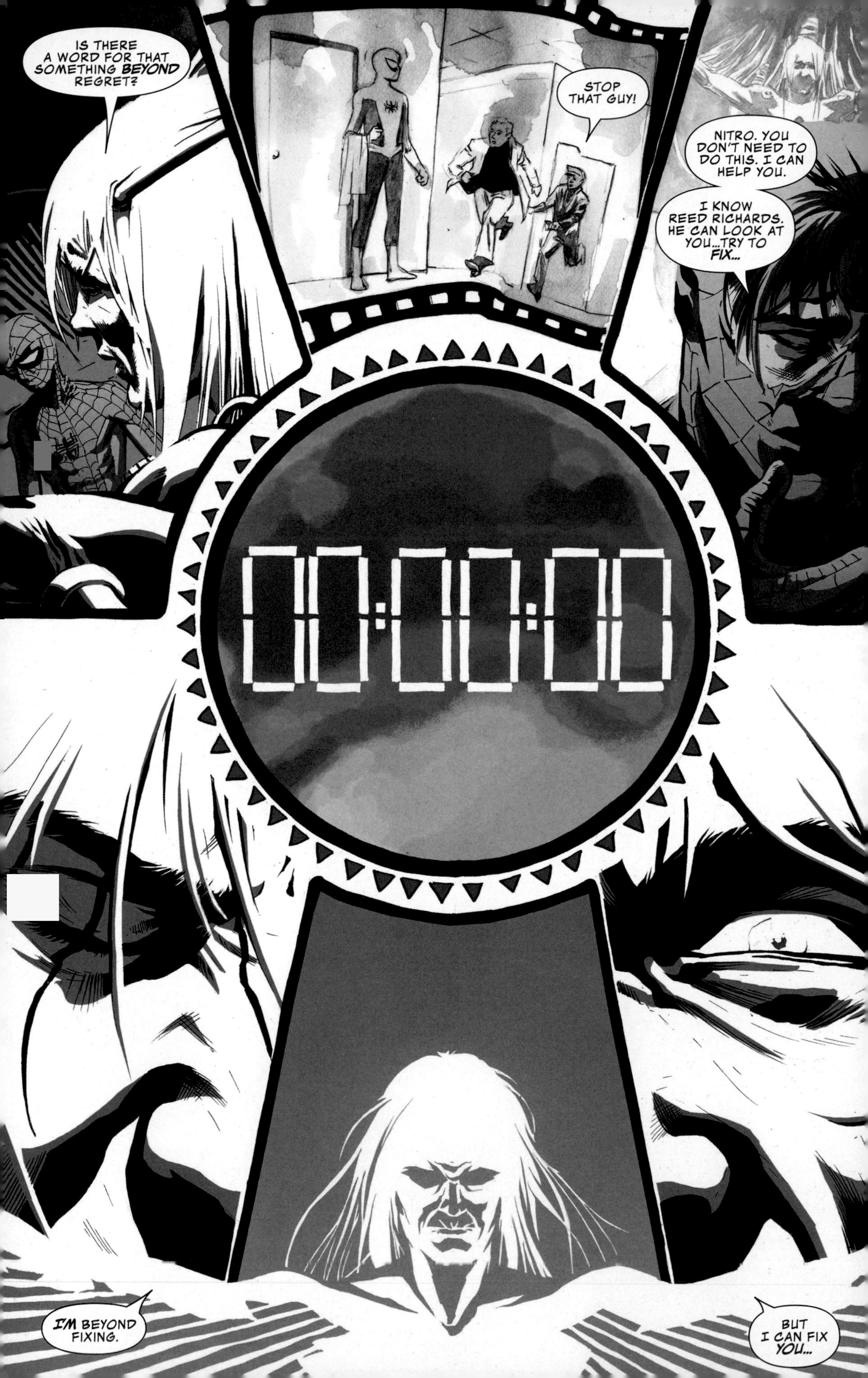
IS THERE A WORD FOR THAT SOMETHING BEYOND REGRET?
STOP THAT GUY!
NITRO. YOU DON'T NEED TO DO THIS. I CAN HELP YOU.
I KNOW REED RICHARDS. HE CAN LOOK AT YOU...TRY TO FIX...
00:00:00
I'M BEYOND FIXING.
BUT I CAN FIX YOU...

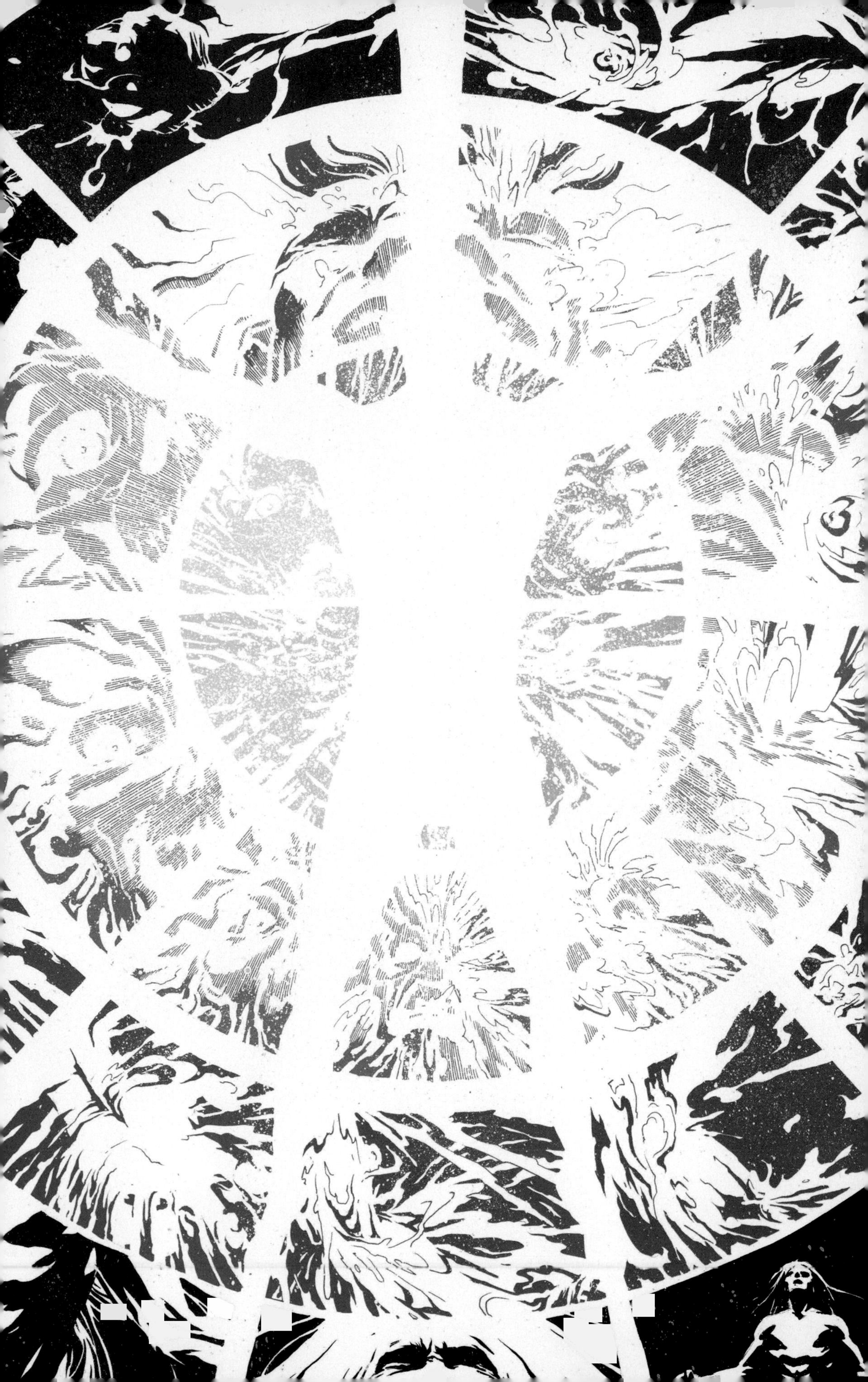

4

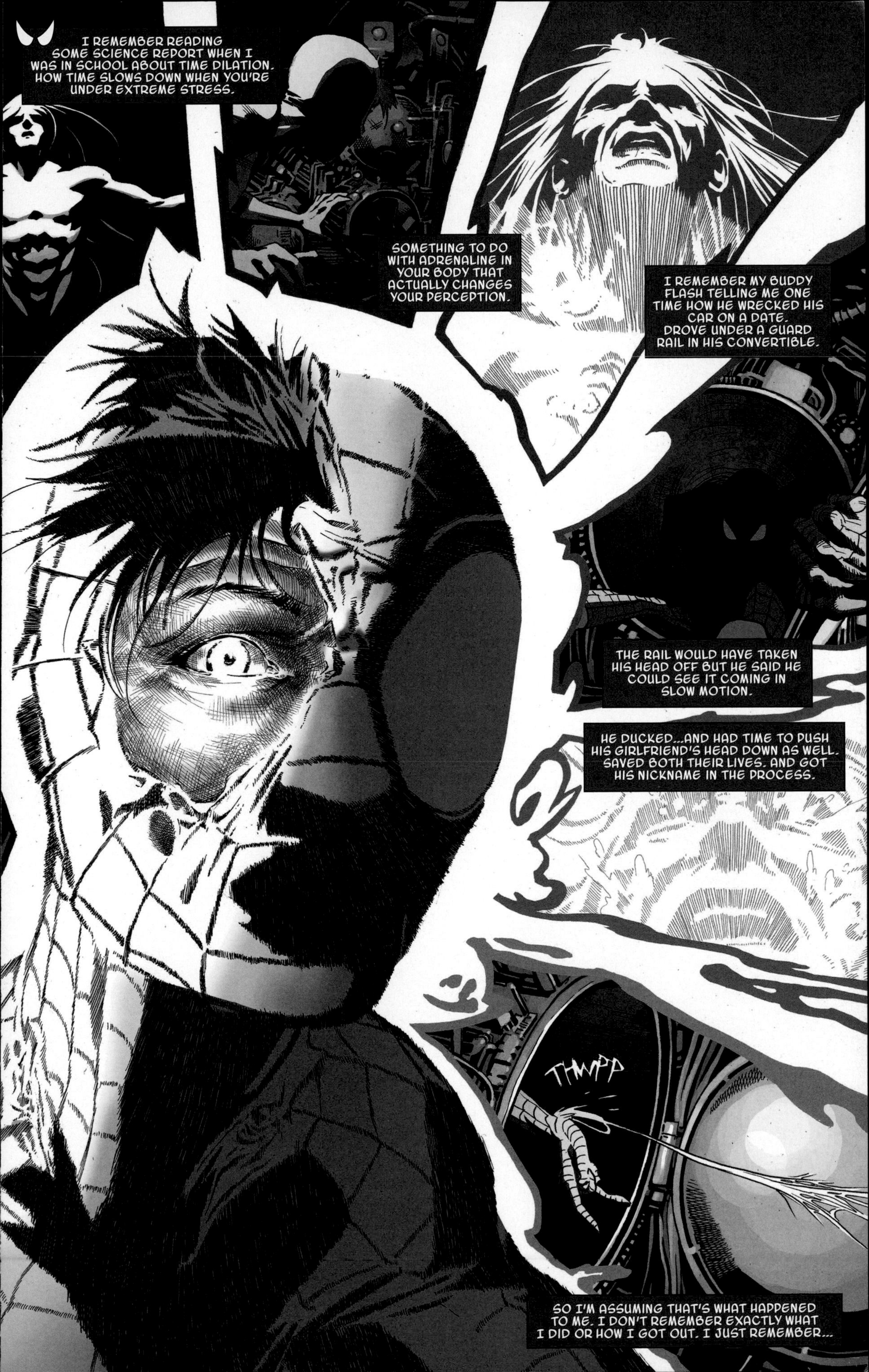
I REMEMBER READING SOME SCIENCE REPORT WHEN I WAS IN SCHOOL ABOUT TIME DILATION. HOW TIME SLOWS DOWN WHEN YOU'RE UNDER EXTREME STRESS.
SOMETHING TO DO WITH ADRENALINE IN YOUR BODY THAT ACTUALLY CHANGES YOUR PERCEPTION.
I REMEMBER MY BUDDY FLASH TELLING ME ONE TIME HOW HE WRECKED HIS CAR ON A DATE. DROVE UNDER A GUARD RAIL IN HIS CONVERTIBLE.
THE RAIL WOULD HAVE TAKEN HIS HEAD OFF BUT HE SAID HE COULD SEE IT COMING IN SLOW MOTION.
HE DUCKED...AND HAD TIME TO PUSH HIS GIRLFRIEND'S HEAD DOWN AS WELL. SAVED BOTH THEIR LIVES. AND GOT HIS NICKNAME IN THE PROCESS.
THWIPP
SO I'M ASSUMING THAT'S WHAT HAPPENED TO ME. I DON'T REMEMBER EXACTLY WHAT I DID OR HOW I GOT OUT. I JUST REMEMBER...

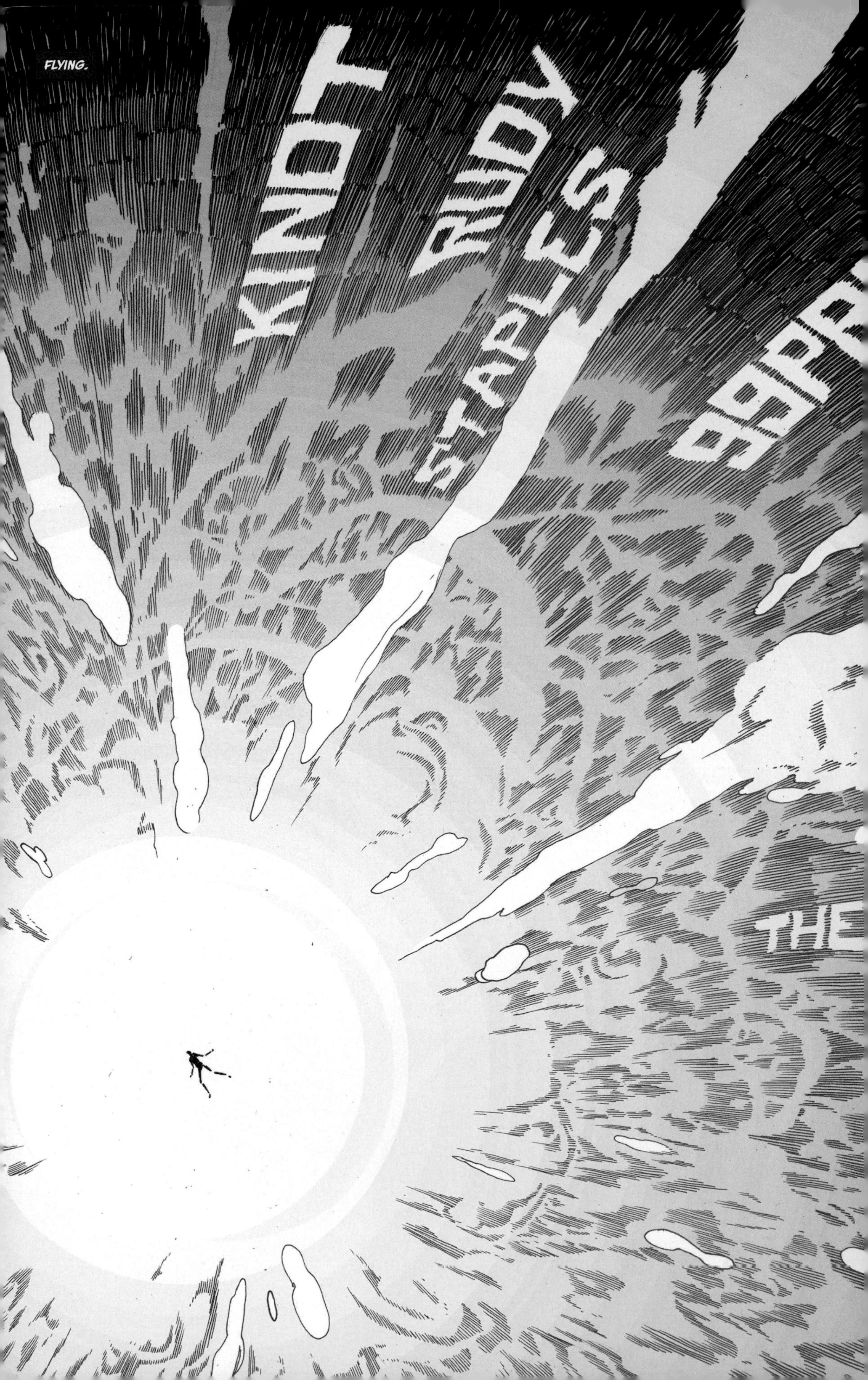
FLYING.
KINDT
RUDY
STAPLES
THE

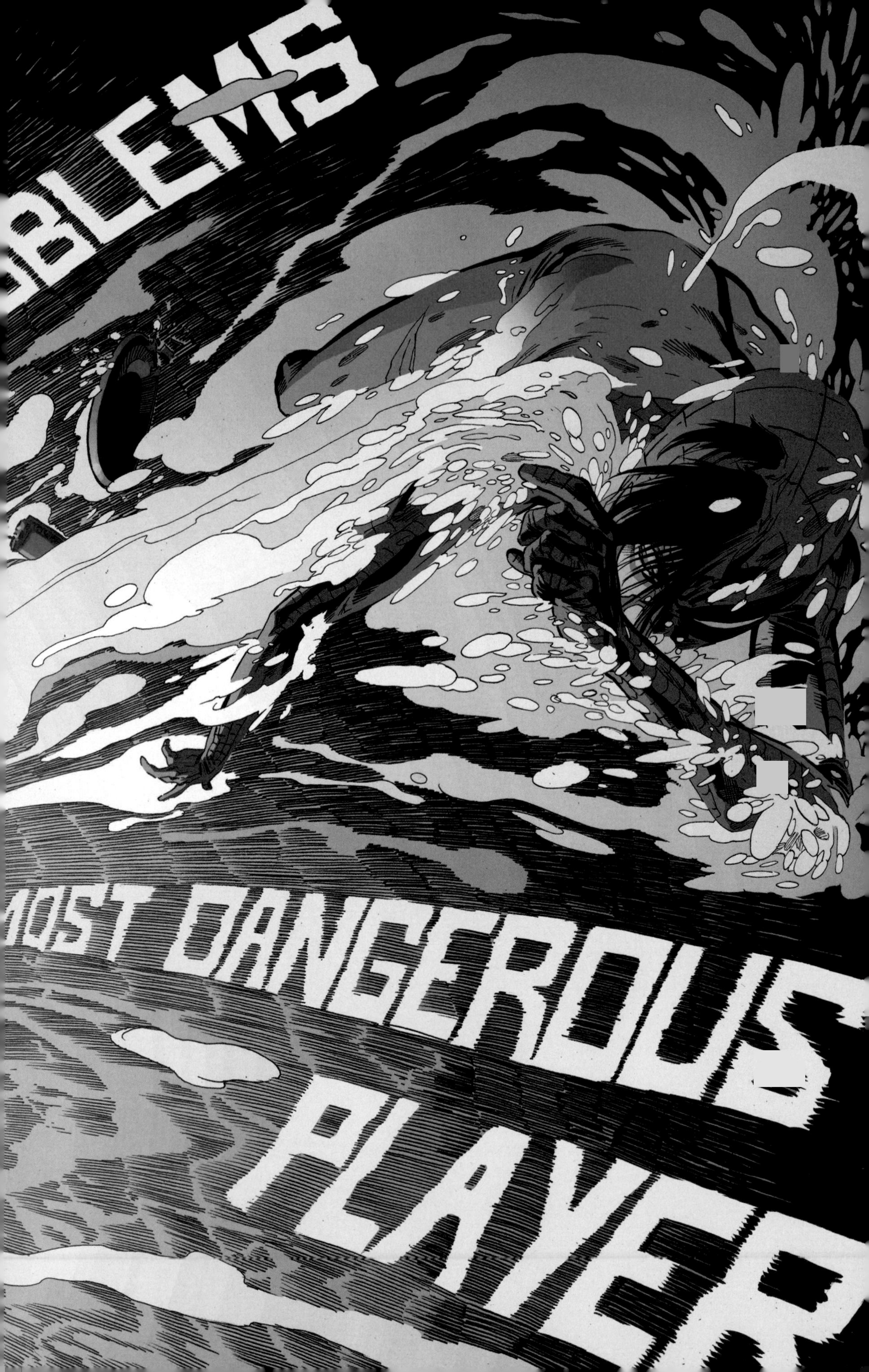

BLEMS
MOST DANGEROUS
PLAYER

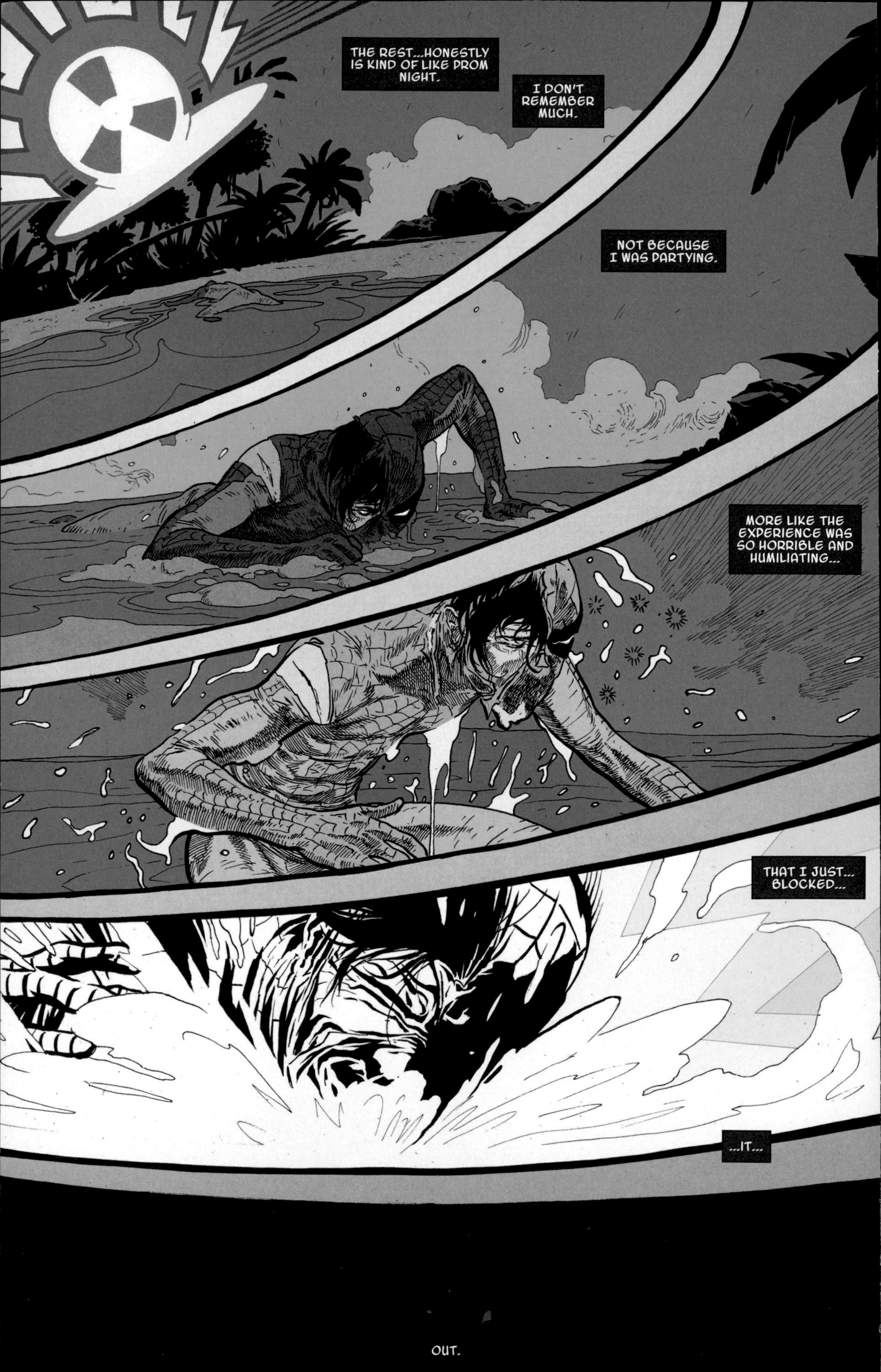
THE REST...HONESTLY IS KIND OF LIKE PROM NIGHT.
I DON'T REMEMBER MUCH.
NOT BECAUSE I WAS PARTYING.
MORE LIKE THE EXPERIENCE WAS SO HORRIBLE AND HUMILIATING...
THAT I JUST... BLOCKED...
...IT...
OUT.

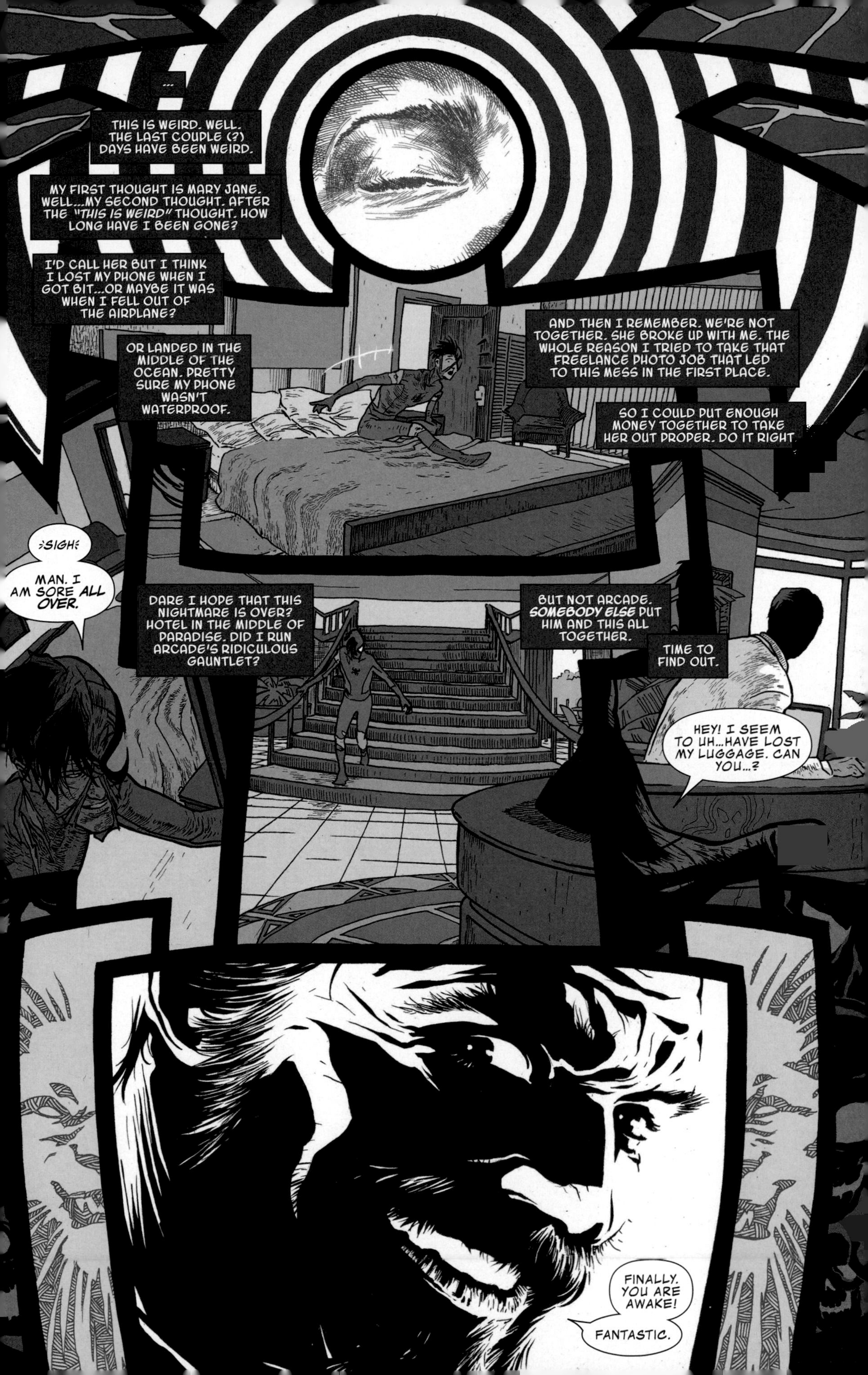
...
THIS IS WEIRD. WELL. THE LAST COUPLE (?) DAYS HAVE BEEN WEIRD.
MY FIRST THOUGHT IS MARY JANE. WELL...MY SECOND THOUGHT. AFTER THE "THIS IS WEIRD" THOUGHT. HOW LONG HAVE I BEEN GONE?
I'D CALL HER BUT I THINK I LOST MY PHONE WHEN I GOT BIT...OR MAYBE IT WAS WHEN I FELL OUT OF THE AIRPLANE?
OR LANDED IN THE MIDDLE OF THE OCEAN. PRETTY SURE MY PHONE WASN'T WATERPROOF.
AND THEN I REMEMBER. WE'RE NOT TOGETHER. SHE BROKE UP WITH ME. THE WHOLE REASON I TRIED TO TAKE THAT FREELANCE PHOTO JOB THAT LED TO THIS MESS IN THE FIRST PLACE.
SO I COULD PUT ENOUGH MONEY TOGETHER TO TAKE HER OUT PROPER. DO IT RIGHT.
SIGH
MAN. I AM SORE ALL OVER.
DARE I HOPE THAT THIS NIGHTMARE IS OVER? HOTEL IN THE MIDDLE OF PARADISE. DID I RUN ARCADE'S RIDICULOUS GAUNTLET?
BUT NOT ARCADE. SOMEBODY ELSE PUT HIM AND THIS ALL TOGETHER.
TIME TO FIND OUT.
HEY! I SEEM TO UH...HAVE LOST MY LUGGAGE. CAN YOU...?
FINALLY. YOU ARE AWAKE!
FANTASTIC.

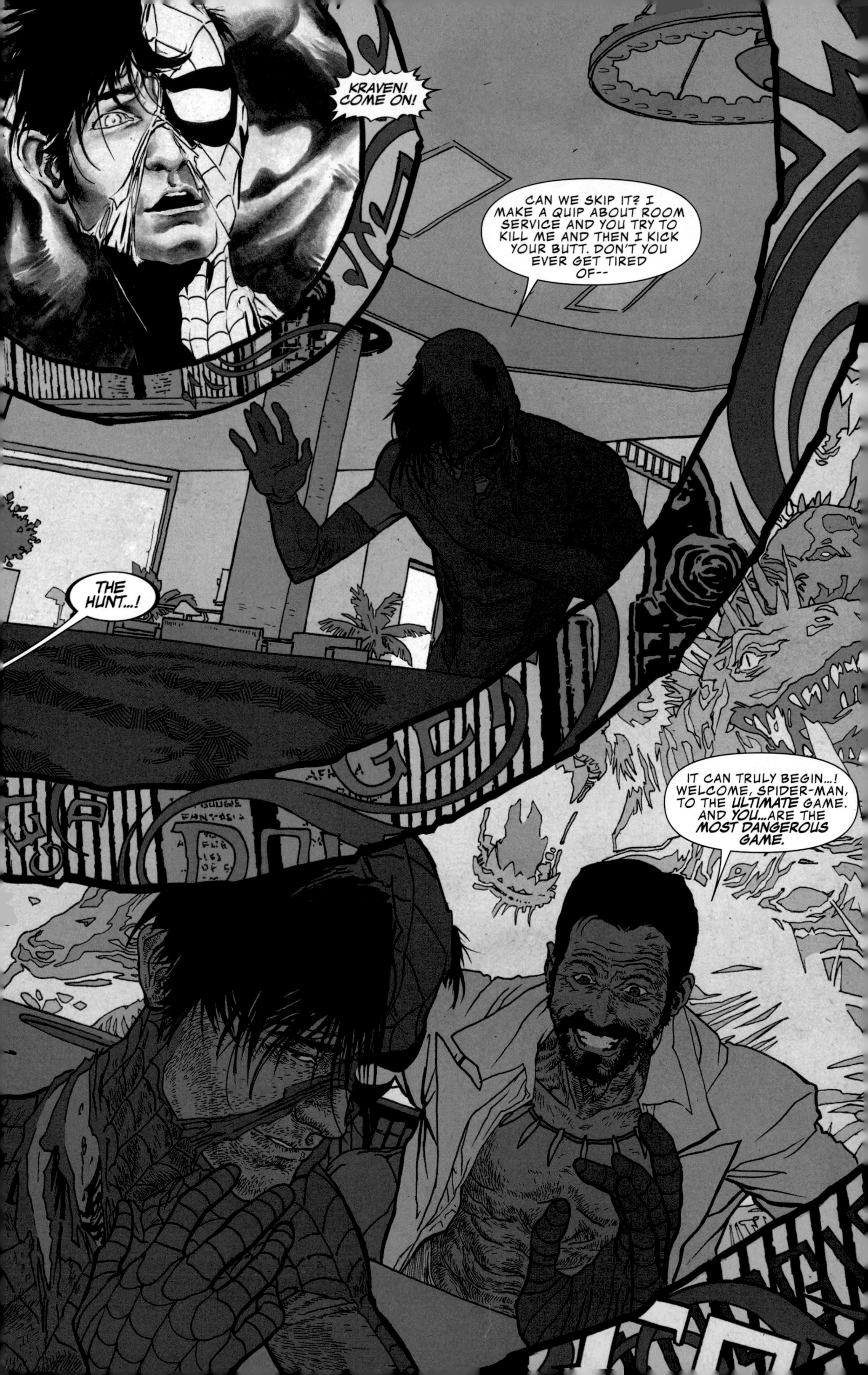
KRAVEN! COME ON!
CAN WE SKIP IT? I MAKE A QUIP ABOUT ROOM SERVICE AND YOU TRY TO KILL ME AND THEN I KICK YOUR BUTT. DON'T YOU EVER GET TIRED OF--
THE HUNT...!
IT CAN TRULY BEGIN...! WELCOME, SPIDER-MAN, TO THE ULTIMATE GAME. AND YOU...ARE THE MOST DANGEROUS GAME.

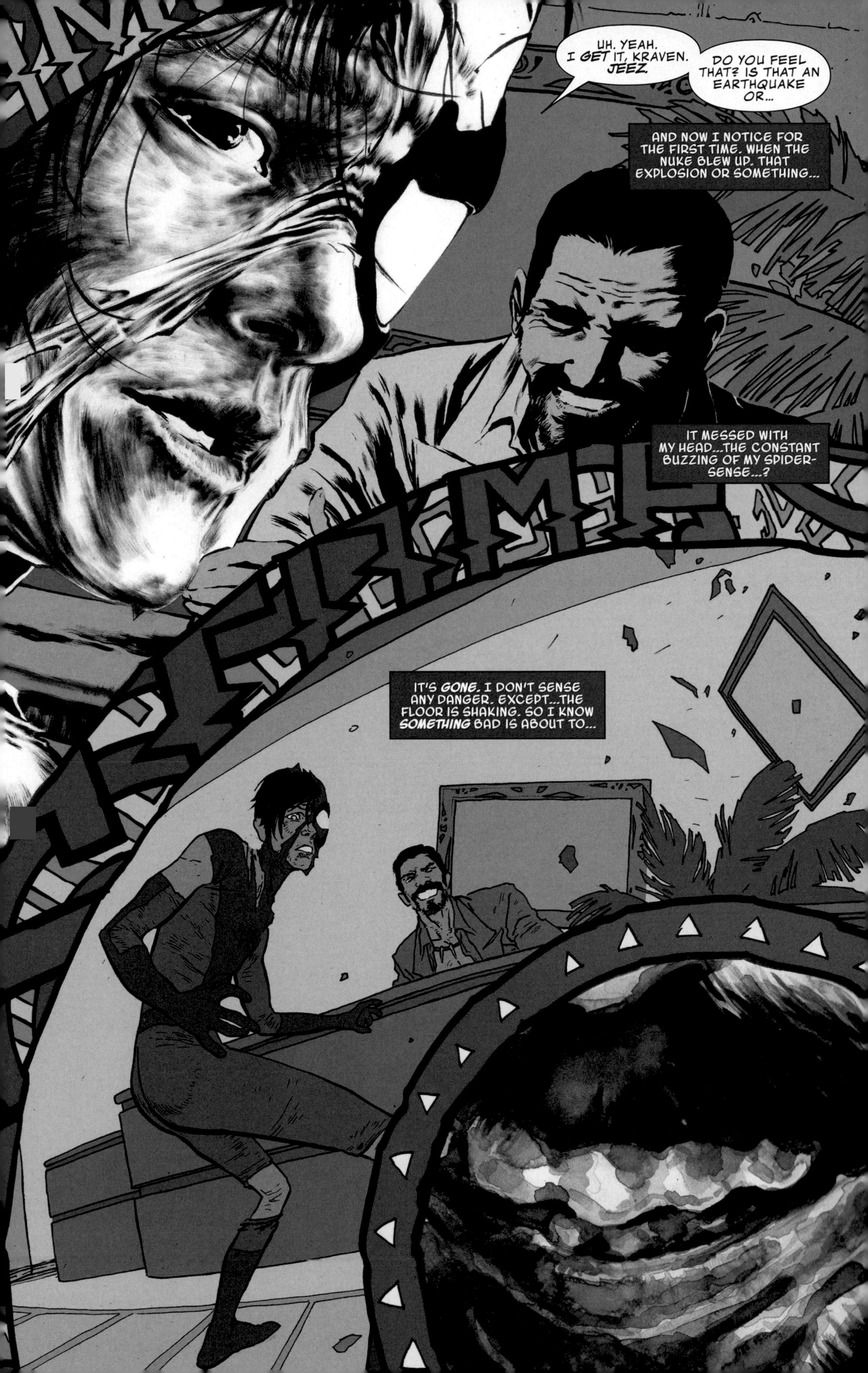
UH. YEAH. I GET IT, KRAVEN. JEEZ.
DO YOU FEEL THAT? IS THAT AN EARTHQUAKE OR...
AND NOW I NOTICE FOR THE FIRST TIME. WHEN THE NUKE BLEW UP. THAT EXPLOSION OR SOMETHING...
IT MESSED WITH MY HEAD...THE CONSTANT BUZZING OF MY SPIDER-SENSE...?
IT'S GONE. I DON'T SENSE ANY DANGER. EXCEPT...THE FLOOR IS SHAKING. SO I KNOW SOMETHING BAD IS ABOUT TO...

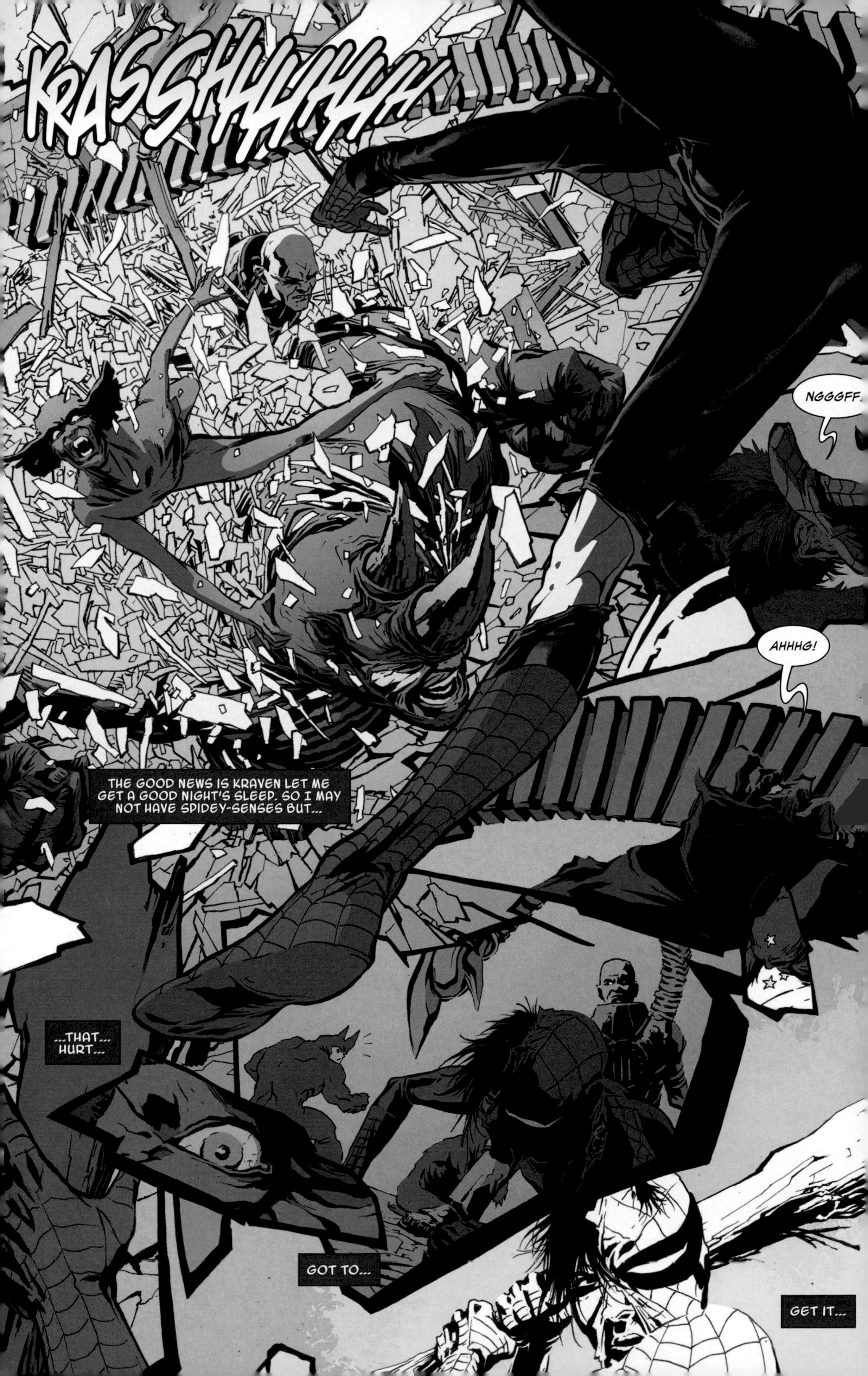
KRASSHHHHHH
NGGGFF.
AHHHG!
THE GOOD NEWS IS KRAVEN LET ME GET A GOOD NIGHT'S SLEEP. SO I MAY NOT HAVE SPIDEY-SENSES BUT...
...THAT... HURT...
GOT TO...
GET IT...

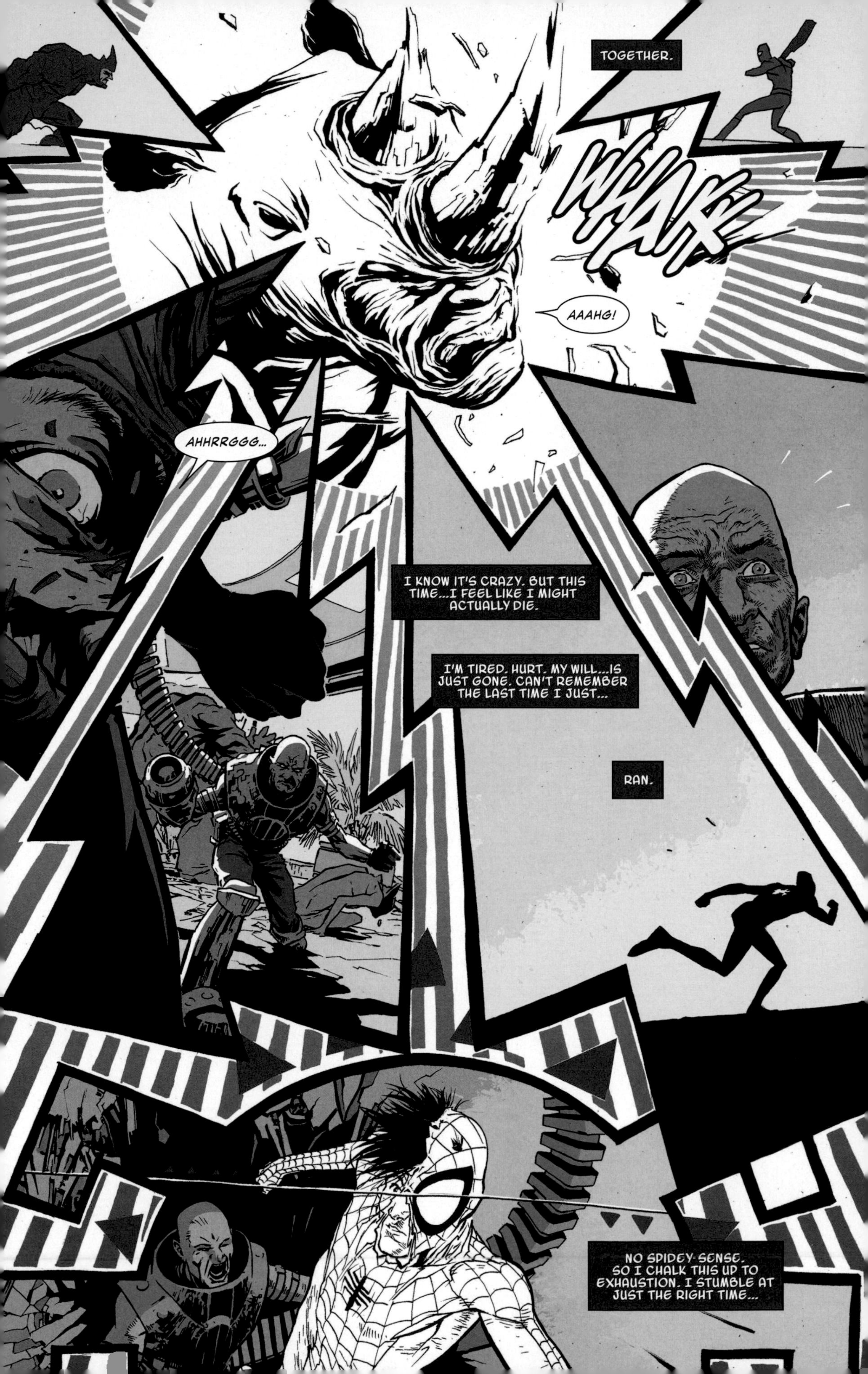
TOGETHER.
WHAK!
AAAHG!
AHHRRGGG...
I KNOW IT'S CRAZY. BUT THIS TIME...I FEEL LIKE I MIGHT ACTUALLY DIE.
I'M TIRED. HURT. MY WILL...IS JUST GONE. CAN'T REMEMBER THE LAST TIME I JUST...
RAN.
NO SPIDEY-SENSE. SO I CHALK THIS UP TO EXHAUSTION. I STUMBLE AT JUST THE RIGHT TIME...

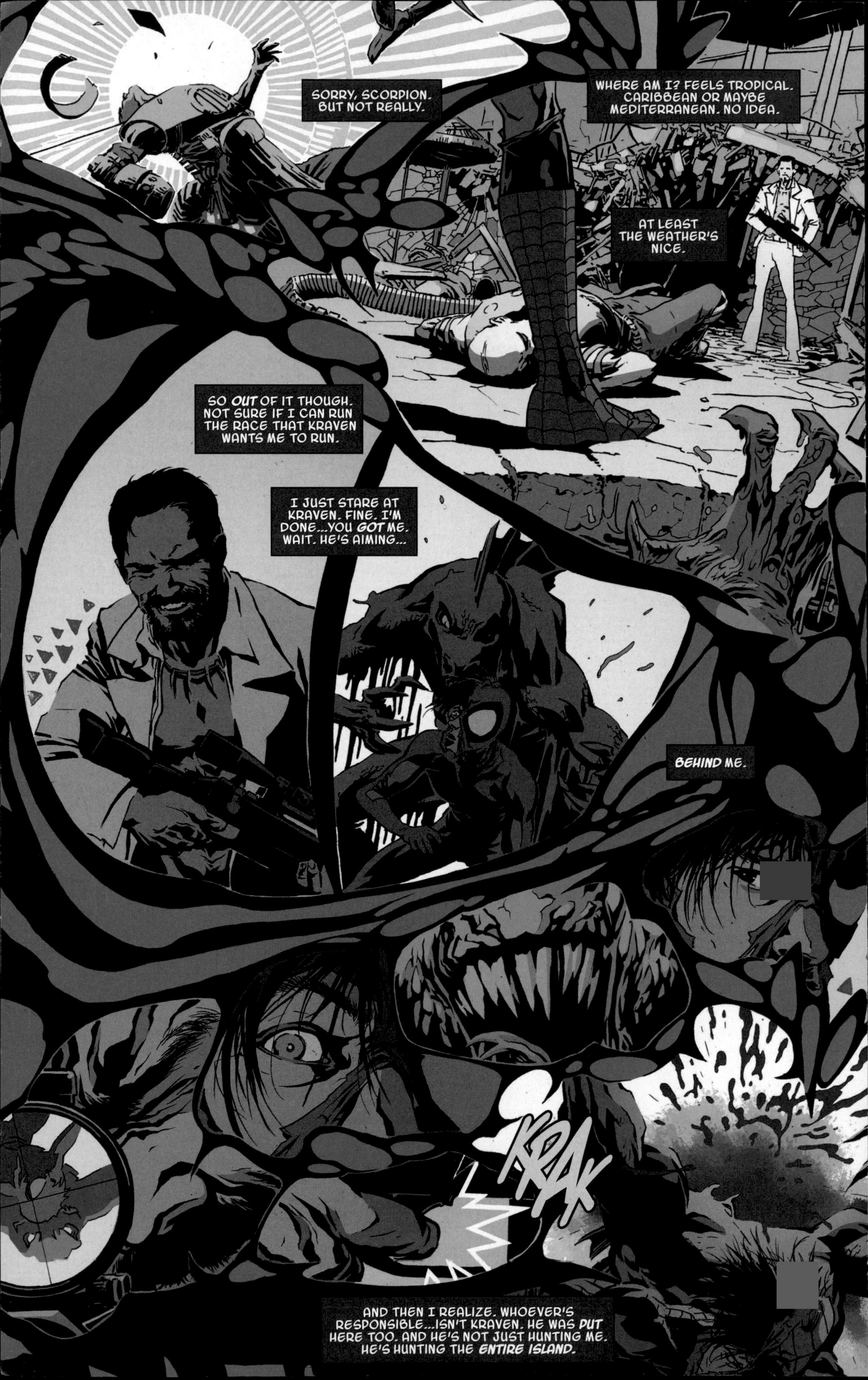
SORRY, SCORPION. BUT NOT REALLY.
WHERE AM I? FEELS TROPICAL. CARIBBEAN OR MAYBE MEDITERRANEAN. NO IDEA.
AT LEAST THE WEATHER'S NICE.
SO OUT OF IT THOUGH. NOT SURE IF I CAN RUN THE RACE THAT KRAVEN WANTS ME TO RUN.
I JUST STARE AT KRAVEN. FINE. I'M DONE...YOU GOT ME. WAIT. HE'S AIMING...
BEHIND ME.
KRAK
AND THEN I REALIZE. WHOEVER'S RESPONSIBLE...ISN'T KRAVEN. HE WAS PUT HERE TOO. AND HE'S NOT JUST HUNTING ME. HE'S HUNTING THE ENTIRE ISLAND.

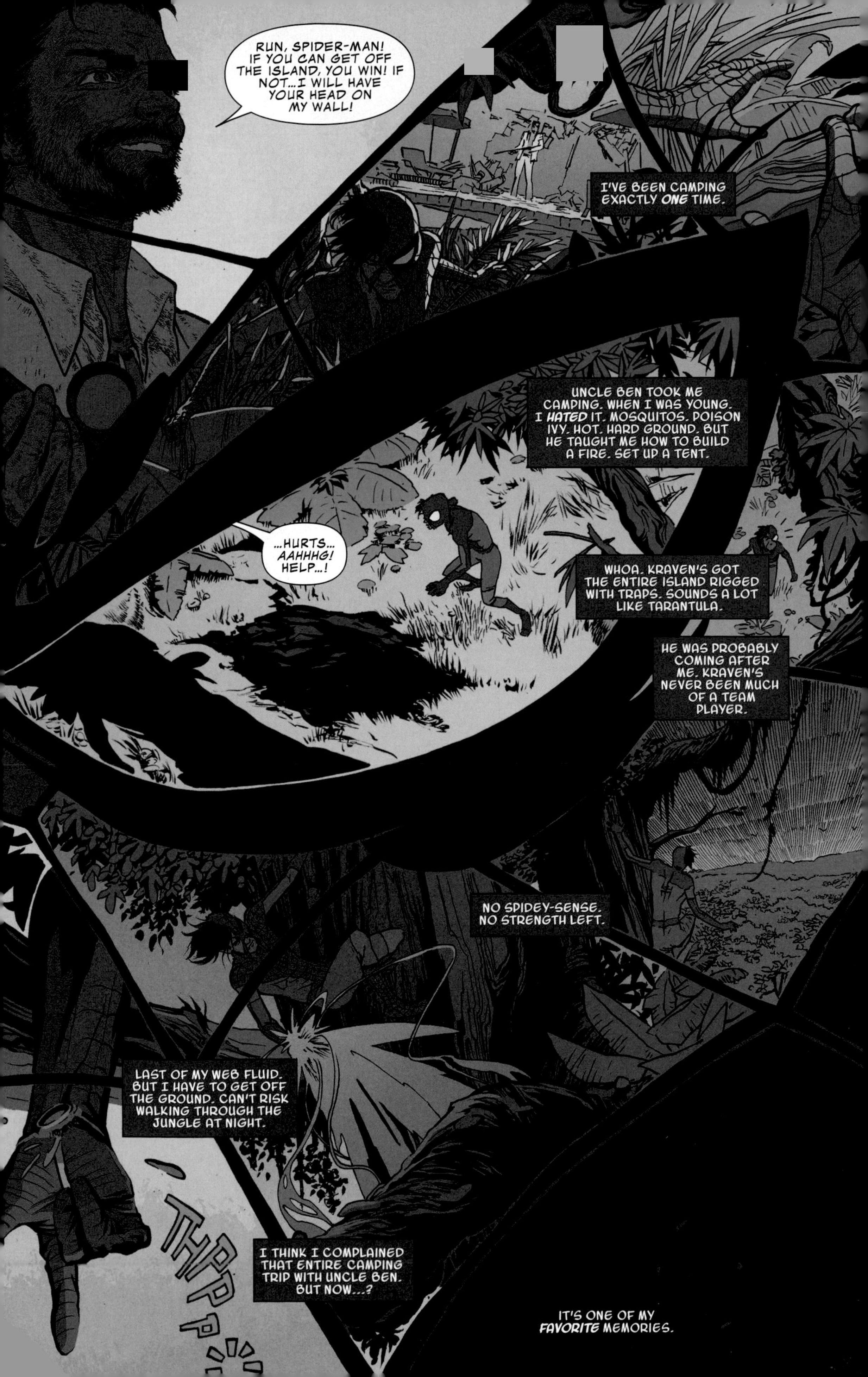
RUN, SPIDER-MAN! IF YOU CAN GET OFF THE ISLAND, YOU WIN! IF NOT...I WILL HAVE YOUR HEAD ON MY WALL!
I'VE BEEN CAMPING EXACTLY ONE TIME.
UNCLE BEN TOOK ME CAMPING. WHEN I WAS YOUNG. I HATED IT. MOSQUITOS. POISON IVY. HOT. HARD GROUND. BUT HE TAUGHT ME HOW TO BUILD A FIRE. SET UP A TENT.
...HURTS... AAHHHG! HELP...!
WHOA. KRAVEN'S GOT THE ENTIRE ISLAND RIGGED WITH TRAPS. SOUNDS A LOT LIKE TARANTULA.
HE WAS PROBABLY COMING AFTER ME. KRAVEN'S NEVER BEEN MUCH OF A TEAM PLAYER.
NO SPIDEY-SENSE. NO STRENGTH LEFT.
LAST OF MY WEB FLUID. BUT I HAVE TO GET OFF THE GROUND. CAN'T RISK WALKING THROUGH THE JUNGLE AT NIGHT.
THPPP
I THINK I COMPLAINED THAT ENTIRE CAMPING TRIP WITH UNCLE BEN. BUT NOW...?
IT'S ONE OF MY FAVORITE MEMORIES.

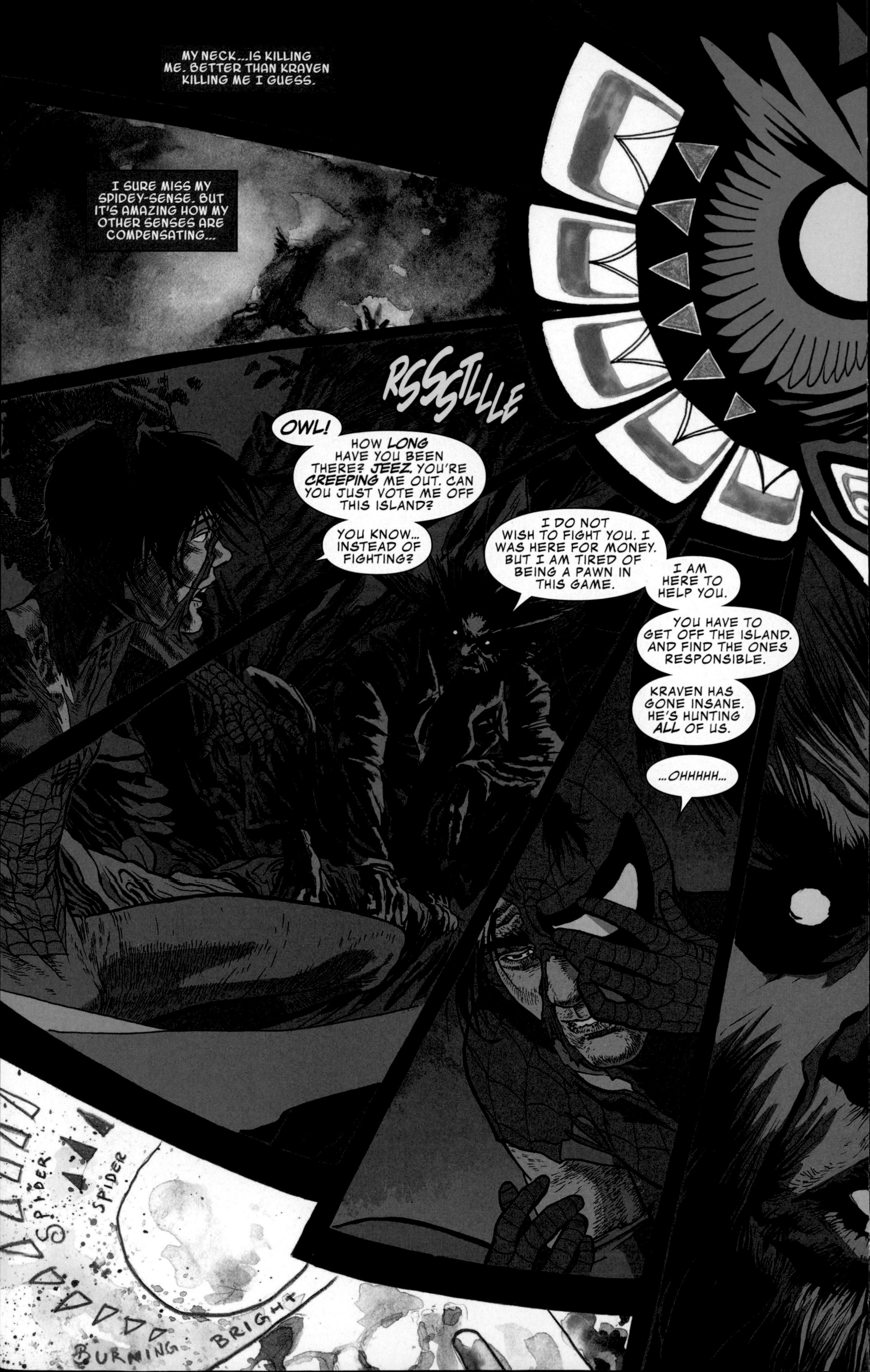

MY NECK...IS KILLING ME. BETTER THAN KRAVEN KILLING ME I GUESS.
I SURE MISS MY SPIDEY-SENSE. BUT IT'S AMAZING HOW MY OTHER SENSES ARE COMPENSATING...
RSSSTLLLE
OWL!
HOW LONG HAVE YOU BEEN THERE? JEEZ. YOU'RE CREEPING ME OUT. CAN YOU JUST VOTE ME OFF THIS ISLAND?
YOU KNOW... INSTEAD OF FIGHTING?
I DO NOT WISH TO FIGHT YOU. I WAS HERE FOR MONEY. BUT I AM TIRED OF BEING A PAWN IN THIS GAME.
I AM HERE TO HELP YOU.
YOU HAVE TO GET OFF THE ISLAND. AND FIND THE ONES RESPONSIBLE.
KRAVEN HAS GONE INSANE. HE'S HUNTING ALL OF US.
...OHHHHH...
SPIDER
SPIDER
BURNING BRIGHT

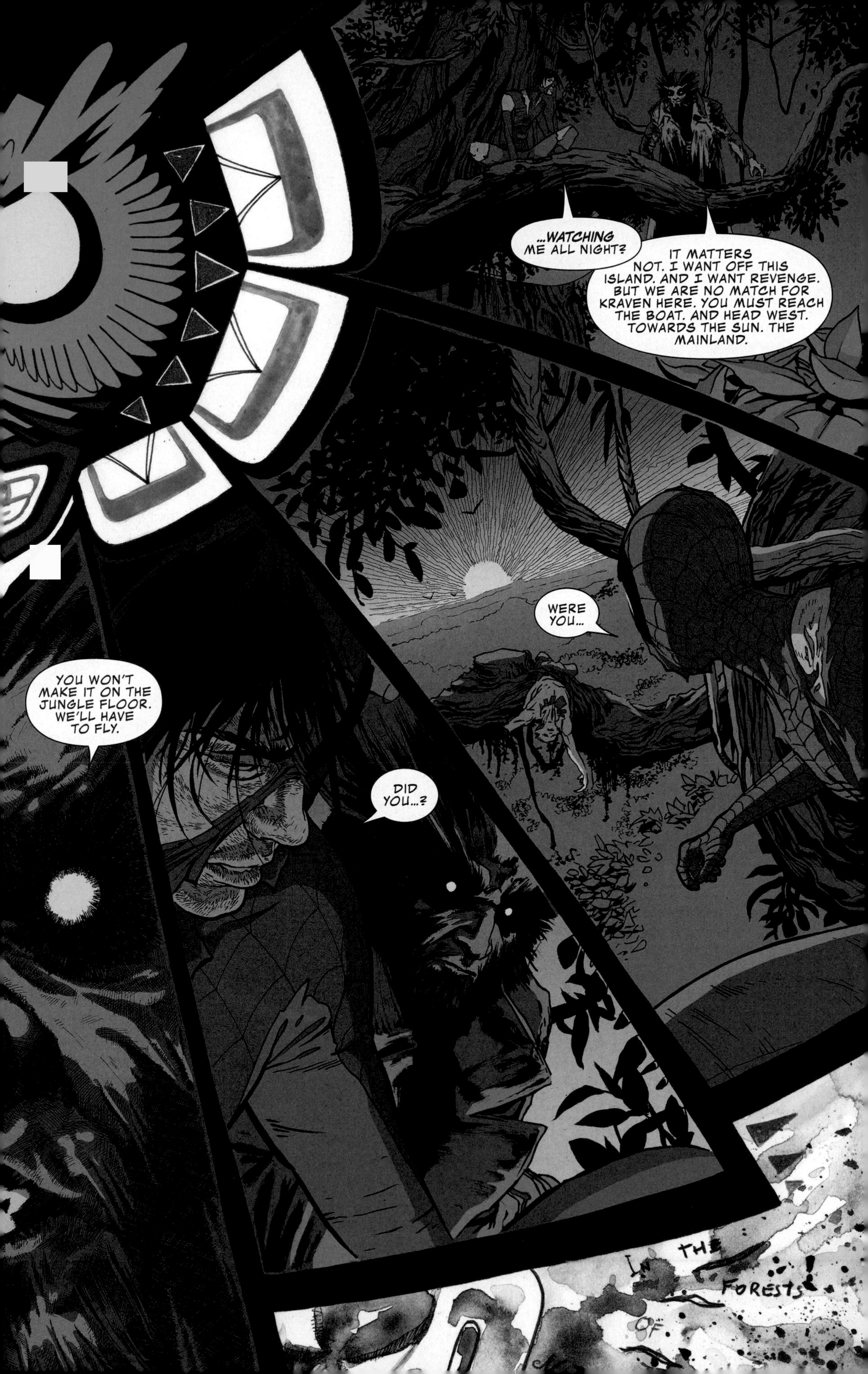
WERE YOU...
...WATCHING ME ALL NIGHT?
IT MATTERS NOT. I WANT OFF THIS ISLAND. AND I WANT REVENGE. BUT WE ARE NO MATCH FOR KRAVEN HERE. YOU MUST REACH THE BOAT. AND HEAD WEST. TOWARDS THE SUN. THE MAINLAND.
DID YOU...?
YOU WON'T MAKE IT ON THE JUNGLE FLOOR. WE'LL HAVE TO FLY.
IN THE
FORESTS
OF

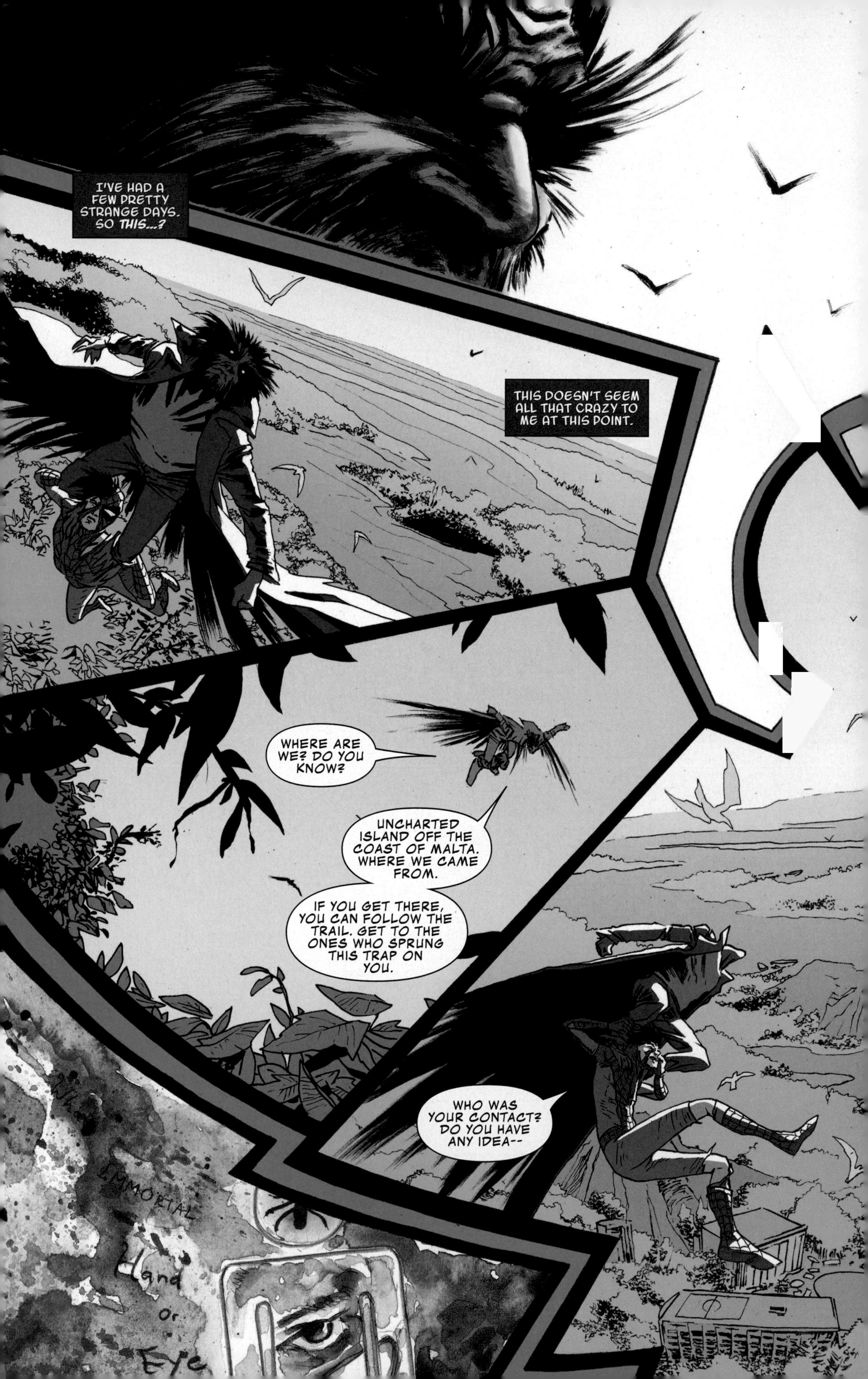
I'VE HAD A FEW PRETTY STRANGE DAYS. SO THIS...?
THIS DOESN'T SEEM ALL THAT CRAZY TO ME AT THIS POINT.
WHERE ARE WE? DO YOU KNOW?
UNCHARTED ISLAND OFF THE COAST OF MALTA. WHERE WE CAME FROM.
IF YOU GET THERE, YOU CAN FOLLOW THE TRAIL. GET TO THE ONES WHO SPRUNG THIS TRAP ON YOU.
WHO WAS YOUR CONTACT? DO YOU HAVE ANY IDEA--
IMMORTAL
Hand
or
Eye

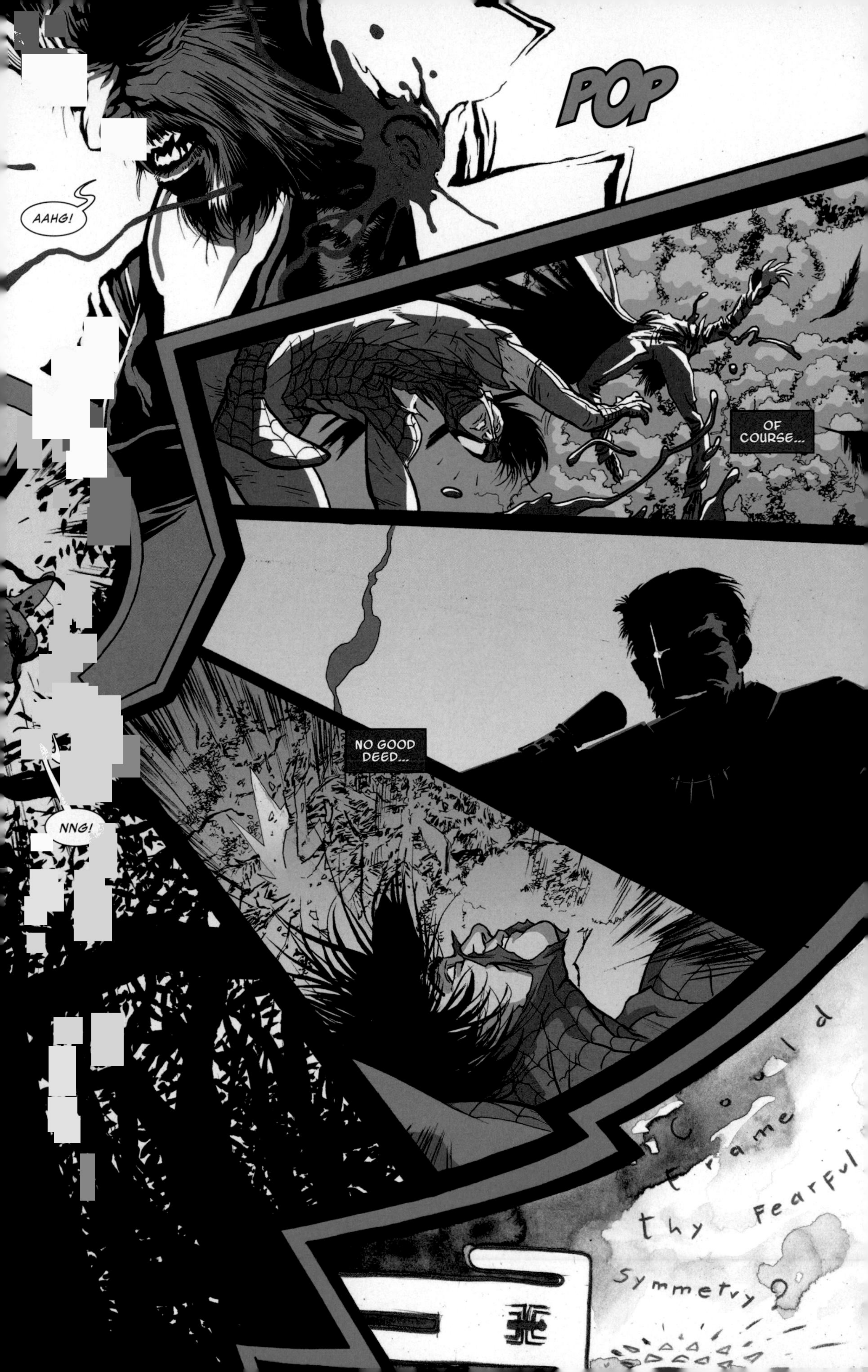
POP
AAHG!
OF COURSE...
NO GOOD DEED...
NNG!
could frame thy fearful symmetry?

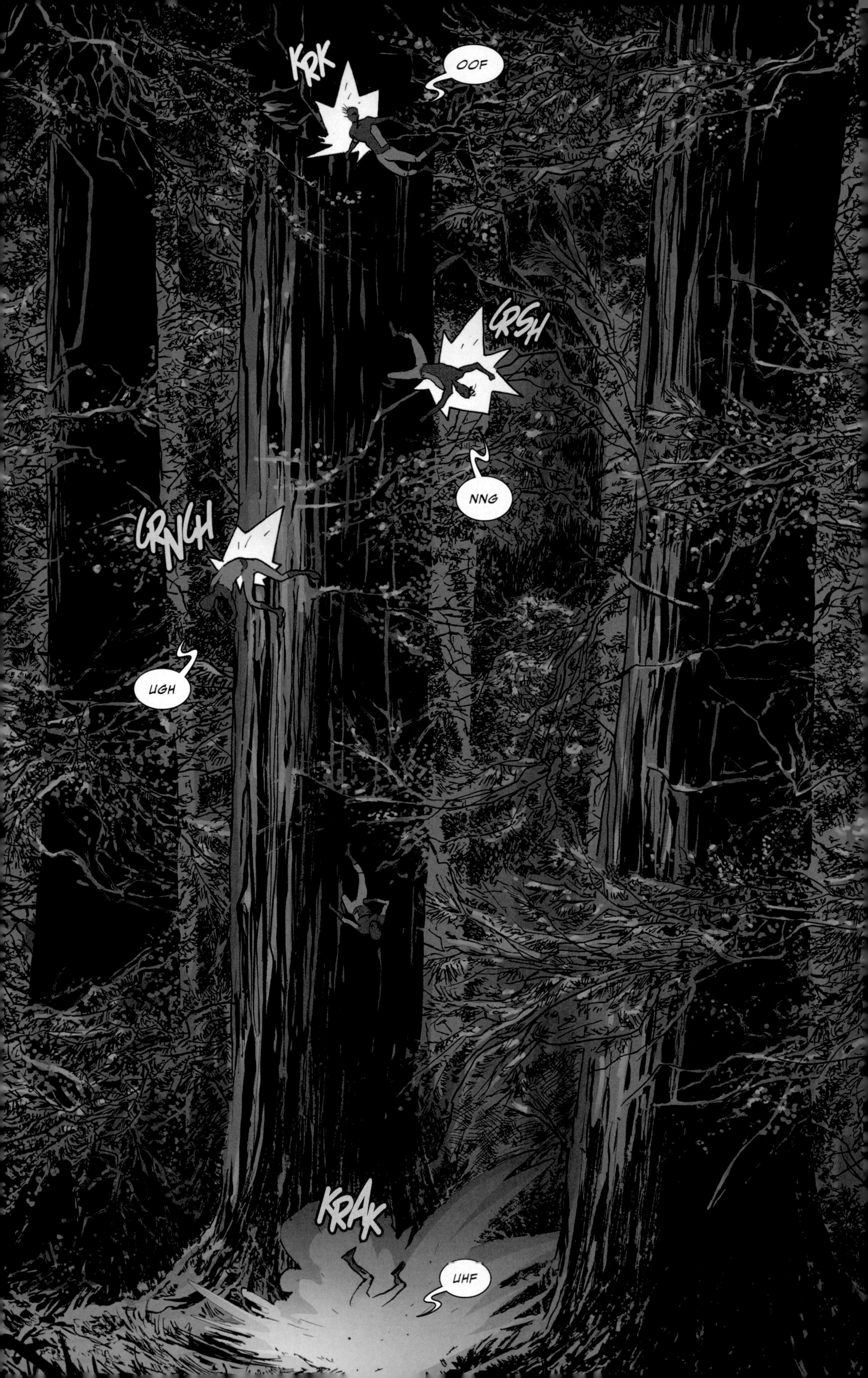
KRK
OOF
CRSH
NNG
CRNCH
UGH
KRAK
UHF

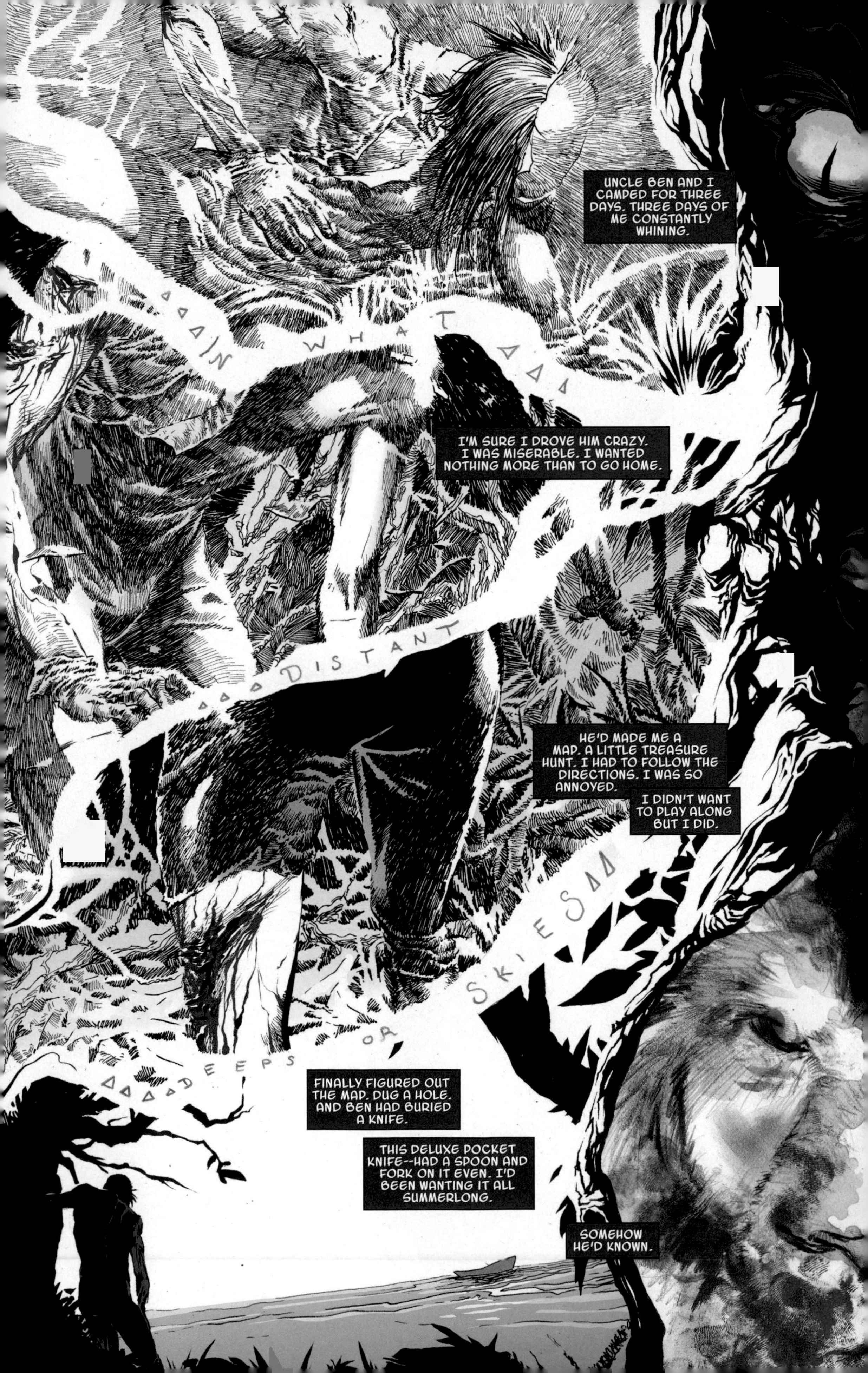
UNCLE BEN AND I CAMPED FOR THREE DAYS. THREE DAYS OF ME CONSTANTLY WHINING.
IN WHAT
I'M SURE I DROVE HIM CRAZY. I WAS MISERABLE. I WANTED NOTHING MORE THAN TO GO HOME.
DISTANT
HE'D MADE ME A MAP. A LITTLE TREASURE HUNT. I HAD TO FOLLOW THE DIRECTIONS. I WAS SO ANNOYED.
I DIDN'T WANT TO PLAY ALONG BUT I DID.
DEEPS OR SKIES
FINALLY FIGURED OUT THE MAP. DUG A HOLE. AND BEN HAD BURIED A KNIFE.
THIS DELUXE POCKET KNIFE--HAD A SPOON AND FORK ON IT EVEN. I'D BEEN WANTING IT ALL SUMMERLONG.
SOMEHOW HE'D KNOWN.

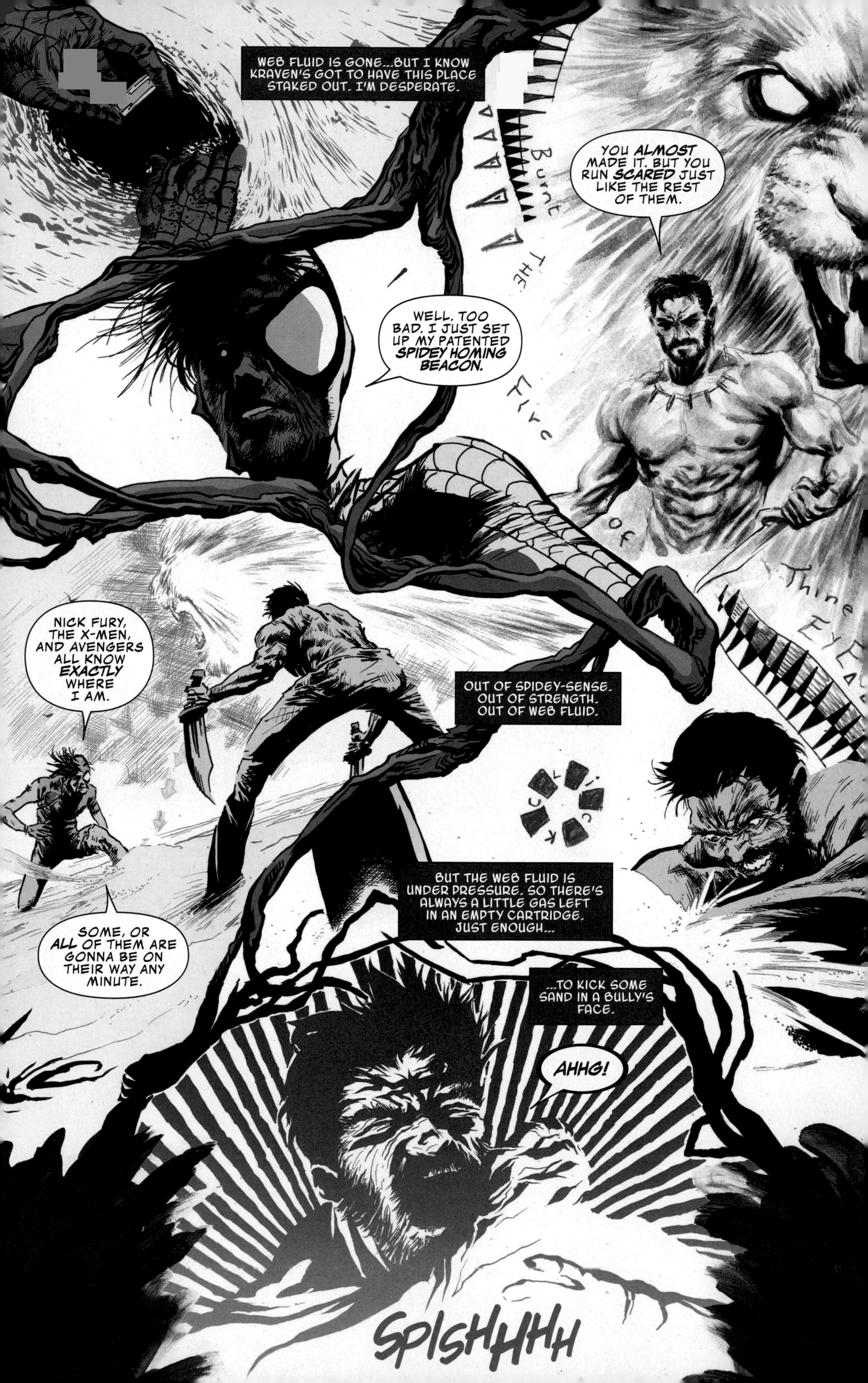

WEB FLUID IS GONE...BUT I KNOW KRAVEN'S GOT TO HAVE THIS PLACE STAKED OUT. I'M DESPERATE.
YOU ALMOST MADE IT. BUT YOU RUN SCARED JUST LIKE THE REST OF THEM.
Burnt THE Fire of Thine
WELL. TOO BAD. I JUST SET UP MY PATENTED SPIDEY HOMING BEACON.
NICK FURY, THE X-MEN, AND AVENGERS ALL KNOW EXACTLY WHERE I AM.
OUT OF SPIDEY-SENSE. OUT OF STRENGTH. OUT OF WEB FLUID.
CLICK
SOME, OR ALL OF THEM ARE GONNA BE ON THEIR WAY ANY MINUTE.
BUT THE WEB FLUID IS UNDER PRESSURE. SO THERE'S ALWAYS A LITTLE GAS LEFT IN AN EMPTY CARTRIDGE. JUST ENOUGH...
...TO KICK SOME SAND IN A BULLY'S FACE.
AHHG!
SPISHHHH

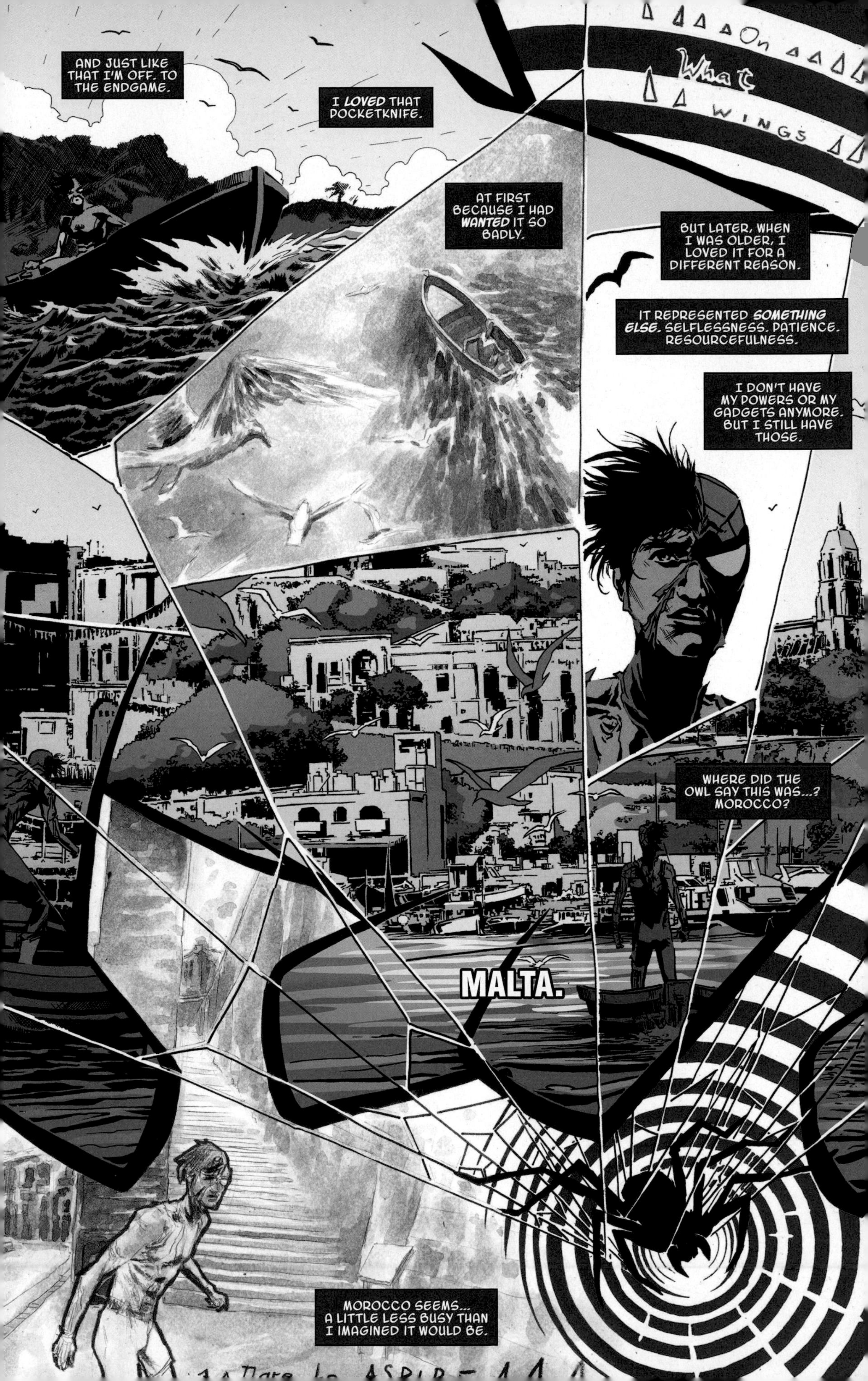
On
What
Wings
AND JUST LIKE THAT I'M OFF. TO THE ENDGAME.
I LOVED THAT POCKETKNIFE.
AT FIRST BECAUSE I HAD WANTED IT SO BADLY.
BUT LATER, WHEN I WAS OLDER, I LOVED IT FOR A DIFFERENT REASON.
IT REPRESENTED SOMETHING ELSE. SELFLESSNESS. PATIENCE. RESOURCEFULNESS.
I DON'T HAVE MY POWERS OR MY GADGETS ANYMORE. BUT I STILL HAVE THOSE.
WHERE DID THE OWL SAY THIS WAS...? MOROCCO?
MALTA.
MOROCCO SEEMS... A LITTLE LESS BUSY THAN I IMAGINED IT WOULD BE.
Dare he ASPIRE

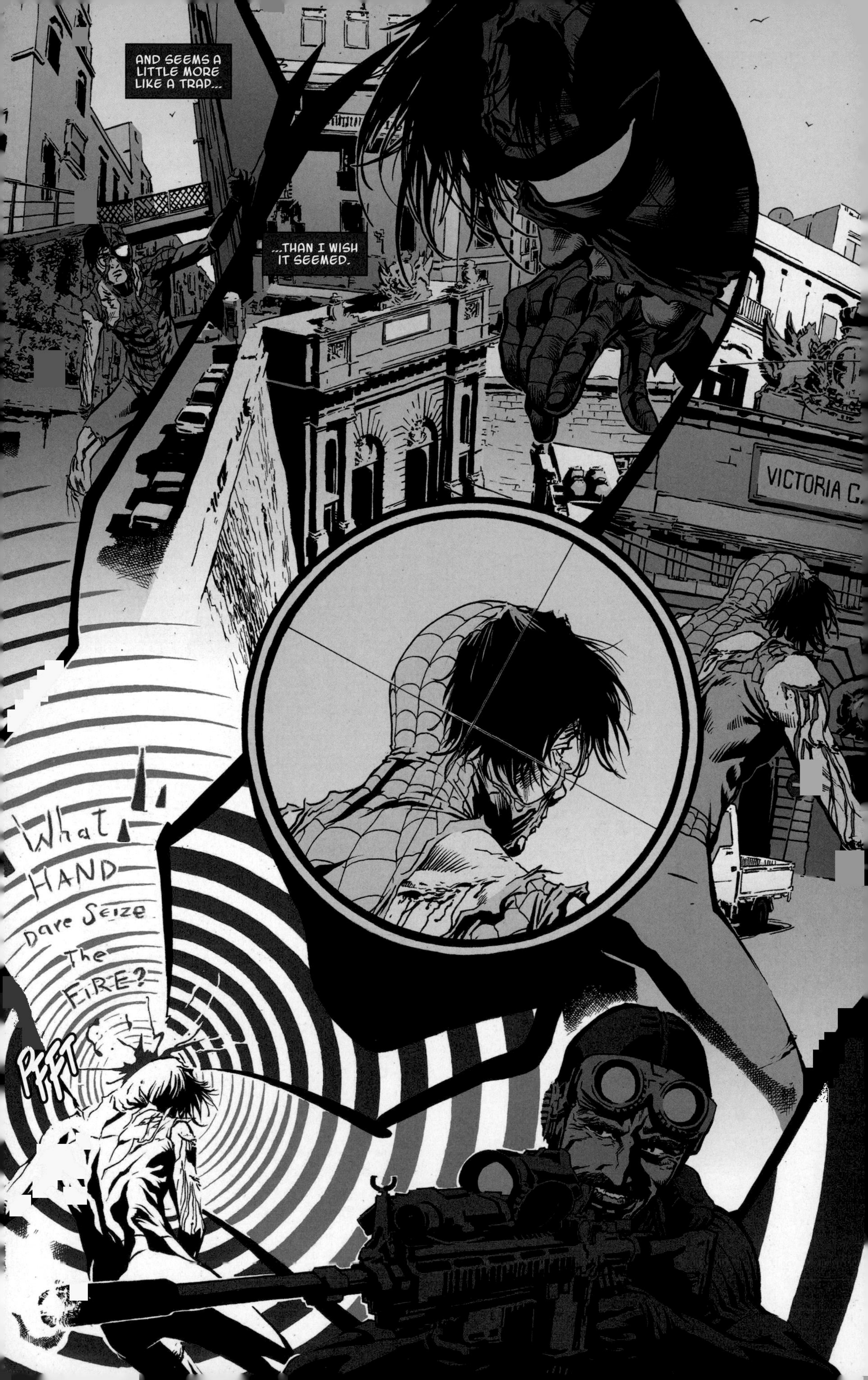
AND SEEMS A LITTLE MORE LIKE A TRAP...
...THAN I WISH IT SEEMED.
VICTORIA
What HAND Dare Seize The FIRE?
PFFT

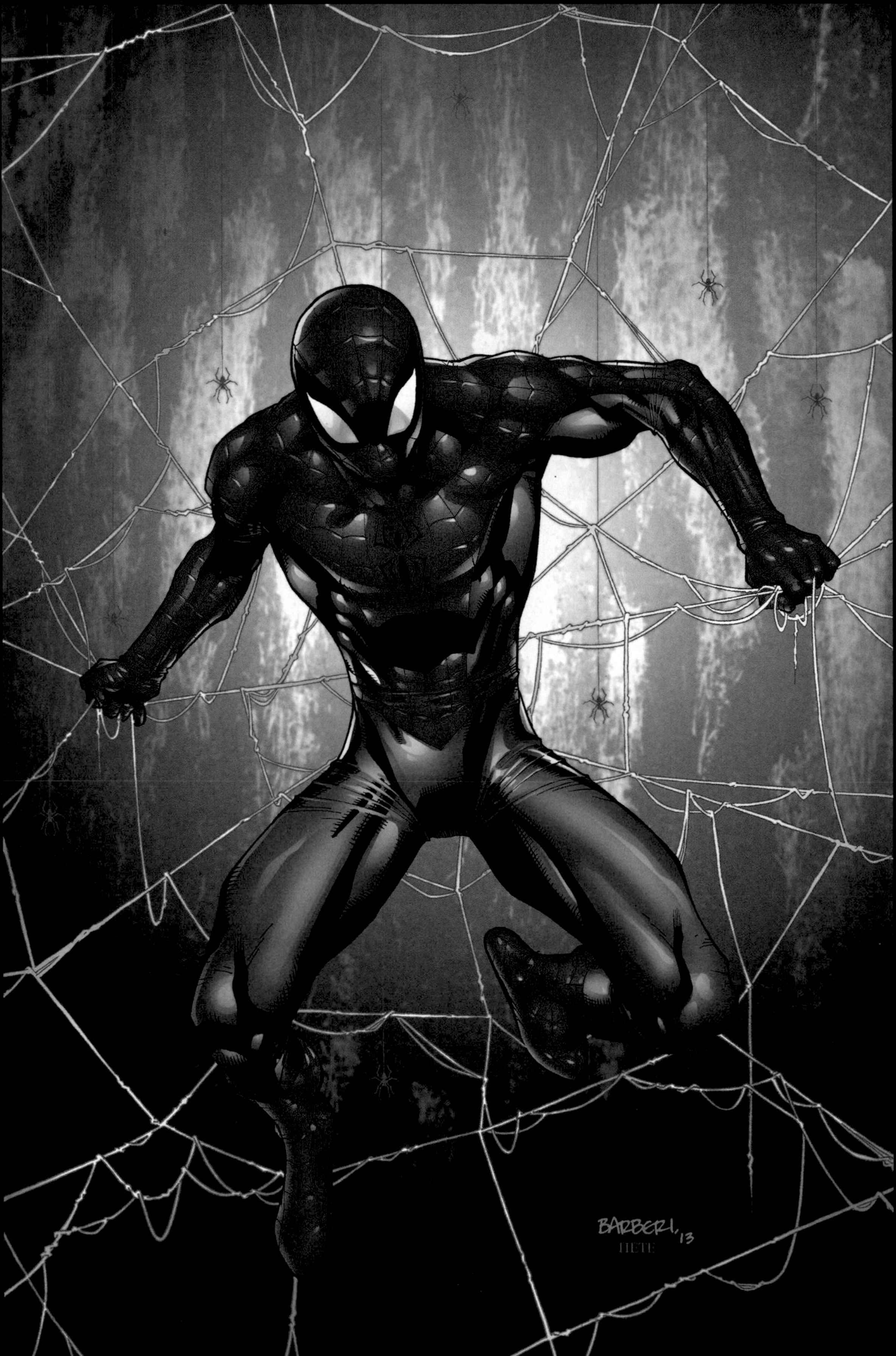
BARBERI, '13
PETE

#1 VARIANT COVER BY CARLO BARBERI & PETE PANTAZIS

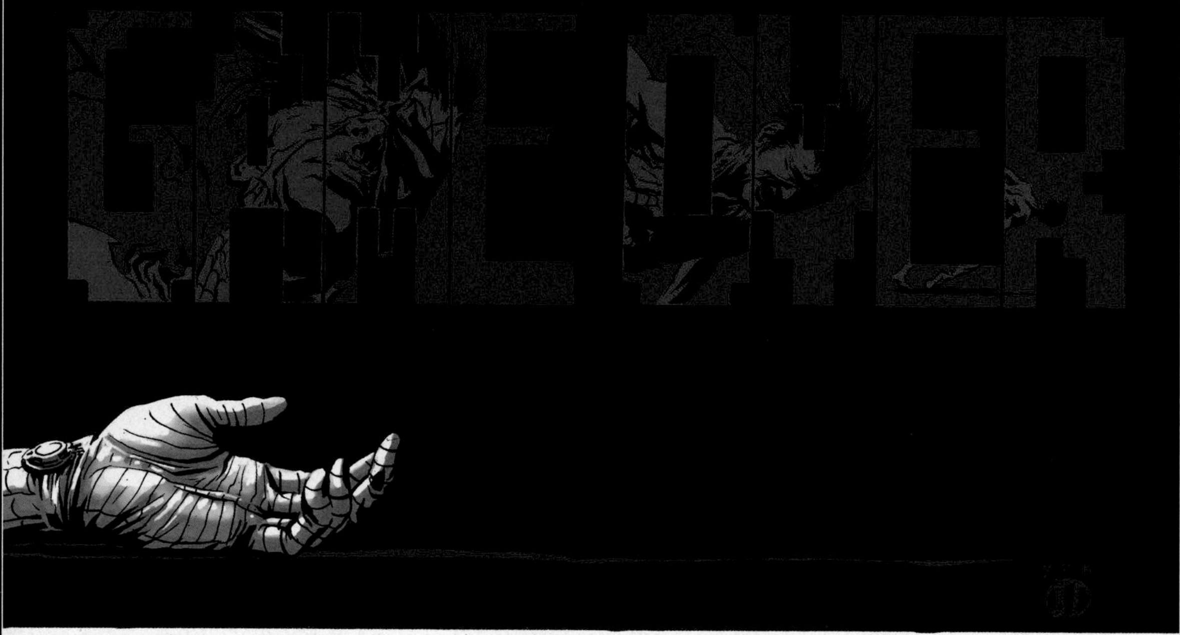
GAME OVER

5

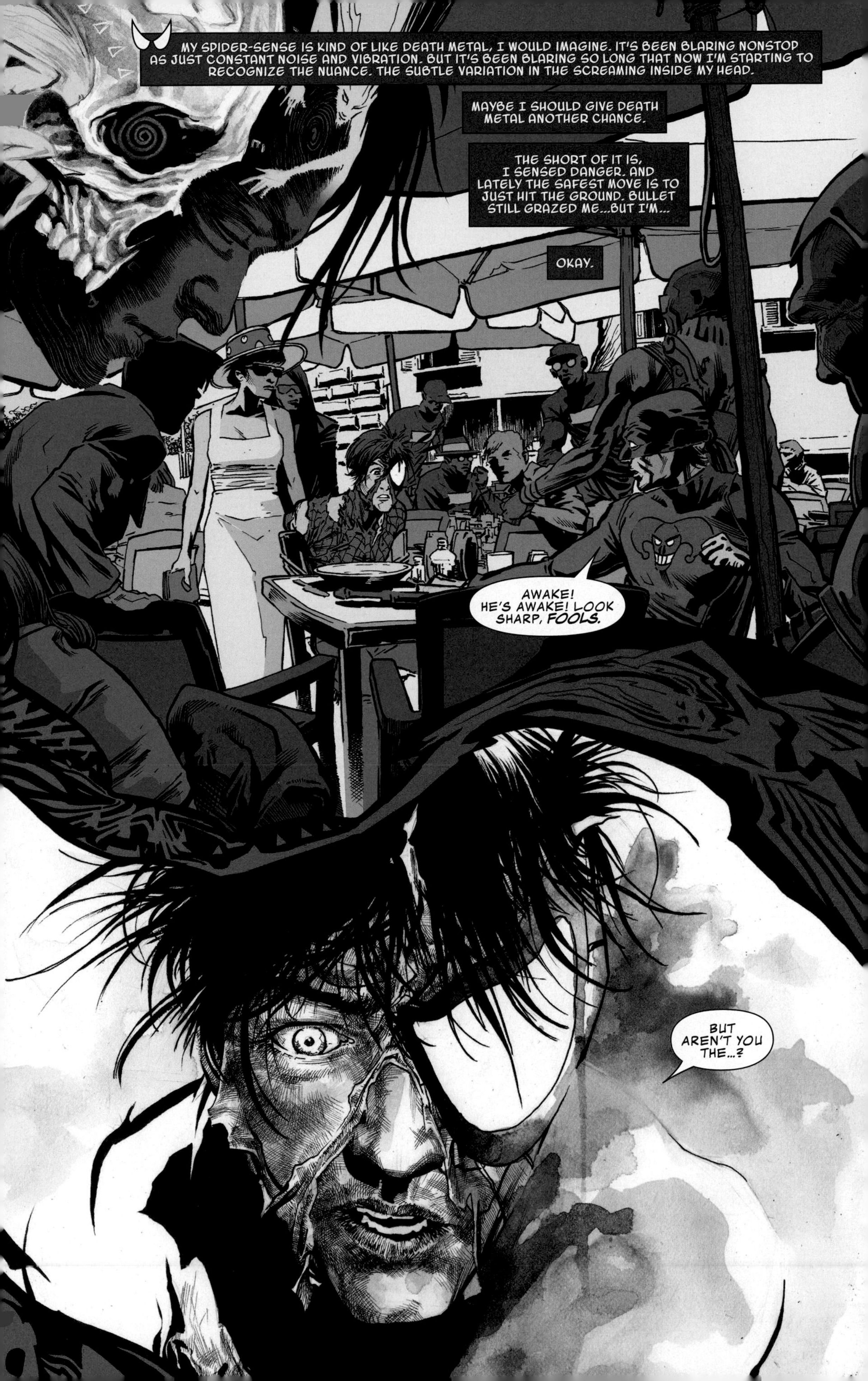
MY SPIDER-SENSE IS KIND OF LIKE DEATH METAL, I WOULD IMAGINE. IT'S BEEN BLARING NONSTOP AS JUST CONSTANT NOISE AND VIBRATION. BUT IT'S BEEN BLARING SO LONG THAT NOW I'M STARTING TO RECOGNIZE THE NUANCE. THE SUBTLE VARIATION IN THE SCREAMING INSIDE MY HEAD.
MAYBE I SHOULD GIVE DEATH METAL ANOTHER CHANCE.
THE SHORT OF IT IS, I SENSED DANGER. AND LATELY THE SAFEST MOVE IS TO JUST HIT THE GROUND. BULLET STILL GRAZED ME...BUT I'M...
OKAY.
AWAKE! HE'S AWAKE! LOOK SHARP, FOOLS.
BUT AREN'T YOU THE...?

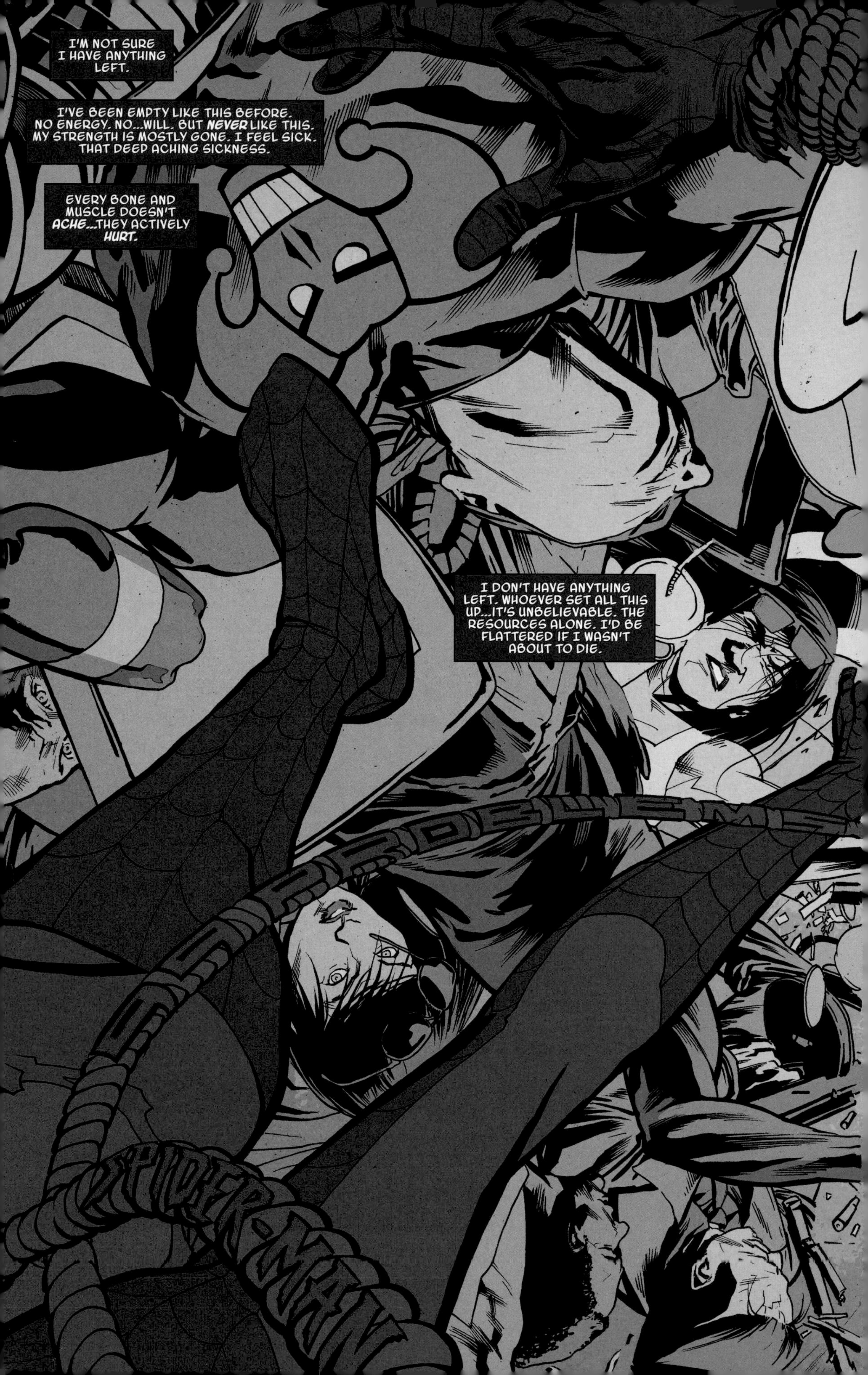
I'M NOT SURE I HAVE ANYTHING LEFT.
I'VE BEEN EMPTY LIKE THIS BEFORE. NO ENERGY. NO...WILL. BUT NEVER LIKE THIS. MY STRENGTH IS MOSTLY GONE. I FEEL SICK. THAT DEEP ACHING SICKNESS.
EVERY BONE AND MUSCLE DOESN'T ACHE...THEY ACTIVELY HURT.
I DON'T HAVE ANYTHING LEFT. WHOEVER SET ALL THIS UP...IT'S UNBELIEVABLE. THE RESOURCES ALONE. I'D BE FLATTERED IF I WASN'T ABOUT TO DIE.

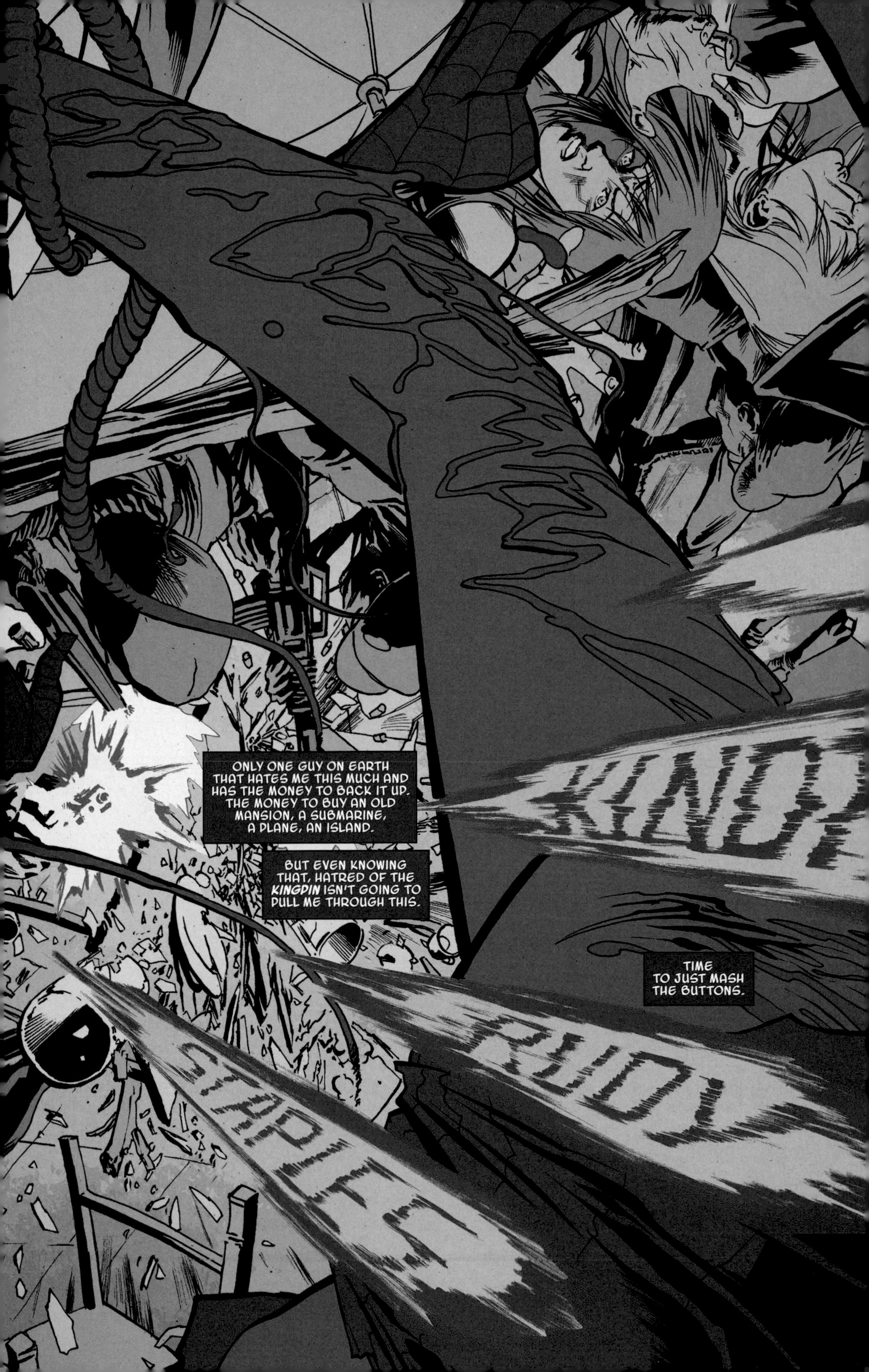

ONLY ONE GUY ON EARTH THAT HATES ME THIS MUCH AND HAS THE MONEY TO BACK IT UP. THE MONEY TO BUY AN OLD MANSION, A SUBMARINE, A PLANE, AN ISLAND.
BUT EVEN KNOWING THAT, HATRED OF THE KINGPIN ISN'T GOING TO PULL ME THROUGH THIS.
TIME TO JUST MASH THE BUTTONS.

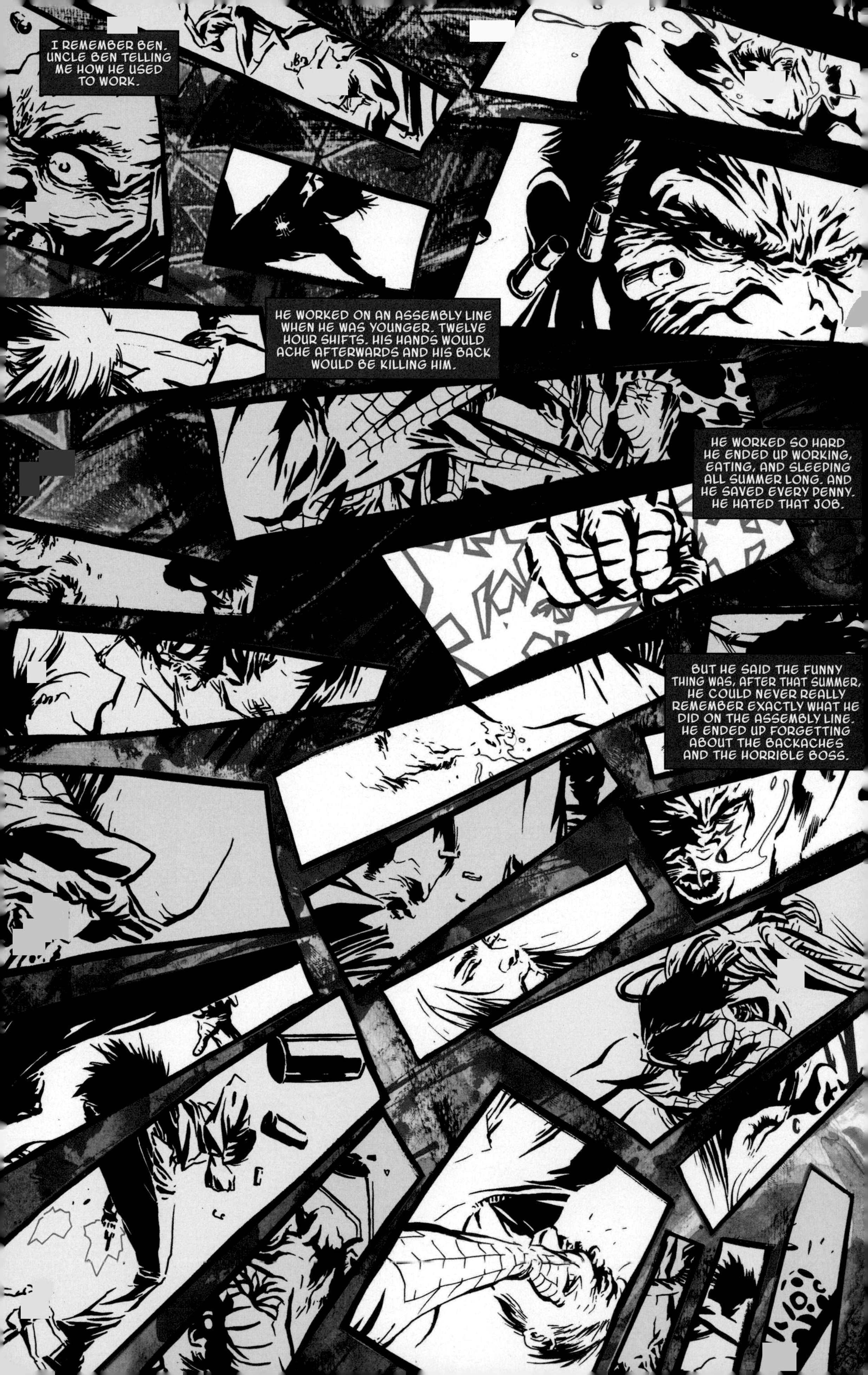
I REMEMBER BEN. UNCLE BEN TELLING ME HOW HE USED TO WORK.
HE WORKED ON AN ASSEMBLY LINE WHEN HE WAS YOUNGER. TWELVE HOUR SHIFTS. HIS HANDS WOULD ACHE AFTERWARDS AND HIS BACK WOULD BE KILLING HIM.
HE WORKED SO HARD HE ENDED UP WORKING, EATING, AND SLEEPING ALL SUMMER LONG. AND HE SAVED EVERY PENNY. HE HATED THAT JOB.
BUT HE SAID THE FUNNY THING WAS, AFTER THAT SUMMER, HE COULD NEVER REALLY REMEMBER EXACTLY WHAT HE DID ON THE ASSEMBLY LINE. HE ENDED UP FORGETTING ABOUT THE BACKACHES AND THE HORRIBLE BOSS.

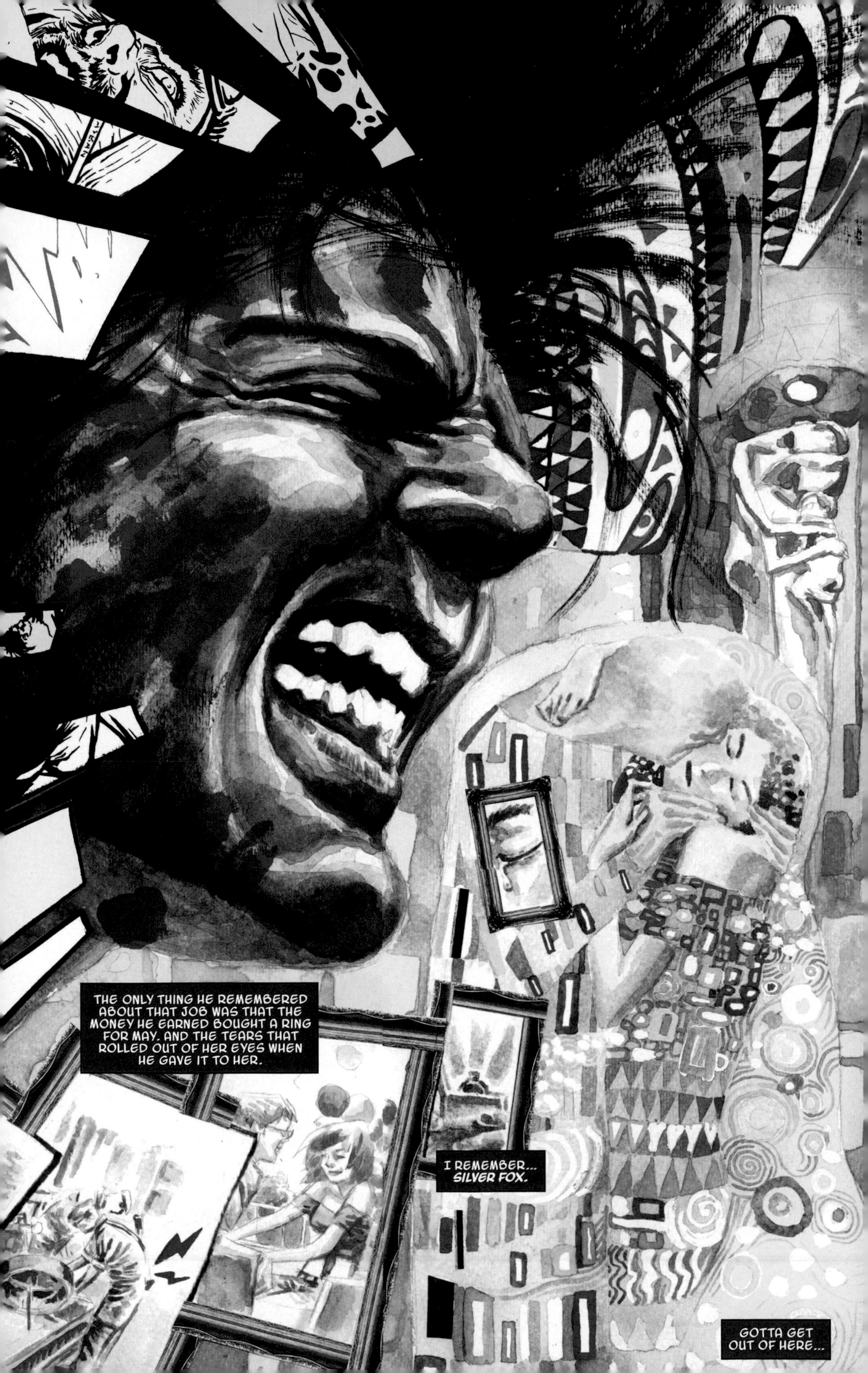
THE ONLY THING HE REMEMBERED ABOUT THAT JOB WAS THAT THE MONEY HE EARNED BOUGHT A RING FOR MAY. AND THE TEARS THAT ROLLED OUT OF HER EYES WHEN HE GAVE IT TO HER.
I REMEMBER... SILVER FOX.
GOTTA GET OUT OF HERE...

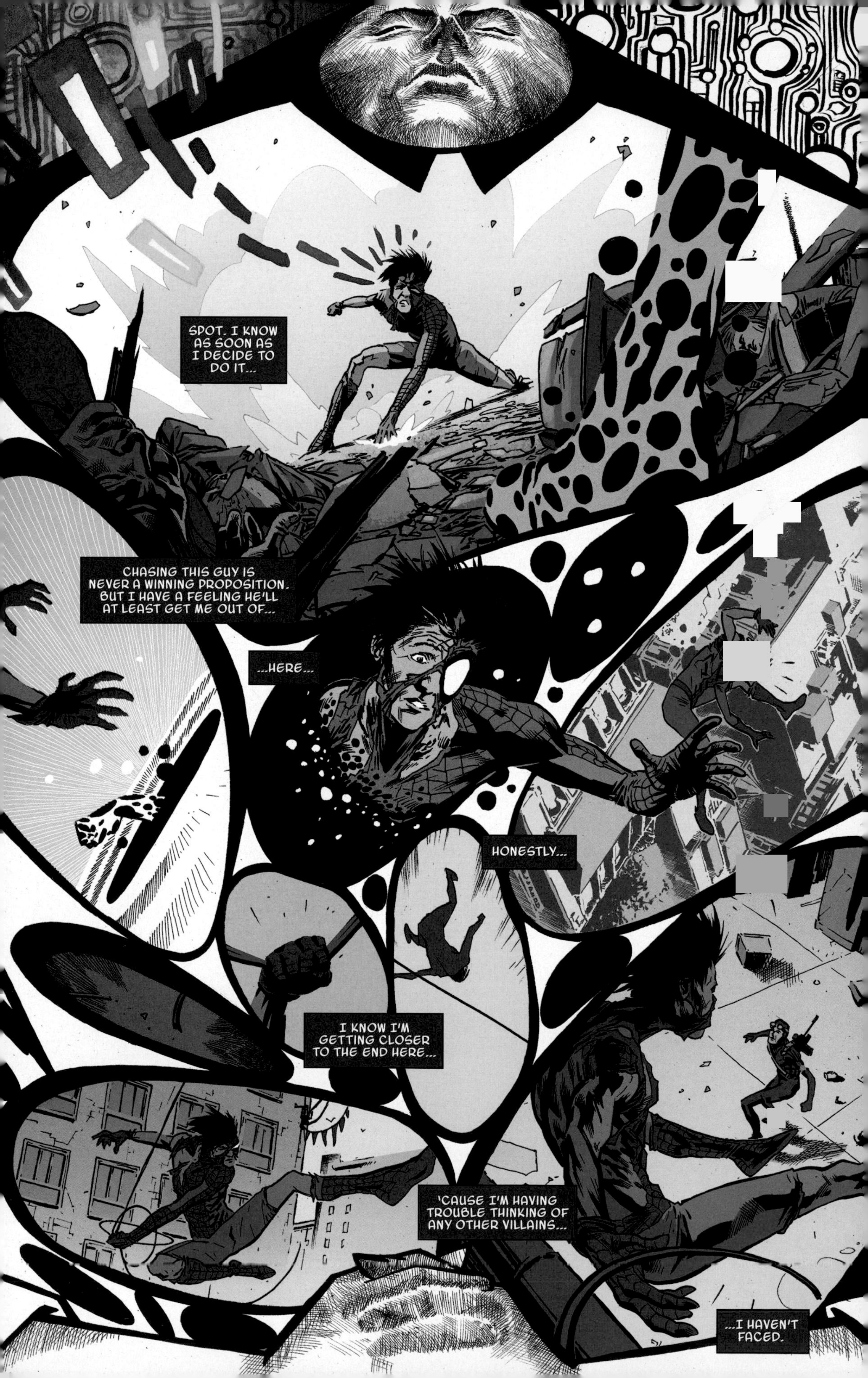
SPOT. I KNOW AS SOON AS I DECIDE TO DO IT...
CHASING THIS GUY IS NEVER A WINNING PROPOSITION. BUT I HAVE A FEELING HE'LL AT LEAST GET ME OUT OF...
...HERE...
HONESTLY...
I KNOW I'M GETTING CLOSER TO THE END HERE...
'CAUSE I'M HAVING TROUBLE THINKING OF ANY OTHER VILLAINS...
...I HAVEN'T FACED.

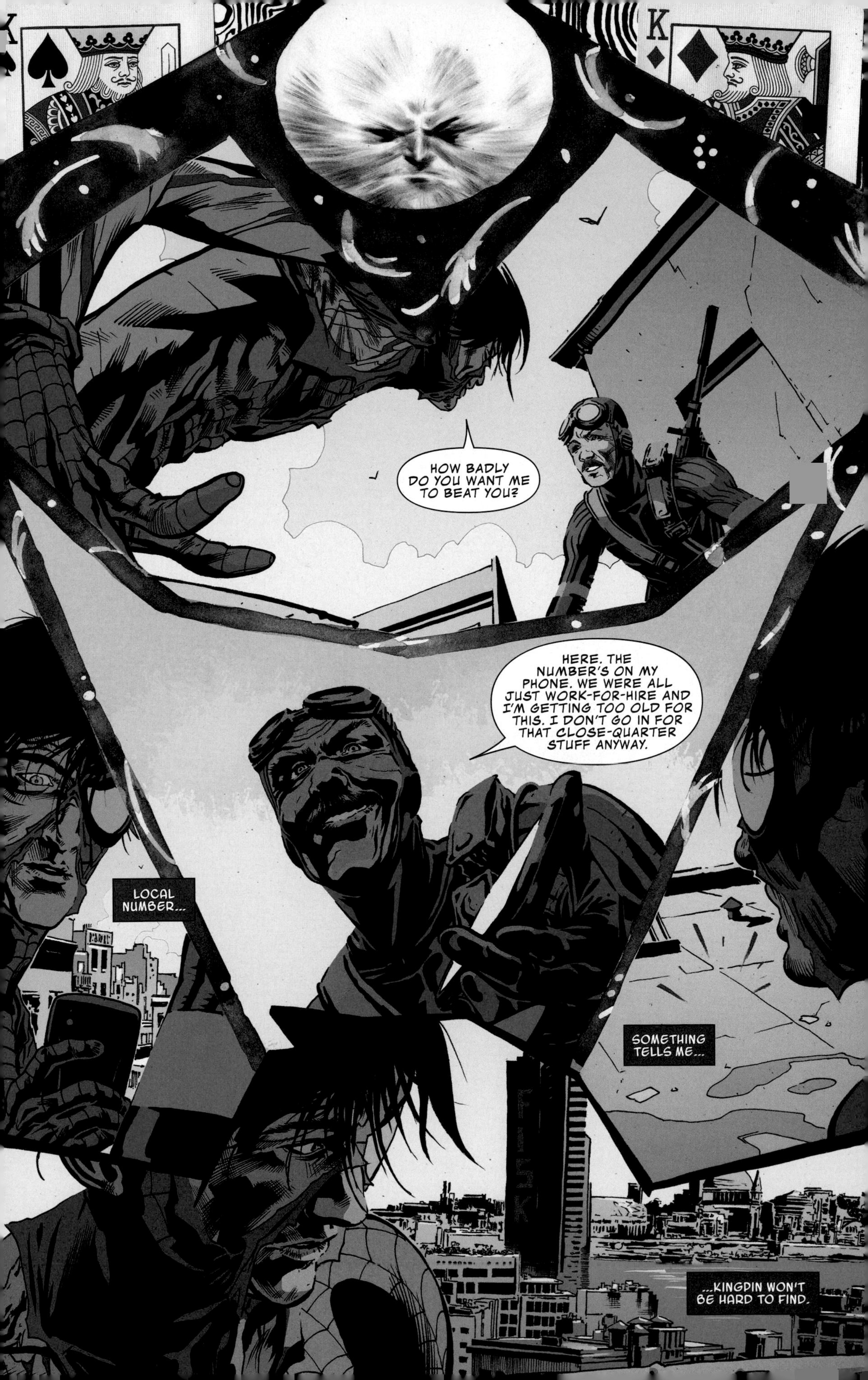
HOW BADLY DO YOU WANT ME TO BEAT YOU?
HERE. THE NUMBER'S ON MY PHONE. WE WERE ALL JUST WORK-FOR-HIRE AND I'M GETTING TOO OLD FOR THIS. I DON'T GO IN FOR THAT CLOSE-QUARTER STUFF ANYWAY.
LOCAL NUMBER...
SOMETHING TELLS ME...
...KINGPIN WON'T BE HARD TO FIND.

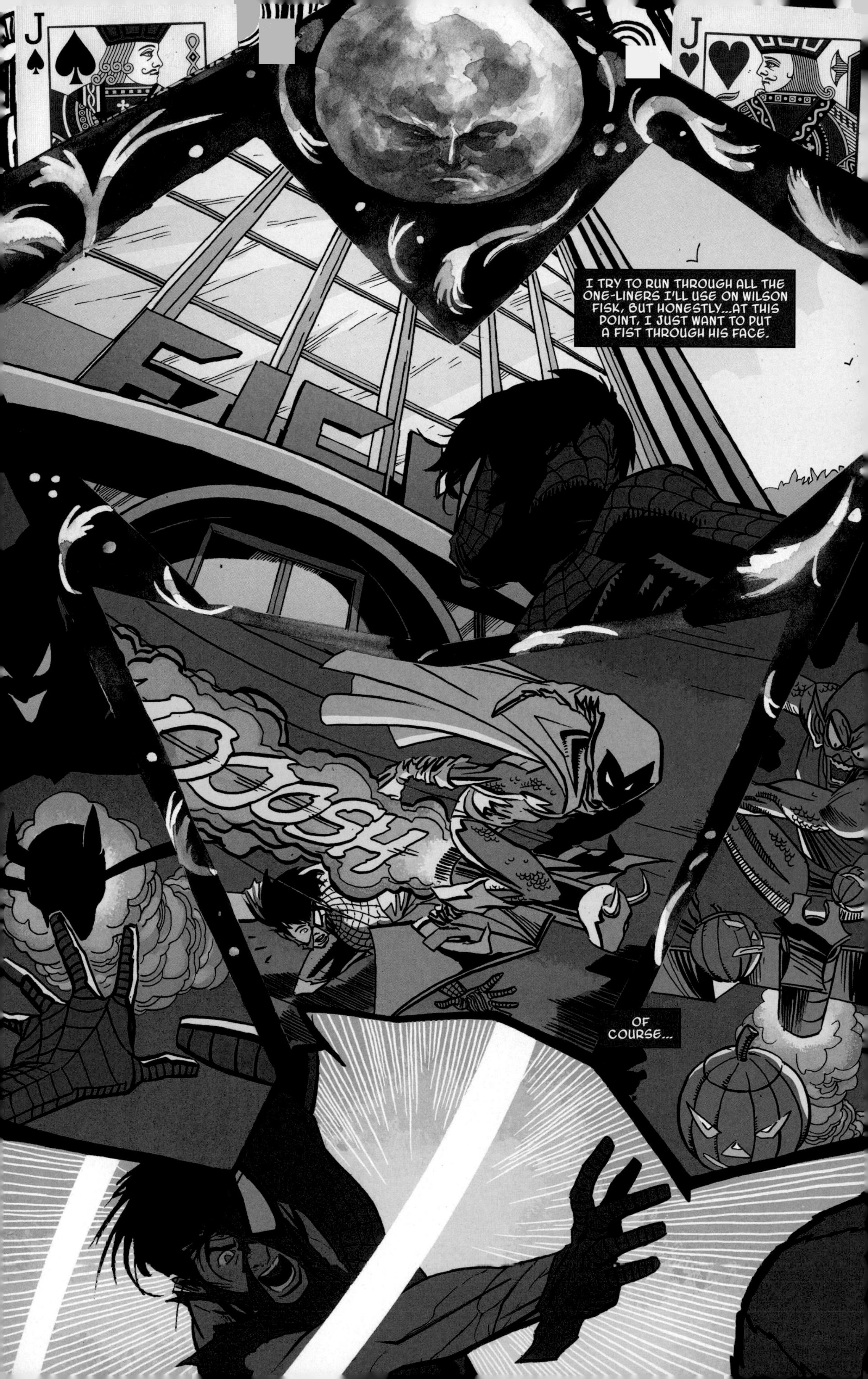

I TRY TO RUN THROUGH ALL THE ONE-LINERS I'LL USE ON WILSON FISK, BUT HONESTLY...AT THIS POINT, I JUST WANT TO PUT A FIST THROUGH HIS FACE.
Poosh
OF COURSE...

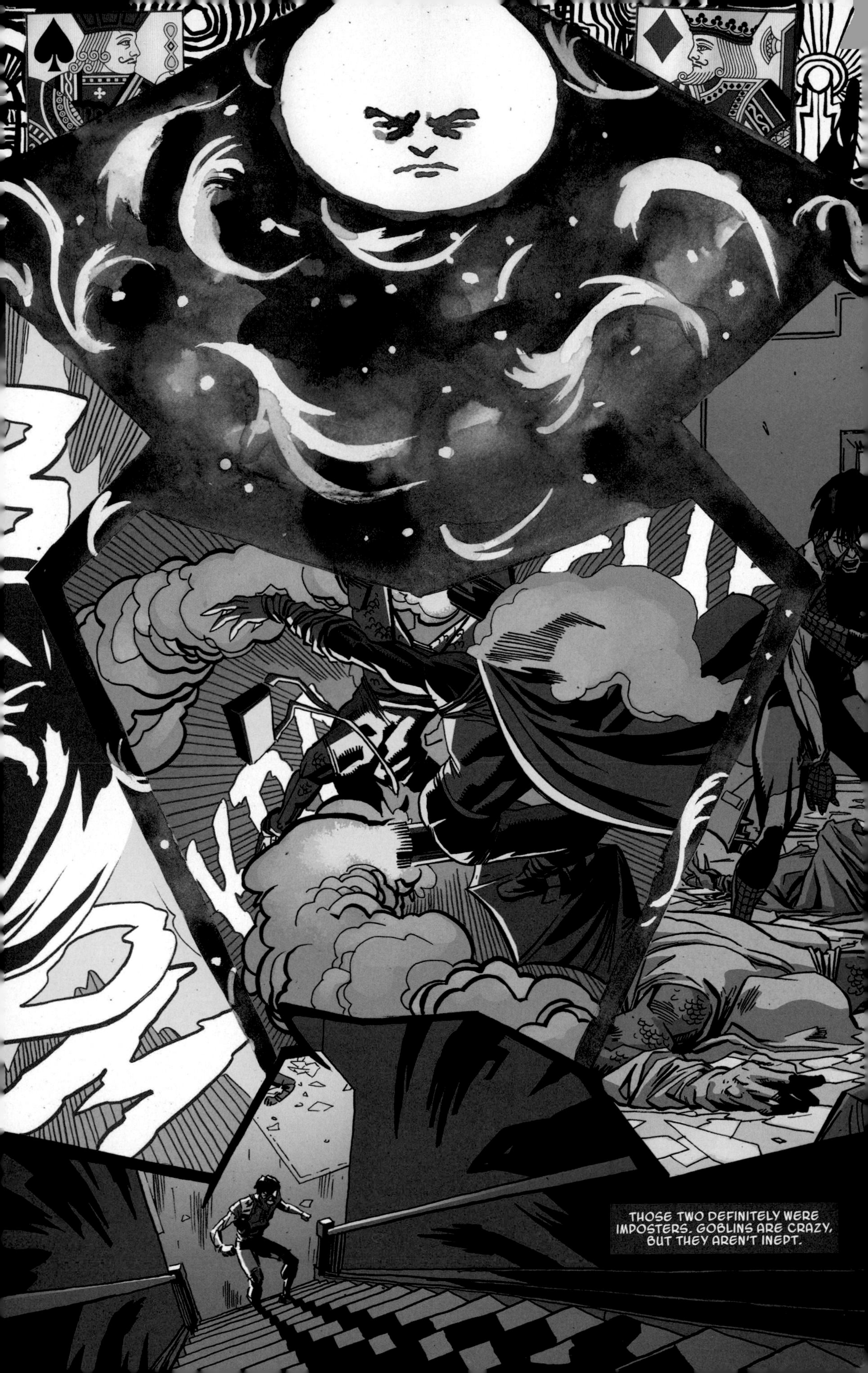
THOSE TWO DEFINITELY WERE IMPOSTERS. GOBLINS ARE CRAZY, BUT THEY AREN'T INEPT.

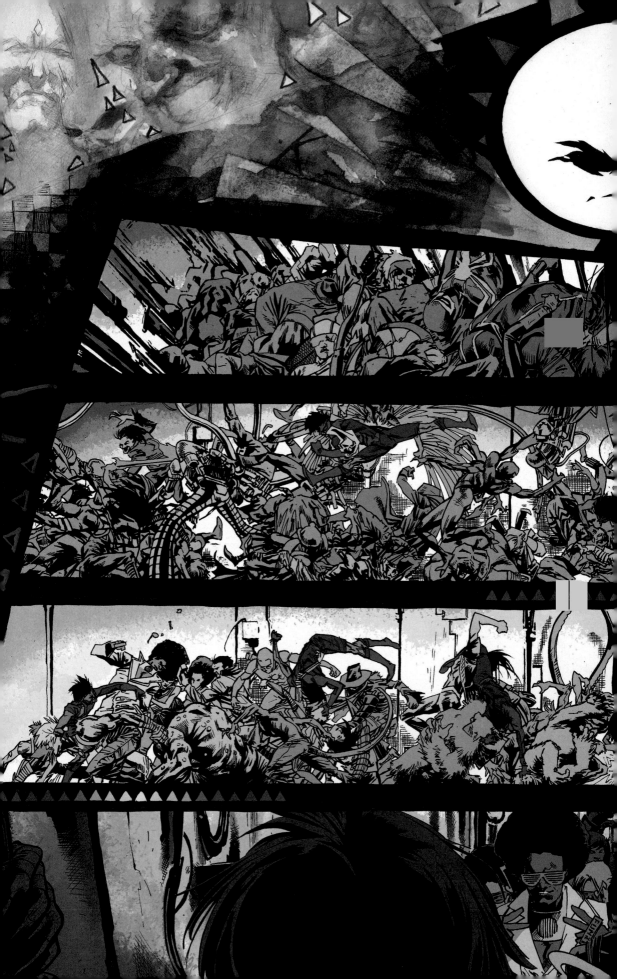

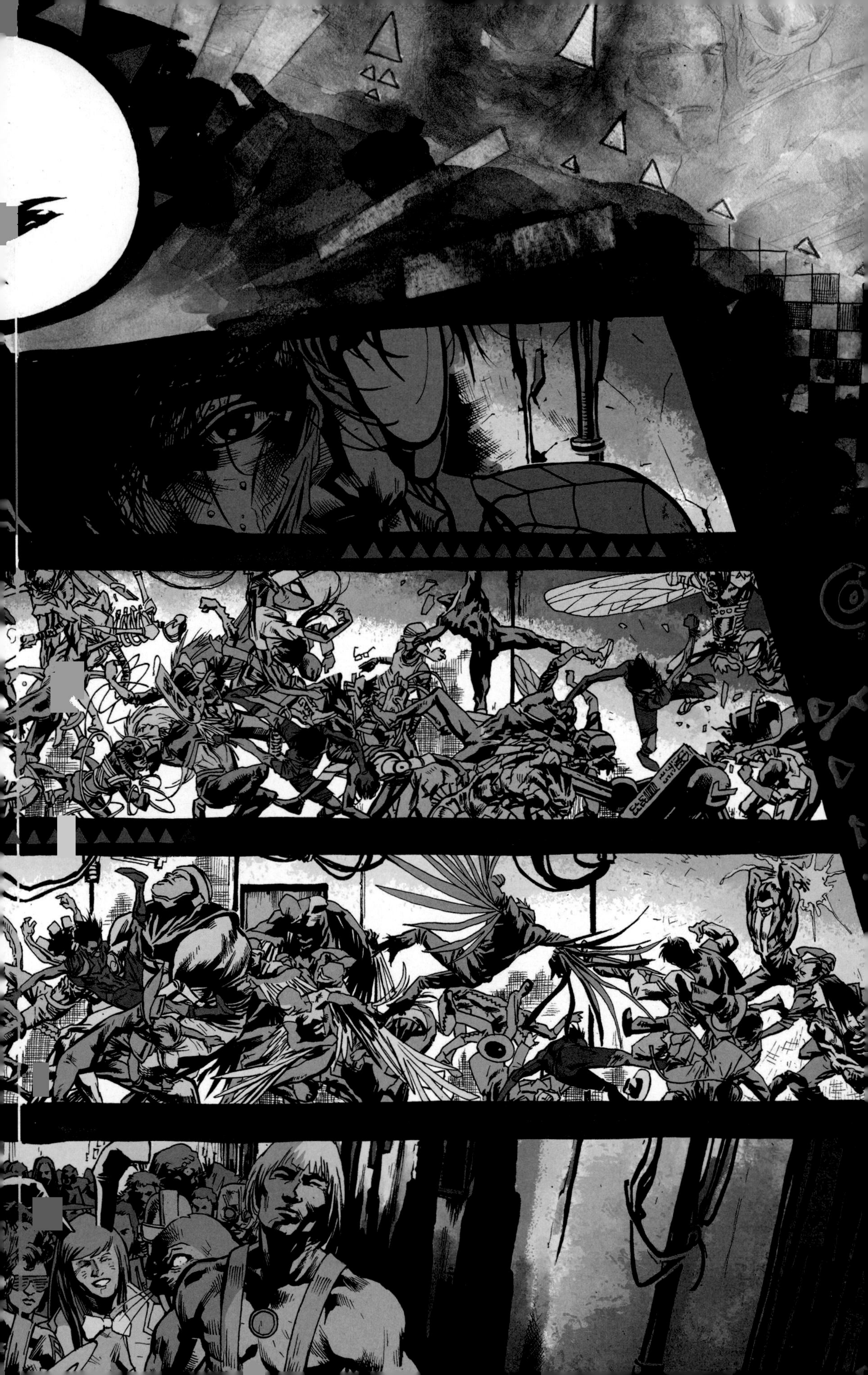

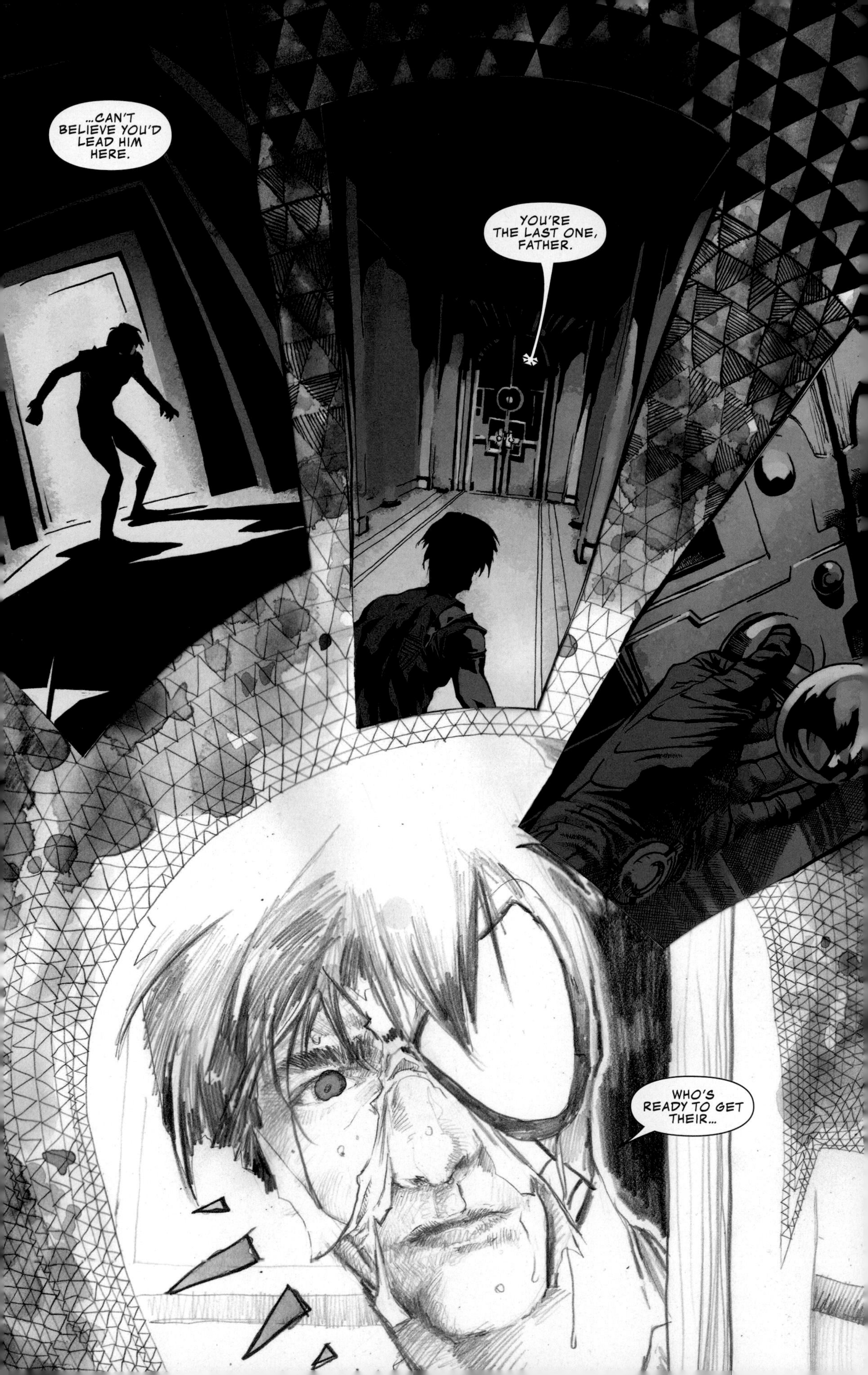
...CAN'T BELIEVE YOU'D LEAD HIM HERE.
YOU'RE THE LAST ONE, FATHER.
WHO'S READY TO GET THEIR...

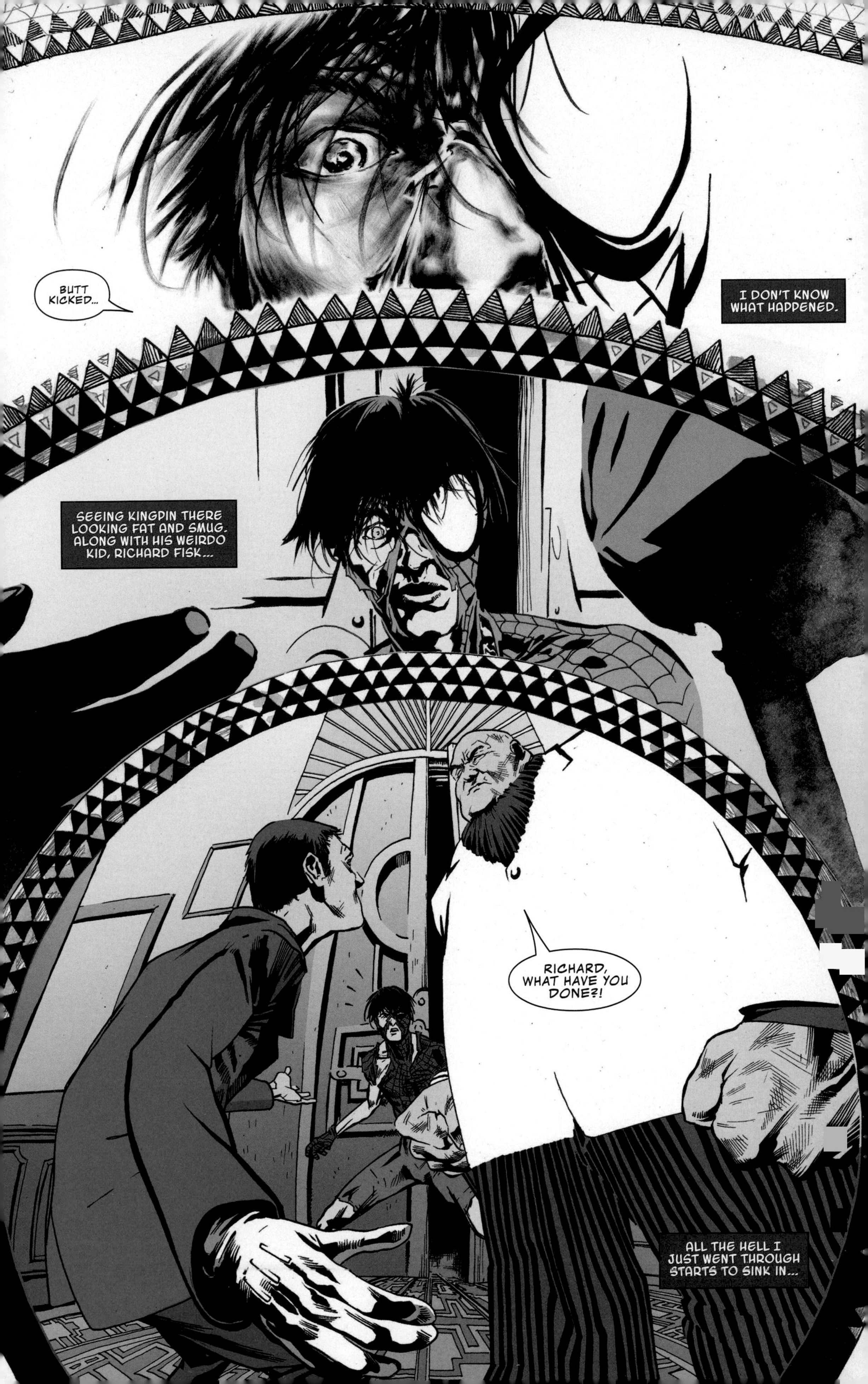
BUTT KICKED...
I DON'T KNOW WHAT HAPPENED.
SEEING KINGPIN THERE LOOKING FAT AND SMUG. ALONG WITH HIS WEIRDO KID, RICHARD FISK...
RICHARD, WHAT HAVE YOU DONE?!
ALL THE HELL I JUST WENT THROUGH STARTS TO SINK IN...

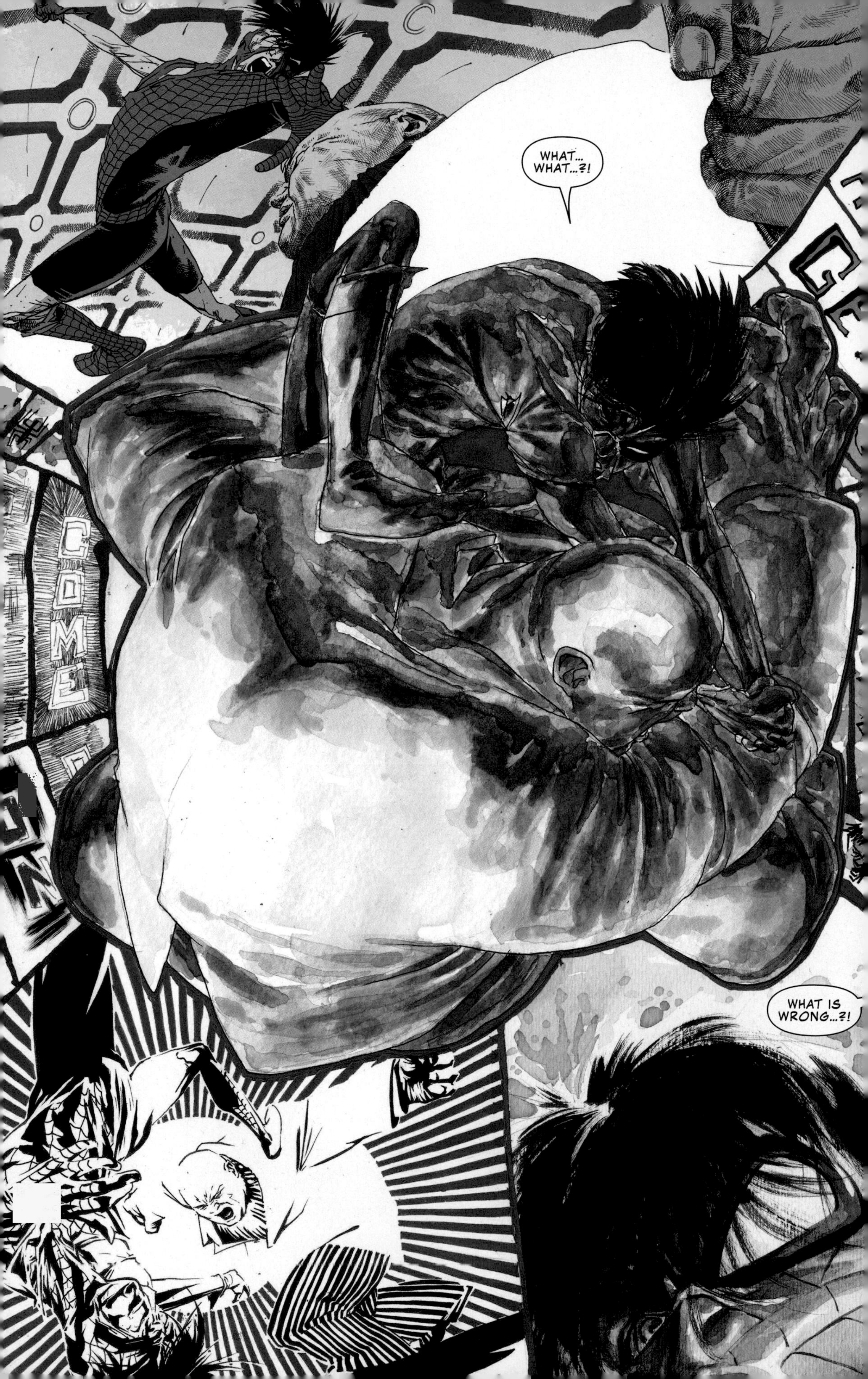
WHAT... WHAT...?!
WHAT IS WRONG...?!

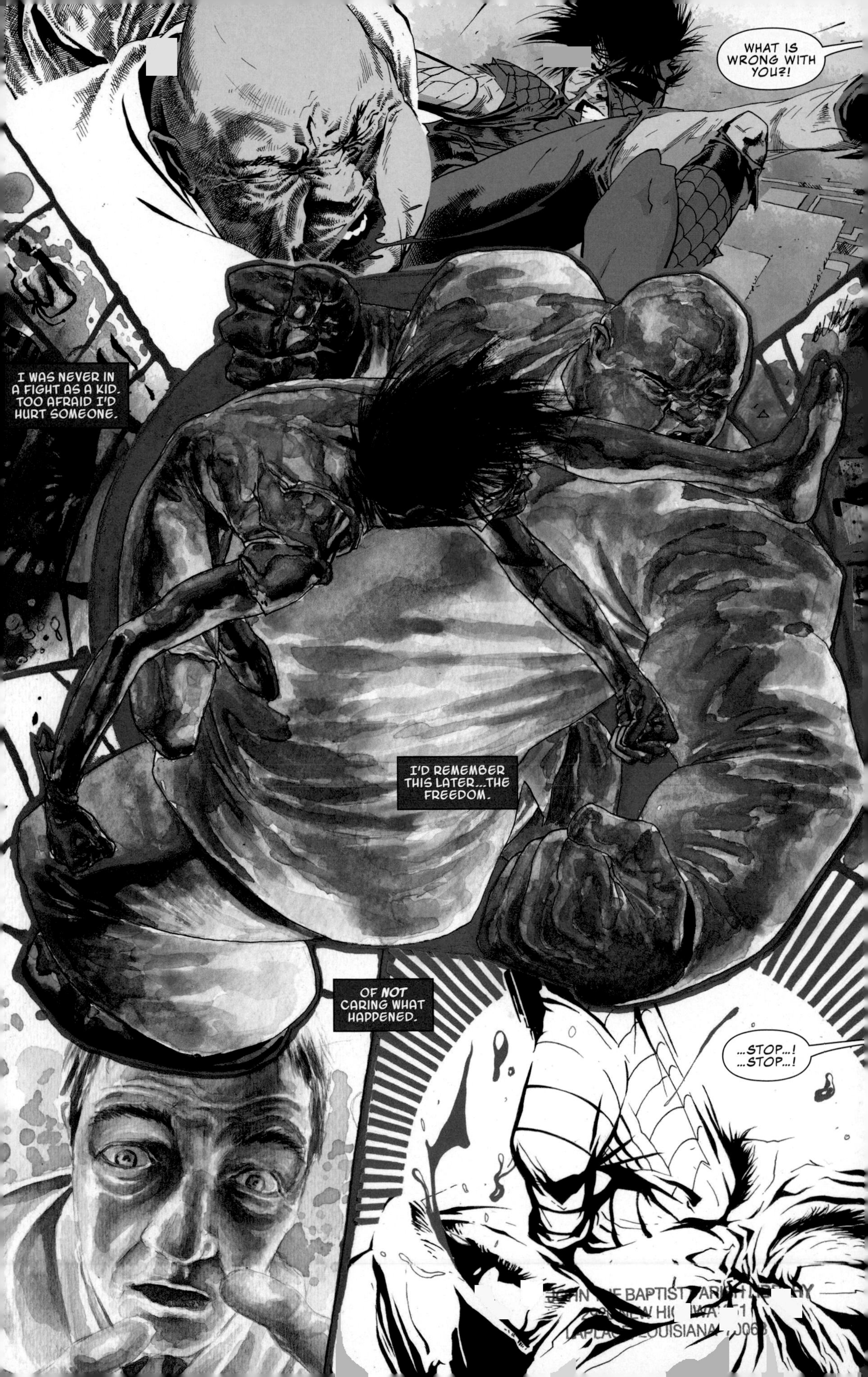
WHAT IS WRONG WITH YOU?!
I WAS NEVER IN A FIGHT AS A KID. TOO AFRAID I'D HURT SOMEONE.
I'D REMEMBER THIS LATER...THE FREEDOM.
OF NOT CARING WHAT HAPPENED.
...STOP...! ...STOP...!

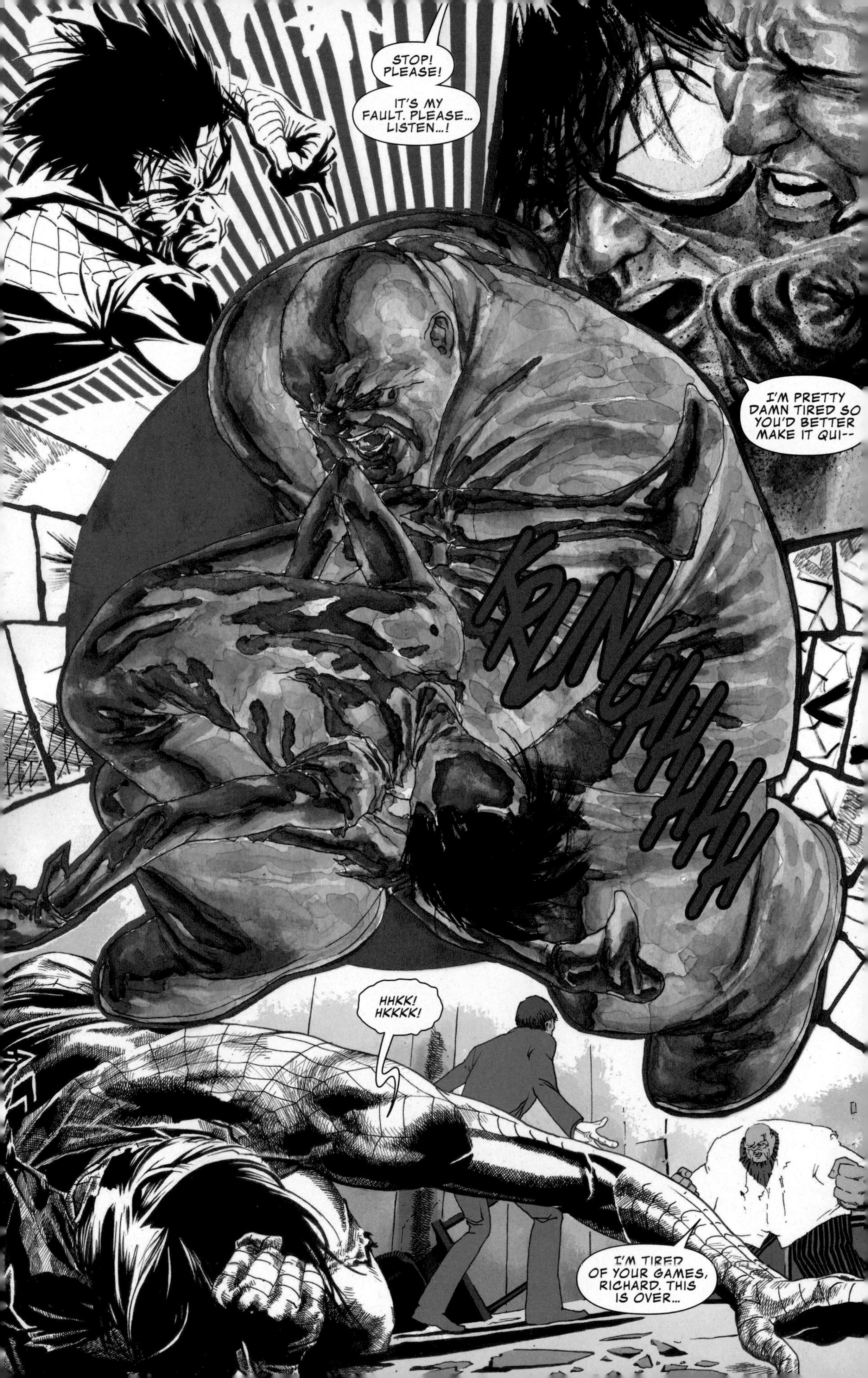

STOP! PLEASE!
IT'S MY FAULT. PLEASE... LISTEN...!
I'M PRETTY DAMN TIRED SO YOU'D BETTER MAKE IT QUI--
KRUNCHHHHH
HHKK! HKKKK!
I'M TIRED OF YOUR GAMES, RICHARD. THIS IS OVER...

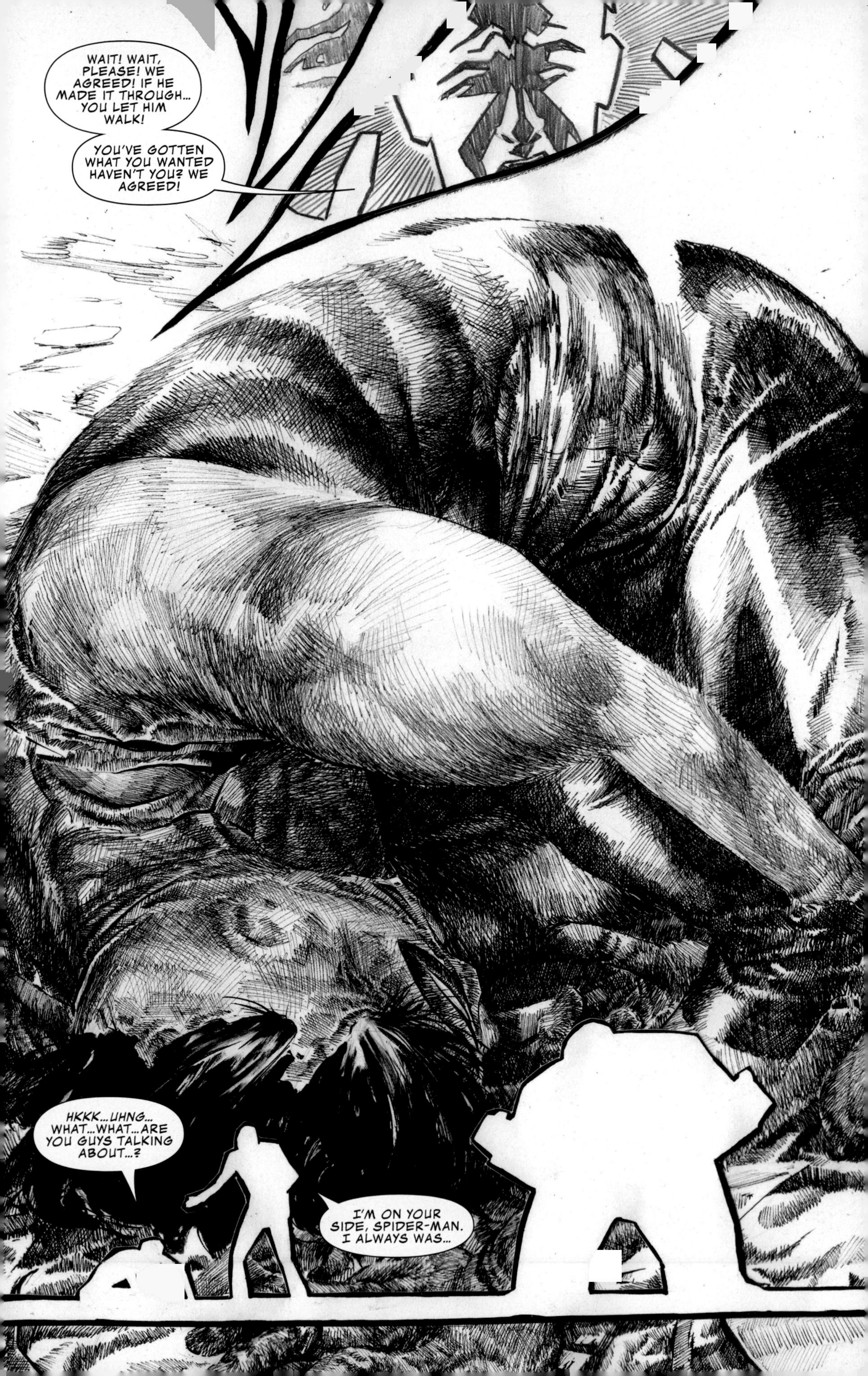
WAIT! WAIT, PLEASE! WE AGREED! IF HE MADE IT THROUGH... YOU LET HIM WALK!
YOU'VE GOTTEN WHAT YOU WANTED HAVEN'T YOU? WE AGREED!
HKKK...UHNG... WHAT...WHAT...ARE YOU GUYS TALKING ABOUT...?
I'M ON YOUR SIDE, SPIDER-MAN. I ALWAYS WAS...

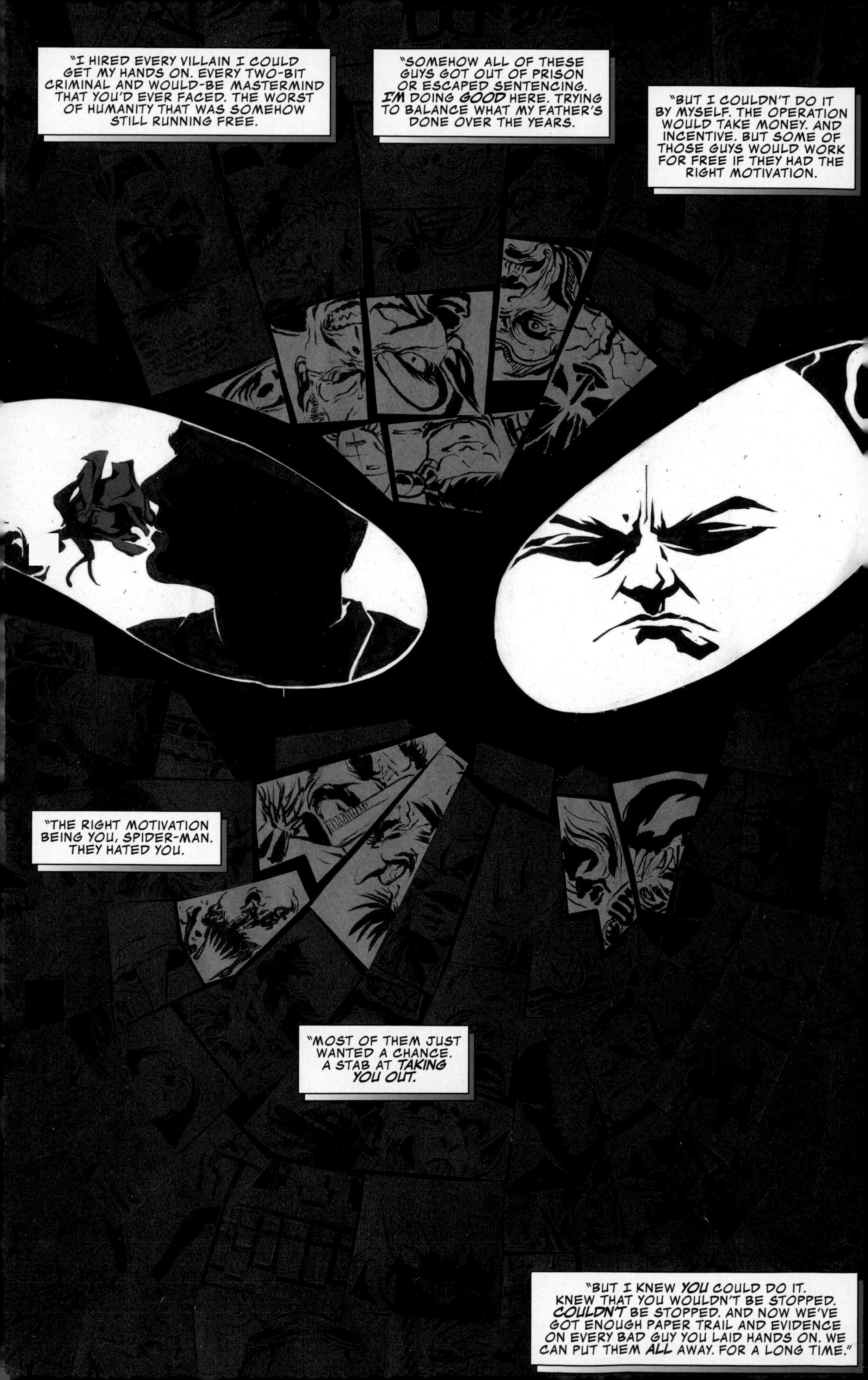
"I HIRED EVERY VILLAIN I COULD GET MY HANDS ON. EVERY TWO-BIT CRIMINAL AND WOULD-BE MASTERMIND THAT YOU'D EVER FACED. THE WORST OF HUMANITY THAT WAS SOMEHOW STILL RUNNING FREE.
"SOMEHOW ALL OF THESE GUYS GOT OUT OF PRISON OR ESCAPED SENTENCING. I'M DOING GOOD HERE. TRYING TO BALANCE WHAT MY FATHER'S DONE OVER THE YEARS.
"BUT I COULDN'T DO IT BY MYSELF. THE OPERATION WOULD TAKE MONEY. AND INCENTIVE. BUT SOME OF THOSE GUYS WOULD WORK FOR FREE IF THEY HAD THE RIGHT MOTIVATION.
"THE RIGHT MOTIVATION BEING YOU, SPIDER-MAN. THEY HATED YOU.
"MOST OF THEM JUST WANTED A CHANCE. A STAB AT TAKING YOU OUT.
"BUT I KNEW YOU COULD DO IT. KNEW THAT YOU WOULDN'T BE STOPPED. COULDN'T BE STOPPED. AND NOW WE'VE GOT ENOUGH PAPER TRAIL AND EVIDENCE ON EVERY BAD GUY YOU LAID HANDS ON. WE CAN PUT THEM ALL AWAY. FOR A LONG TIME."

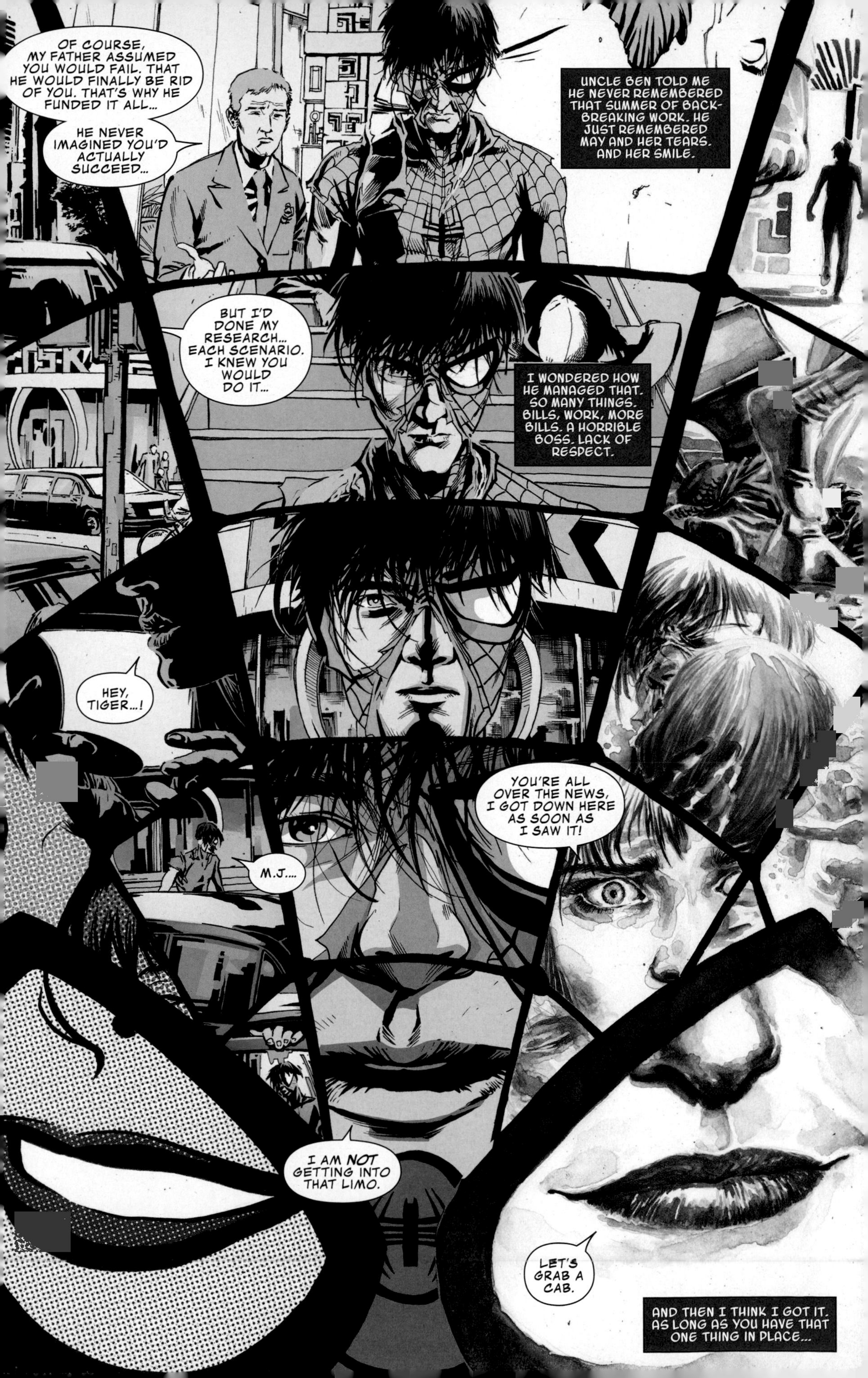
OF COURSE, MY FATHER ASSUMED YOU WOULD FAIL. THAT HE WOULD FINALLY BE RID OF YOU. THAT'S WHY HE FUNDED IT ALL...
HE NEVER IMAGINED YOU'D ACTUALLY SUCCEED...
UNCLE BEN TOLD ME HE NEVER REMEMBERED THAT SUMMER OF BACK-BREAKING WORK. HE JUST REMEMBERED MAY AND HER TEARS. AND HER SMILE.
BUT I'D DONE MY RESEARCH... EACH SCENARIO. I KNEW YOU WOULD DO IT...
I WONDERED HOW HE MANAGED THAT. SO MANY THINGS. BILLS, WORK, MORE BILLS. A HORRIBLE BOSS. LACK OF RESPECT.
HEY, TIGER...!
YOU'RE ALL OVER THE NEWS, I GOT DOWN HERE AS SOON AS I SAW IT!
M.J....
I AM NOT GETTING INTO THAT LIMO.
LET'S GRAB A CAB.
AND THEN I THINK I GOT IT. AS LONG AS YOU HAVE THAT ONE THING IN PLACE...

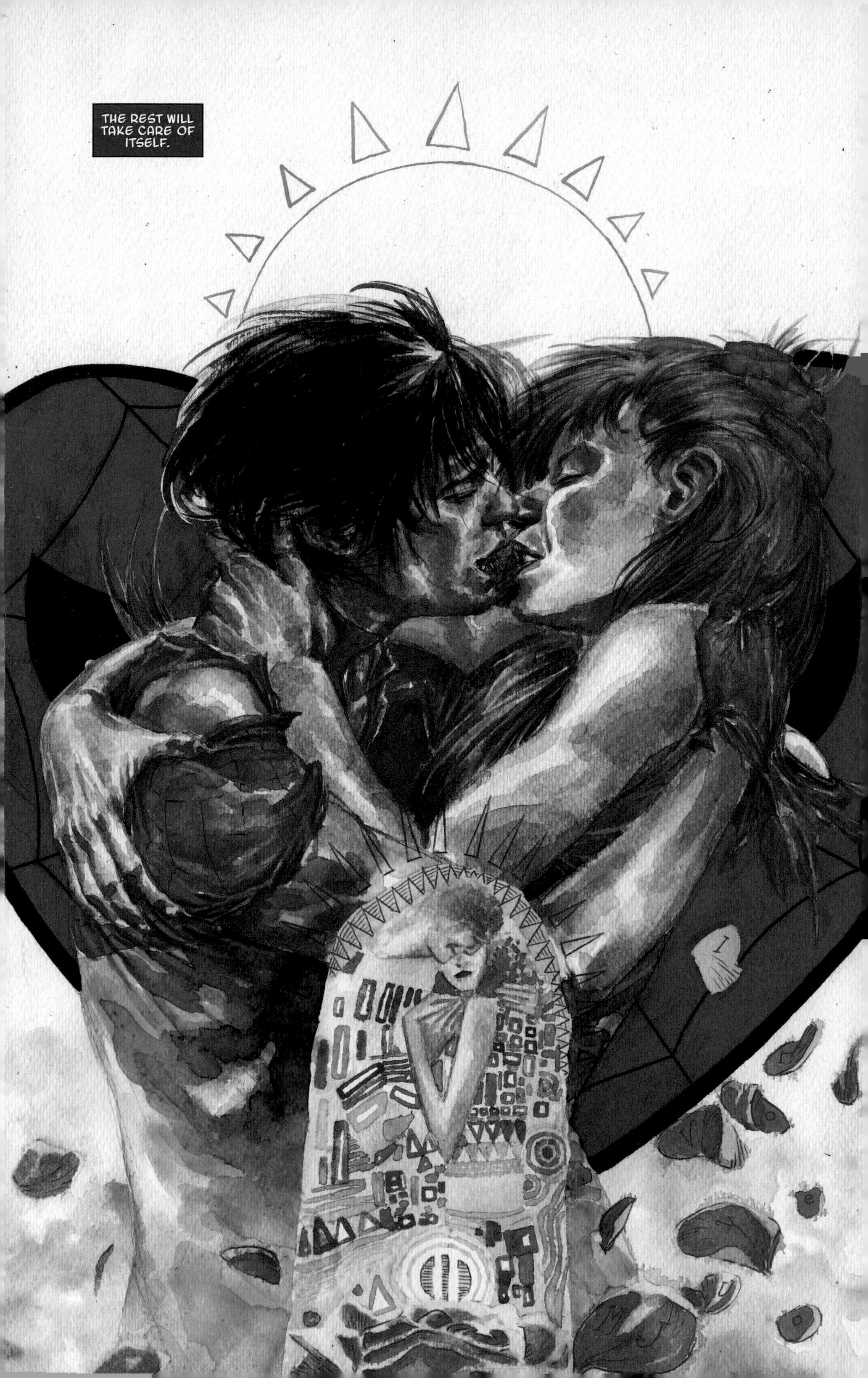
THE REST WILL TAKE CARE OF ITSELF.